DØ422346

LAMP UNTO MY FEET

LAMP UNTO MY FEET

A Verse-a-Day Devotional

 HarperSanFrancisco
An Imprint of HarperCollins*Publishers*

HarperCollins Web Site: http://www.harpercollins.com
HarperCollins®, ♣ ®, and HarperSanFrancisco™ are trademarks of HarperCollins Publishers Inc.

FIRST EDITION

ISBN 0–06–067961–1 (CLOTH)

97 98 99 00 01 ❖ RRD(H) 10 9 8 7 6 5 4 3 2 1

CONTENTS

➤   **xi**

ACKNOWLEDGMENTS

Deepest thanks to my wife, Karen, for holding the standard high for this endeavor and for her many sacrifices for me to pursue this dream. Thanks to my daughter, Kaeli, for her two- to five-year-old way of rejuvenating my soul.

Thanks to my mother, Opal, and my late father, Art, for loving me into adulthood; thanks to my in-laws, Junius and Leila Kendrick, for adding to that love.

Thanks to those who have facilitated this project, including Laura Tucker at Richard Curtis Associates, who found it a publishing home, and Patricia Klein at Harper San Francisco, whose editing strengthened it, as did Anne Collins's copy editing. Thanks to my Baptist Press co-workers, Herb Hollinger, Polly House, and Betty Kemp, and all the writers in the Baptist Press system for the quality Christian journalism that makes my job truly enjoyable and, often, exhilarating.

Thanks to all the publicists, secretaries, executive assistants, congressional press secretaries, receptionists, spouses, and friends who first fielded and then forwarded my requests for a Bible verse reflection to the person I was seeking to contact. I think, for instance, of Linda Rose, a real estate agent in Tallahassee, Florida, who made two trips to the home of her good friend, Ann Bowden, wife of Florida State head football coach Bobby Bowden, to help Ann get her Bible verse reflection in just at deadline time. Thanks also to numerous reference librarians, especially those at the Public Library of Nashville and Davidson County, for ever-patiently fielding requests for information covering the gamut of human endeavor.

Finally, a special thanks to every individual who shared a comment on Scripture, giving of his or her heart and time to make this witness to the Word of God truly possible.

INTRODUCTION

In 1992, astronaut Dave Leestma carried a microfiche Bible on the space shuttle *Atlantis*'s nine-day mission. I was stirred. Off and on for days, the thought came to mind of this astronaut— a real person; moreover, a highly trained professional, a scientist—carrying Scripture into space. He must have a strong belief in the Bible's value and relevance, I reasoned; I was moved by the courage it took to make that kind of statement of faith.

Perhaps with a divine nudge, I began wondering what verse or verses in Scripture this astronaut might cite as pivotal to his life.

Then I began wondering what Scriptures might be pivotal to other Christians in the sciences—and in the entertainment industry, government, business, sports, the arts, education, and other fields.

I put out a few queries and got my earliest responses from Tom Lester, Kenneth Cooper, Carl F. H. Henry, Glen Keane, Barbara Mandrell, Max Lennon, Bobby Richardson, Sam Rutigliano, and Andre Thornton. Slowly the number grew to 24, to 50, 75, 100, 150, and now more than 350 who wrote or telephoned to share a reflection for *Lamp Unto My Feet: A Verse-a-Day Devotional.*

Some responses gripped my heart; some made me pause to ponder the words their contributors had shared. I had asked folks to share something from their hearts—and they were doing just that, some with straightforward, simple words in just a sentence or two, others with sentences that soared with eloquence.

What's my own favorite verse?

It's Romans 5:10: "For if, when we were God's enemies, we were reconciled to him through the death of his Son, how much more, having been reconciled, shall we be saved through his life!" (NIV).

My family had driven from Ohio to visit our relatives in Mississippi during the summer of 1971. One evening, I learned that my grandmother was going to a revival. How quaint, I thought. Attending a revival in rural Mississippi would surely be something to tell my college friends about back in Ohio.

The evening started out as everything I had hoped for. The preacher looked somewhat like fiery Alabama governor George Wallace. He seemed to yell up a storm. But then my soul began to urge me to listen to what this fellow had to say. The essence of his message was that, compared to any of the world's social systems, philosophies, or religions, Christ offers the most hope of changing people's hearts. Good point, I admitted. My heart sure needed changing. But when the altar call was given, I was much too sophisticated to go forward.

The next day, to my surprise, the preacher—Cliff Estes, now of Shreveport, Louisiana—dropped by my grandmother's house. Deep down, I was glad to see him. As we talked, he asked me, straightforwardly yet in a caring way, whether I was a Christian. No, I said, because, to be honest, I had always wondered whether Christ had really existed, whether He was as real as Abraham Lincoln or as mythical as Paul Bunyan.

I must have hit on one of Cliff's specialties, because he relayed more evidence for Christ's historical existence than I had ever heard before. Then I was ready. Cliff and I prayed; just like countless others who have turned to Jesus Christ, I told Him I was repenting and asking Him to forgive my sin and my sinfulness; I asked Him to come into my life and change it as my Lord and Savior.

I was saved. I knew I had a personal relationship with Him. Yet little did I know how saved I was. Then a few years later came the words of Romans 5:10: "how much more shall we be saved by his life." His life. Hmm, what did it mean? Yeah, Jesus' life in me! His Holy Spirit in me—giving me peace and joy; transforming me; urging me to continually confess my sins and be cleansed of guilt; energizing me to the things of God; stirring me to holy courage to step out in faith daily; giving me a wondrous dose of heaven while I'm still here on earth.

On the following pages you can experience a multitude of doses of heaven through the Scripture reflections of people in all walks of life. It can be, as one friend put it, "like counting the stars in the sky!"

What if, someone once asked me, one of these people falls into some sort of disgrace? My answer is this: That person's Bible verse reflection should become a reminder to us to extend prayer and grace to that individual, a reminder that "there but for the grace of God, go I." Whatever other thoughts might come to mind regarding that person, there's no better way to utilize those moments than in prayer.

Art Toalston

JANUARY

January 1

NANCY ALCORN, founder and president, Mercy Ministries of America, which operates nonprofit homes for unwed expectant mothers in Nashville, Tennessee, and Monroe and West Monroe, Louisiana, offering a Christian environment, counsel, and training in life skills as they decide whether to keep their babies or choose adoption; author of *Echoes of Mercy*, chronicling her vision for launching and leading Mercy Ministries; former athletic director at a Tennessee correctional facility for delinquent girls.

". . . For I know the plans I have for you," declares the LORD, "plans to prosper you and not to harm you, plans to give you hope and a future. . . ." (Jeremiah 29:11, NIV)

In my work with unwed mothers and troubled girls, I have been so blessed to see how the Spirit of God has used this verse in the lives of seemingly hopeless people in seemingly hopeless situations. Through this verse, many young women on the brink of suicide and destruction have realized that God loves them and that He really does have a purpose for their lives and future. I think, for instance, of Sherry, who came to us at age eighteen after finding out she was pregnant. Confused, hurting, and ashamed, Sherry knew she needed to make a brand-new commitment of her life to Christ. While at Mercy Ministries, Sherry chose to make Jesus the Lord of her life, and she also very lovingly chose adoption. Now, seven years later, God is still blessing the choices Sherry made. After leaving Mercy Ministries, she met a wonderful young man named Dale who eventually became her husband. It was Dale who encouraged Sherry to go after her dream of becoming a nurse. Sherry trusted God to see her through a four-year nursing program, from which she recently graduated. To top that, Sherry became the OB-GYN nurse in the labor and delivery room where the young women from Mercy Ministries in Nashville deliver their babies. Isn't that incredible? I'm also happy to note that Sherry and Dale have been blessed with a beautiful baby boy named Cole. God's mercy is truly a path to restoration, and Sherry by God's grace is walking that path.

January 2

SHARON ANDERSON, professional interior designer; "Design Solutions" columnist for *Draperies and Window Coverings* monthly magazine; instructor in the nationally accredited interior design program at Learning Tree University, Thousand Oaks, California.

> *Shout for joy to the LORD, all the earth.*
> *Serve the LORD with gladness;*
> *come before him with joyful songs.*
> *Know that the LORD is God.*
> *It is he who made us, and we are his;*
> *we are his people, the sheep of his pasture.*
> *Enter his gates with thanksgiving*
> *and his courts with praise;*
> *give thanks to him and praise his name.*
> *For the LORD is good and his love endures forever;*
> *his faithfulness continues through all generations.*
> *(Psalm 100, NIV)*

I first came across this chapter when I was asked to memorize it as a twelve-year-old. Little did I know it would be the promise that would stay with me through my Christian experiences. The

Lord tells us to worship with gladness. I *know* that the Lord is God; He has proved Himself over and over again; and I have always remembered to praise His name. His love endures forever and ever. And we have to pass this on to our children. They need to know that the Lord's love endures, that this is His promise. The Lord also promises us that His faithfulness will continue through all generations. This means our children and our children's children will experience the faithfulness of the Lord. What a promise!

January 3

BROTHER ANDREW, founder and president, Open Doors International, known for its forty-year ministry of encouraging the persecuted church in more than sixty countries, transporting Bibles into the former Soviet Union and Eastern Bloc, China, Vietnam, Cuba, and now, the Muslim world of the Middle East, Africa, and Asia—undergirded by international around-the-clock campaigns "Seven Years of Prayer for the Soviet Union" begun in 1983 and "Ten Years of Prayer for the Church in the Muslim World" begun in 1990; author of *God's Smuggler,* 10-million-seller now translated into thirty languages, *Ethics of Smuggling,* and several other books; several years after his first Bible-smuggling trip from his native Netherlands, into Eastern Europe in 1955, he adopted the "Brother Andrew" code name for his travels.

Awake and strengthen what remains, which is at the point of death. (paraphrase of Revelation 3:2)

My world was radically changed, redirected, and, in retrospect, definitely guided when God spoke so clearly to me that day in July 1955 as I watched the masses of Communist young people parading, carrying their red banner, preparing for worldwide revolution, singing and chanting "We are ragged and we are poor, but we will conquer and change the world." And I stood there, my Bible grasped in my hand, pressed to my heart, wondering, "Where is the church, where are God's children in this place, where is the answer of the rest of the world to the awful challenge of communism?" Then God spoke that verse that has been my lodestar ever since, Revelation 3:2: "Awake and strengthen what remains, which is at the point of death." Not suddenly, yet clearly I knew and began to understand. "Awake," wake up, we are asleep, and the world goes to hell, "and strengthen what remains," not a pleasant ministry, you have got to seek them, because they are at the point of death. The down-and-outers, I know you'll find them on the streets of New York, but you'll find them by the millions in Eastern Europe, Russia, Central Asia, Siberia, China, Vietnam. I found them gradually as I started and continued to travel along the pathway of the Communist revolution around the world: Africa, Latin America, and, now, very much in the Middle East. There is still a suffering church in these regions, and we have to find its members. But first we have to wake up to the need for our own survival, for which God has given us all the resources. Then we can strengthen them. How will we stand before the judgment seat of Christ, when one day we say we have squandered all the God-given resources? We did not wake up in time. There is a suffering church to be reached in the areas of persecution—and today there is more persecution than forty years ago when I began. Ten years from now there will be more persecution than today. Wake up, brother and sister, please wake up and strengthen what remains, which is at the point of death.

January 4

JOHN ANTHONY, Metropolitan Opera baritone; one of the soloists in the world premiere of Leonard Bernstein's *Mass* for the September 5, 1971, opening of the John F. Kennedy Center for the Performing Arts in Washington.

Remove far from me falsehood and lying; give me neither
poverty nor riches; feed me with the food that is needful
for me. . . . (Proverbs 30:8, RSV)

I was in sort of a crisis situation over making ends meet when I heard a Baptist pastor in Washington, D.C., preach on this verse. It was a fabulous sermon, especially considering he was making an appeal for the church budget. He commended the small congregation for giving everything the church had ever needed, far beyond what might be expected of a congregation that size. Then he enumerated several examples from history of individuals who had grabbed after money, property, power, who accumulated all sorts of things and ended up paying a very dear price for their greed. The sermon imparted to me a very helpful point of view about our needs in life: Hey, what are you worrying about? Just relax. Strive to do your very best, be sure it's all right in the eyes of God, and your needs will be taken care of.

January 5

BILL ARMSTRONG, U.S. senator from Colorado, 1979–91; member, U.S. House of Representatives, 1973–79; member, Colorado Senate, 1965–73, also serving as majority leader, and Colorado House of Representatives, 1963–65; currently, chairman of three mortgage banking firms, a title insurance company, and a residential real estate firm; formerly president for more than twenty-five years of Denver-area radio stations KOSI and KEZW.

But they that wait upon the LORD shall renew their
strength; they shall mount up with wings as eagles; they
shall run, and not be weary; and they shall walk, and not
faint. (Isaiah 40:31, KJV)

We live in a time of decadence, a time when traditional values and especially traditional Christian values are under attack. And it is a time of discouragement and cynicism, a time when many conscientious people are just tempted to give up. But the assurance we have from this passage of Scripture is that if we wait upon the Lord, He will give us strength beyond human understanding.

January 6

ELLEN ARMSTRONG, wife of former Colorado Senator Bill Armstrong; during her eighteen years in Washington, she was among the organizers of the Senate Wives Bible Study, with other involvements including Congressional Wives Fellowship, Congressional Wives for Soviet Jewry, Federation of Parents for Drug-Free Youth, and Campus Crusade for Christ; recent involvements include PRIIME TIIME Today (Parents Responsibly Involved in Media Excellence and Teens Involved in Media Excellence) board member and National Coalition Against Pornography advisory board member.

> *Jesus looked at them and said, "With man this is impossible, but not with God; all things are possible with God."* *(Mark 10:27, NIV)*

This verse has helped me become confident in believing that the God who calls me to certain assignments is the one who provides for their accomplishment. If the task is from God, He will not cause me to fail.

January 7

MARY KAY ASH, chairwoman emeritus, Mary Kay Cosmetics, Inc., which she founded in 1963 in a Dallas storefront and guided to Fortune 500 status as the largest direct seller of skin-care products in the United States, topping $1 billion in annual retail sales since 1991; twice listed in *The 100 Best Companies to Work for in America,* the company now encompasses more than 475,000 independent beauty consultants in twenty-five countries and has pioneered in discontinuing animal testing, in recycling, and in skin-care products for men; member of the Texas Business Hall of Fame and Texas Women's Hall of Fame; the Mary Kay Museum opened in Dallas in 1993.

> *What time I am afraid, I will trust in thee.*
> *(Psalm 56:3, KJV)*

There are so many Scripture verses I love, but if I have to choose, I suppose I would have to start with the one I learned when I was just a little girl in Sunbeams at Tabernacle Baptist Church in Houston, Texas. This verse has helped me all my life in times of trouble and fear. It always quiets my fears and helps me through whatever crisis there might be.

January 8

JOHN ASHCROFT, U.S. senator from Missouri, elected in 1994; governor of Missouri, 1985–93; chairman, National Governors' Association, 1991–92; chairman, Education Commission of the States, 1987–88; Missouri attorney general, 1976–85; president, National Association of Attorneys General, 1981–82, and 1983 recipient of its highest honor, The Wyman Award; named 1991 Layperson of the Year by the National Association of Evangelicals.

> *For God hath not given us the spirit of fear; but of power,*
> *and of love, and of a sound mind. (2 Timothy 1:7, KJV)*

The spirit of fear is the most paralyzing, immobilizing spirit that ever grips our being. The recipe for activity, as opposed to immobility, is power, love, and a sound mind. If we are indeed to be salt and light in the world, this is God's assurance: when the spirit of fear comes, that's not His Spirit; rather, He gives us the capacity to act constructively by having authority, compassion, and reasonability.

January 9

JENNIFER AZZI, member of 1996 gold medal U.S. Olympic women's basketball team; 1990 Naismith winner as women's college basketball player of the year who led Stanford University to a 32–1 record and the NCAA championship; member of U.S. women's team that won the 1994 Goodwill Games and finished third in the World Championship; member of 1994 Swedish champion pro women's team in Arvika, Sweden.

> *But they that wait upon the* LORD *shall renew their strength; they shall mount up with wings as eagles; they shall run, and not be weary; and they shall walk, and not faint. (Isaiah 40:31, KJV)*

This is the Bible verse that I read most frequently for inspiration as a professional athlete. For me, basketball has become an expression of my faith. When I put all my hope in God, I don't worry about my performance. He gives me the strength to play, so I just use it as best I can. If you just let yourself go, His power can allow you to reach your potential.

January 10

TED BAEHR, chief executive officer, Christian Film and Television Commission, Atlanta, which he founded in 1986 as a liaison to the entertainment industry in behalf of family entertainment; publisher and radio commentator, *Movieguide* family periodical and broadcast applying biblical values to entertainment choices; author of several books; former positions include president, Episcopal Radio-Television Foundation, and director, Television Center at the City University in New York.

*For though we walk in the flesh, we do not war according
to the flesh. For the weapons of our warfare are not carnal
but mighty in God for pulling down strongholds, casting
down arguments and every high thing that exalts itself
against the knowledge of God, bringing every thought
into captivity to the obedience of Christ. . . .*
(2 Corinthians 10:3–5, NKJV)

These verses have guided our corporate ministry at the Christian
Film and Television Commission as well as my personal growth
as a Christian. I see these verses calling us individually and cor-
porately to redeem our thought life and our culture, freeing
them from bondage to the idols of our age into the peace that is
a hallmark of a relationship with Jesus Christ. Using these
verses as a guide, I have been impressed at how they help redeem the values of those we minister to in mass media communications.

January 11

LAURIE BALBACH-TAYLOR, formerly a police, fire, and rescue communications officer with the Hamilton County Communication Center, Cincinnati, and, earlier, the Silverton, Ohio,
Police Department; author, *Unit 6–George–90, Signal 44* (police
lingo for "Oh God, Please Tell Me Where You Are"); currently,
general manager, Faith Publishing Company, Milford, Ohio.

*I will make with them a covenant of peace; it shall be an
everlasting covenant with them, and I will multiply them,
and put my sanctuary among them forever. My dwelling
shall be with them; I will be their God, and they shall be
my people. Thus the nations shall know that it is I, the
LORD, who make Israel holy, when my sanctuary shall be
set up among them forever.*
(Ezekiel 37:26–28, NAB, Saint Joseph ed.)

When Satan seems to have taken over the world with wars, injustices, and atrocious crimes multiplying daily, it is comforting to remember the words of our Lord, promising that He is with us in the most loving way—dwelling with us. Out of love for His people, He chooses His home among us. We are not alone with evil because God lives with us. The horrors of this world can then be seen in a new light. God knows our sufferings firsthand because He lives with us. He will comfort us through them, if we are open to Him. He will give us the guidance of His Holy Spirit in making decisions for our personal lives and for our roles in developing peace among people. He leads us in our daily battles against the powers of darkness. Comforting as these thoughts are, however, it can be tempting for us to become "victims" of our times, resting in complacency and becoming indifferent to the plight of our neighbors. Especially at such times, we must remember that a *covenant* implies responsibility from all parties involved. It is not just God's responsibility, but ours as well. We realize His fidelity to His covenant with us when we also demonstrate our fidelity to it. We do this by acknowledging and welcoming God's presence among us and demonstrating our love for Him by obeying His laws. Then the peace He promises grows—first in our hearts, then spreading to the world—through people of God uniting in their love for Him and dedication to upholding His covenant. We have a long way to go to realize the fullness of God's presence in our midst throughout the world. But each of us holds a part of the responsibility to turn to Him, working with and through Him, to bring about His kingdom of peace on earth.

January 12

JAY BARKER, New England Patriots quarterback; winningest quarterback in University of Alabama history, with thirty-five wins as a starter from 1991 to 1994, including the 1992 national championship, a 34–13 victory over the University of Miami in the Sugar Bowl, capping a 13–0 season; 1994 Southeastern Conference Player of the Year and Johnny Unitas Golden Arm Award winner as nation's top senior quarterback; subject of 1995 biography, *In Due Time: The Struggles and Triumphs of Alabama Quarterback Jay Barker,* by Wayne Atcheson.

And we know that all things work together for good to them that love God, to them who are the called according to his purpose. (Romans 8:28, KJV)

When I'm on the field, to me it's a way to worship the Lord. My objective is to play for the Lord, to praise Him, to win for Him. The other stuff will take care of itself. I rely on the Lord's support and I realize I am nothing without Him. My ritual is that every night before a game, I have a quiet time with the Lord, studying the Bible and praying, not to win the game, but that His name will be lifted up and that I will be an influence on the field for Him. That influence sometimes is awesome. When we played the Gamecocks in '93 in South Carolina, I signed an autograph for a little boy, among many that day. I always add Romans 8:28 below my name. I later received a letter from the boy's father saying that at first they thought I had put down my room number. Then he noticed it was a Scripture verse. The man stated that he had not read the Scriptures in quite a while. So he opened his Bible, looked the verse up, and began to read more of the Scriptures. Now, he said, he was in touch with his wife and felt more than ever that they might be getting back together, and he wanted me to know how much that autograph and Scripture verse had meant to his life.

January 13

FRONIA CONNELL BARNARD, Birmingham, Alabama, poet and author of two books, *100 Years of Memories,* released in 1994 when she was 103 years of age, and *Dear Folks: Letters and Diary of a World War II GI,* based on letters from her son during the war and entries in his diary, released when she was 100; named Alabama Poetry Society's Poet of the Century.

> *. . . lo, I am with you alway, even unto the end of the world. (Matthew 28:20, KJV)*

This verse was a great blessing to my husband and me in a very traumatic situation in our lives. In September 1942 our then-eighteen-year-old son, Boyd, entered the University of Alabama. In December he joined the Army enlisted reserve corps and on April 6, 1943, he was called to active duty. He served as a radio operator/mechanic during his more than three years in service. When he left home, he carried a brass-covered New Testament and a letter from our family physician, Dr. Lelis Kirby, in the left pocket of his shirt. The letter related the experience we had with Boyd when he was eight years old and he and a playmate were exposed to scarlet fever. Boyd was given a shot, which soon evidenced that he was allergic to the horse serum in it. On the way home from the doctor's office, Boyd wanted to sit with me and lean against my shoulder, complaining of hurting and feeling strange. He wouldn't eat anything and went to bed. After checking him and finding that he had difficulty moving his arms, we called Dr. Kirby. This was back when physicians made house calls, and he came immediately. He gave Boyd a shot and sat with us all night, massaging his body and limbs. I had called our pastor, family members, and friends and asked them to help us pray for Boyd. The next morning, Boyd began to move his limbs. In a few days, he was much better. Then the doctor told us the chilling news that only twice before had he had patients react in such a manner. Once a man's arm was permanently paralyzed. The other patient was a child with whom he worked all night until the child died.

When Boyd went to Army basic training, he was told he would have to take a tetanus shot. Horse serum had been used in tetanus shots, and he called us and was frantic. We reassured him all we could and, of course, we prayed. Boyd went to the Army doctor and presented the letter. The doctor read it, patted Boyd on the shoulder, and said, "Don't worry, buddy. I happen to have the same allergy you have. In fact, quite a number of people are allergic to horse serum, so we now use rabbit serum in tetanus shots. It will not hurt you." At the end of the war, Boyd returned home and finished college, majoring in business administration and marketing. He's a strapping six-foot-two-inch man with a nice business and is happily married with a daughter and three fine grandsons.

January 14

PSHON BARRETT, assistant U.S. attorney, Southern District of Mississippi, Department of Justice, since 1980, and chief of the Civil Division's Financial Litigation Unit; blind since birth, she is a member of the American Blind Lawyers Association's board of directors; former general counsel, Mississippi Governor's Office of Job Development and Training; she also holds a master of arts in marriage and family therapy from Reformed Theological Seminary and is a volunteer counselor with the Addie McBryde Rehabilitation Center for the Blind, Jackson, Mississippi; pianist and vocalist in various church and civic settings.

"And why do you worry about clothes? See how the lilies of the field grow. They do not labor or spin. Yet I tell you that not even Solomon in all his splendor was dressed like one of these. If that is how God clothes the grass of the field, which is here today and tomorrow is thrown into the fire, will he not much more clothe you, O you of little faith? So do not worry, saying, 'What shall we eat?' or 'What shall we drink?' or 'What shall we wear?' For the pagans run after all these things, and your heavenly Father

knows that you need them. But seek first his kingdom and his righteousness, and all these things will be given to you as well. Therefore do not worry about tomorrow, for tomorrow will worry about itself. Each day has enough trouble of its own. . . ." (Matthew 6:28–34, NIV)

This passage gives me assurance and comfort that our loving heavenly Father provides for, and is interested in, the minute details of my life. As a person who has always found security in planning and organizing my life, I am challenged by this passage to live today to the fullest, without spending needless time and energy being anxious and projecting about the future, over which I have no control. Only when I surrender control over people, opportunities, and events in my life can God begin to plant, cultivate, and harvest the fruits of His will so that I may be equipped for usefulness in His kingdom.

January 15

DAVID M. BEASLEY, governor of South Carolina; member of the South Carolina House of Representatives, 1979–92, first winning office at the age of twenty and later holding the posts of majority whip, speaker pro tempore, and majority leader.

Call unto me, and I will answer thee, and shew thee great and mighty things, which thou knowest not.
(Jeremiah 33:3, KJV)

The discipline of prayer is vital in the life of a believer. Through prayer, we are able to communicate directly with God in times of trial and triumph, knowing He is faithful to provide answers beyond our human understanding. We only have to ask. I am consistently humbled by the hundreds of friends across the nation who have my wife, Mary Wood, and me on their prayer lists. In my opinion, there's no more important list to make. Prayer strengthens my eyes of faith to see God's hand working out every daily detail and situation that may affect our entire state to His honor and glory.

January 16

MINDY BEATY, student, Georgia State University; 1994 graduate, Alexander High School, Douglasville, Georgia, whose activities included spearheading a committee that organized safety programs in Douglas County schools over a two-year period after four friends not wearing seat belts were killed in two separate car crashes; launching two community food drives for the needy and workshops on nutrition and hunger-related issues; and producing a newsletter on local pollution issues; named Douglas County 4-H'er of the Year, 1993, 1991, 1990.

> For the Lord says, "Because he loves me, I will rescue him; I will make him great because he trusts in my name. When he calls on me I will answer; I will be with him in trouble, and rescue him and honor him. I will satisfy him with a full life and give him my salvation."
> (Psalm 91:14–16, TLB)

Several years ago, when I was in the ninth grade, I was recovering from a back injury sustained in a car accident. I had been active in several sports, but after the injury, I couldn't engage in the sports anymore and probably not excessively for the rest of my life. I felt like a lot of doors had been closed. I still trusted in the Lord, and it was at this time that I first became really familiar with these verses and pulled strength from them, because they state that when we love God, He'll take care of us and give us a full life. That really affected me because at the time I seemed to be very weak physically and a little bit spiritually. I soon found ways to engage in new activities, like community service, to share my love for God and His love for everyone. I had always been somewhat involved in community service, but now it was like a constant flow of motivation. One thing led to another, and I'd see a problem and do something about it, like learning about worldwide hunger at summer camp and initiating a community food drive after I got home. When I go to the nursing home and folks tell me about their backs hurting, I can really relate and understand their hurts. Anytime I find myself getting down or if my back becomes especially painful, I turn to these verses. They comfort me and remind me that God is in control. It's hard to look at a permanent back injury as a blessing, but it really has been.

January 17

DAVID BECKMANN, president since 1991, Bread for the World, 44,000-member grassroots Christian citizens' movement founded in 1974, lobbying in Washington for U.S. policies to address root causes of hunger and poverty in the United States and overseas; the previous fifteen years, he was an economist with the World Bank, working in more than seventy countries; Lutheran minister and former relief and development worker in Bangladesh; coauthor, with Richard A. Hoehn, of *Transforming the Politics of Hunger.*

> "... if you have faith as a grain of mustard seed, you will say to this mountain, 'Move hence to yonder place,' and it will move; and nothing will be impossible to you."
> *(Matthew 17:21, RSV)*

I am reassured that God asks so little of us and promises so much. We need only look to God with a mustard seed of faith, and God works through us mightily.

January 18

LOU B. BEVILL, wife of former U.S. Congressman Tom Bevill of Alabama; concert pianist who performs a number of times each year in Washington and Alabama and also performs duo-piano programs with partner Doris Vance Harmon; member and past president, Congressional Wives Fellowship Group; member, Congressional Wives Mental Health Group, and frequent speaker on mental health matters.

If I take the wings of the morning, and dwell in the uttermost parts of the sea; Even there shall thy hand lead me, and thy right hand shall hold me. (Psalm 139:9–10, KJV)

These verses have been my guide and comfort for most of my life. They tell me that through anguish or indecision—or whatever my troubles—He is with me. He directs and enables me. If I should fall, He will pick me up and set me on the right path. In life or death, He is with me. That is all I need to know.

January 19

LONISE BIAS, mother of Len Bias, University of Maryland basketball star and first-round Boston Celtics pick in 1986 who died of a drug overdose two days after the draft at age twenty-two; one of her other three children, Jay, was murdered at a Washington-area mall in 1990 at age twenty; after Len's death, she became a public speaker emphasizing in schools, community and church appearances, and TV interviews that young people are "reachable, teachable, lovable, and savable."

For God so loved the world, that he gave his only begotten Son, that whosoever believeth in him should not perish, but have everlasting life. (John 3:16, KJV)

In my grieving period after Len's death, I was asking the Lord, "Why, why, why, why, why?" I remember being in our family room and a minister was on TV. I heard him say something so profound—the words of John 3:16—though I had known this Scripture all along. But it was revealed anew in my heart that the Lord had given His only begotten Son for humanity to be redeemed. Because He had given His Son, I would be able to see my son again in eternity. The Lord also reminded me, "You lost

Len, but you still have a husband and three children you can love." That particular Scripture helps me when I think of the price that was paid for us to embrace and have a part of eternity. Something had to be willfully given. His Son was given unto us. When we go through things that hurt us, we often don't understand how God's love operates. We just want life to be hunky-dory, sweet and smooth. But God has a love that sometimes can be very hard. We often think of the characteristics of God as kindness, gentleness, and so on—and God does have those characteristics—but He also has a love that can come in many forms. All that God had placed in me before the death of my son, for example, and all that was taught to me while I was going through his death—there were spiritual treasures God was storing up within me, and it was a sweet fragrance, but only I was getting the fragrance. In order for the fragrance to come out, I had to be broken. The alabaster box, so to speak, had to be broken. And that brokenness was God's love, even though it hurt. God gave His Son and because of all that His Son went through, we can have eternal life. One thing I think hinders the body of Christ is that we get too hung up in this life; we don't think eternal or walk in the eternal. Even though we are saved and we love the Lord, we know our Scriptures, and we're involved in the church, we still have not really embraced the eternal—that whoever believes in Him should have life everlasting.

January 20

BRIAN BIRD, producer, ABC series *Step by Step;* with partner John Wierick, penned the 1993 Paramount Pictures film *Bopha!* and wrote for the CBS series *Evening Shade* and *The Family Man;* former director of public relations, World Vision relief organization; former reporter, *San Gabriel Valley Tribune.*

Though I am free and belong to no man, I make myself a slave to everyone, to win as many as possible. To the Jews

I became like a Jew, to win the Jews. To those under the law I became like one under the law (though I myself am not under the law), so as to win those under the law. To those not having the law I became like one not having the law (though I am not free from God's law but am under Christ's law), so as to win those not having the law. To the weak I became weak, to win the weak. I have become all things to all men so that by all possible means I might save some. (1 Corinthians 9:19–23, NIV)

As our culture becomes increasingly polarized over the issue of faith—whether it be caused by our society's drift toward secularism or by our own failed example of what Christianity is all about—this passage speaks to the urgent need for Christians to come down off their self-righteous soapboxes and try getting their hands dirty for a change. We need to stop expecting lost people to find their own way into our church pews and start taking the gospel to them, whether they live in cardboard boxes on skid row or in the high-rises of Hollywood's media elite. Nonbelievers will not be bludgeoned, guilted, shamed, or boycotted into the kingdom. But they will respond to people who truly care about them. Even Christians.

January 21

TULLY BLANCHARD, evangelist and director of men's and prison ministries, Central Church of God, Charlotte, North Carolina; president, Ring of Truth Ministries, Inc.; former wrestler with National Wrestling Alliance, noted as one of the "Four Horsemen," and World Wrestling Federation, winning tag team championships in both organizations.

But as many as received him, to them gave he power to become the sons of God, even to them that believe on his name: Which were born, not of blood, nor of the will of the flesh, nor of the will of man, but of God. (John 1:12–13, KJV)

Every time a decision has to be made, large or small, I have to go back to 4:00 A.M., November 13, 1989. Is it real . . . or just a psychological game I'm playing? The answer is the same every time. God chose me. God saved me. God changed me. I belong to God; therefore, my decision making has to line up with God's Word and God's plan for Tully. Tully shouldn't be lord anymore.

Back in August 1989, my partner and I were one of the main events—the Brain Busters versus Demolition—for the World Wrestling Federation tag team championship at Madison Square Garden. That was the mecca of sports stadiums, in my opinion, and I got to walk the aisle, with 21,000 screaming people on hand. My name was on the marquee. But not long after that, instead of worrying about making money and paying my bills, I let my greed take over. I didn't think the WWF was paying me enough, and I struck a deal to go to World Championship Wrestling on Turner Broadcasting for $5,000 a week for three years, $750,000 in all. I had to give a sixty-day notice, and about thirty days into it, I got careless. I failed a drug test and the WWF suspended me on November 2. But I didn't think that was a problem because I'd already made the deal with World Championship Wrestling. I went home for eleven days, played golf, worked out, and thought life was coming up roses.

And then on November 13, at one o'clock in the morning, I got a phone call from fellow wrestler Ric Flair and he said, "They're not going to honor their agreement with you because of what happened with the WWF. They're not going to hire you." At one o'clock in the morning, that $5,000 a week was gone. I lay in my bed and tossed and turned and tossed and turned—until four o'clock when the words "Jesus Christ, take over my life" came out. You might think that was understandable, but this is a man who had never been to church, except maybe five times with my grandma when I was a little boy. I didn't have the knowledge to say, "Jesus Christ, take over my life." God, in the power of the Holy Spirit, came down and put the words in my mouth and in my brain, and the peace of God that passes all understanding came over me, and God lulled me to sleep.

At 7:30 that morning when I woke up, I didn't question what I had said. I didn't say, "Whoa, wait just a minute. What am I doing?" I went to the closet and got out a Bible that my parents had mailed me, and I started reading it. I pulled out the tapes they had been mailing me and listened to sermons three times a day. God came down with a mighty move of the Holy Spirit and changed my heart and changed my life. No man can describe the feeling that is in you when Jesus Christ comes into your heart and you know you're going to heaven. You know because you know, because you know, because you know.

January 22

HERBERT BLOMSTEDT, music director, San Francisco Symphony, 1986–95; 1992 Grammy winner, best performance of a choral work, conducting the San Francisco Girls/Boys Chorus, SFS Chorus, and San Francisco Symphony in Carl Orff's *Carmina Burana;* former music director, Germany's Dresden Staatskapelle, the world's oldest orchestra, the Oslo Philharmonic, Danish Radio Symphony, Swedish Radio Symphony, and Sweden's Norrkoping Symphony.

Thus will I bless thee while I live: I will lift up my hands in thy name. (Psalm 63:4, KJV)

Psalm 63:4 is a fine motto for a symphony conductor. The conductor serves the music, and together we serve the Creator. What a privilege! We are on holy ground.

January 23

MARTHA BOLTON, staff writer for Bob Hope the past thirteen years who also writes for Phyllis Diller, Ann Jillian, and Mark Lowry; author of twenty-three books of humor, beginning with *A Funny Thing Happened to Me on My Way Through the Bible;* "The Cafeteria Lady" columnist for *Brio* teen girls' magazine.

> . . . *the cheerful heart has a continual feast.*
> *(Proverbs 15:15, NIV)*

This Scripture doesn't say that the cheerful heart has joy only in the good times. It says it has a *continual* feast—in the good times, the bad times, when we get that grocery cart with all four wheels going in opposite directions, when that instant teller machine pretends it's never heard of us and swallows our card, when we get a flat tire in front of our child's school (and we're in our bathrobe and reindeer slippers). We can have a feast of joy twenty-four hours a day, no matter what comes our way. God created each of us with a sense of humor. This Scripture has been a great reminder to me of the importance of using it.

January 24

PAT BOONE, national chairman and host of the Easter Seal Society Telethon since 1981; National Day of Prayer cochairman; singer whose recordings, such as "Love Letters in the Sand" and "Ain't That a Shame," have passed 45 million in sales and, during the rock and roll era, kept him on Billboard's charts a record 200 consecutive weeks; featured in fifteen films, including *State Fair* and *All Hands on Deck;* author of ten books, including million-seller *A New Song,* and coauthor of two books with wife Shirley; host of *The Gospel America* weekly Trinity Broadcasting Network telecast; 1979 recipient of the Israel Cultural Award, the nation's highest honor for non-natives.

*. . . work out your own salvation with fear and trembling;
for it is God who works in you both to will and to do for
His good pleasure. (Philippians 2:12–13, NKJV)*

This Scripture literally changed my life. For thirty years I knew
and tried to obey verse 12, with diminishing results. It seems
cold and forbidding, like much "religion." Finally I read verse
13, and everything changed. God will do it! All we have to say is
"yes" to Him, and He will work His salvation, His joy, and His
purpose through every part of our lives by His Spirit. Simply
and quietly permitting Him, inviting Him to work His will in and
through me has made all the exciting difference.

January 25

ANN BOWDEN, wife of Bobby Bowden, head football coach,
Florida State University, mother of Terry Bowden, head coach at
Auburn University in Alabama, and three other sons, two of
whom are in coaching, and two daughters; civic activities include public affairs chairperson, Florida Association of Child
and Family Agencies, which lobbies for legislation and funding
for residential homes for abused and neglected children.

*A wife of noble character who can find?
She is worth far more than rubies.
Her husband has full confidence in her
and lacks nothing of value. . . .
She is clothed with strength and dignity;
she can laugh at the days to come.
She speaks with wisdom,
and faithful instruction is on her tongue.
She watches over the affairs of her household
and does not eat the bread of idleness.
Her children arise and call her blessed;
her husband also, and he praises her. . . .
(Proverbs 31:10–11, 25–28, NIV)*

I think that just as we choose God as our personal Savior, He chooses us for certain tasks here on earth. I felt that God called me first to be a wife and mother and a good support system for my family. I always wanted to be the best wife and mother I could be. In these verses, Solomon describes what a good wife and mother should be. I pray that in some small way I have fulfilled God's calling to me. Other passages of Scripture have spoken to me over the years as well. I was a very young wife and mother. There were many days when I didn't know which way to turn, and I found comfort in Proverbs 3:5–6: "Trust in the Lord with all your heart. . . ." I tried very hard to raise my children in the right way, heeding Proverbs 22:6: "Train up a child in the way he should go. . . ." Caring for a family of six children can be difficult at times, to say the least. I found a lot of encouragement in Paul's letter to the Philippians, chapter 4, verse 13: "I can do everything through him who gives me strength." I have never doubted God's words spoken through Paul in Romans 8:28: ". . . in all things God works for the good of those who love him, who have been called according to his purpose." Maybe one of the most important verses of all is 1 John 4:16: ". . . God is love. Whoever lives in love lives in God, and God in him." God's love is the most important ingredient in life; it is humankind's greatest need, the answer to so many of the world's problems.

January 26

BOBBY BOWDEN, head football coach, Florida State University, since 1977; national champions, 1993; second among active college coaches in career victories, 259 in twenty-nine seasons; the only NCAA Division 1 coach to post nine consecutive ten-win seasons, 1987–95, finishing in the AP poll's top four each year; father of Auburn University head coach Terry Bowden; author, with Bill Smith, of autobiography, *It's More Than Just a Game.*

*I can do all things through Christ which strengtheneth
me. (Philippians 4:13, KJV)*

No man can be the ultimate without the strength of a higher
source. That source comes from God in Christ. If it is God's
will, no man nor power on earth can stop me.

January 27

TERRY BOWDEN, head football coach, Auburn University,
who led the Tigers to an 11–0 record in 1993, the first coach to
post an undefeated, untied record in his first season in Division
IA; 1993 Football News Coach of the Year; son of Bobby
Bowden, head football coach at Florida State University; former
head coach at Salem College in West Virginia and Samford
University in Alabama.

*I can do all things through Christ which strengtheneth
me. (Philippians 4:13, KJV)*

I believe in having a positive attitude that instills belief in yourself, your talents, your purpose here on earth, and the fact that
God wants us to boldly make a difference with our lives. This
verse tells us exactly that.

January 28

FORREST BOYD, news director, UNI (United News and
Information) radio network and "Another View" radio commentator for UPI; former chief correspondent, Standard News
radio network, Washington, D.C.; cofounder of the former
International Media Service, the first radio news network for
Christian radio stations; previously White House correspondent, Mutual Broadcasting System, eleven years.

*Try to realize what this means—the Lord is God! He
made us—we are his people, the sheep of his pasture.
(Psalm 100:3, TLB)*

This verse has caused me to think about how great and powerful God is . . . how awesome. And then to realize that He is my Lord, my friend, and my redeemer. The very suggestion that such a great God takes a personal interest in me is food for thought and wonder for the rest of my life.

January 29

SID BREAM, Houston Astros infielder whose twelve-year career also includes a World Series with the Atlanta Braves, 1992, and National League Championship Series with the Braves, 1991, and Pittsburgh Pirates, 1990, when he also won the major leagues' Hutch Award as the player who best overcame adversity, after three knee surgeries in 1989; major league record holder for assists by a first baseman in a season, 166 in 1986.

Trust in the LORD with all thine heart; and lean not unto thine own understanding. In all thy ways acknowledge him, and he shall direct thy paths. (Proverbs 3:5–6, KJV)

These verses have meant a lot to me over the years, because of the circumstances I have gone through in my baseball career. When the future looked bleak because of my injuries and I was struggling in my mind and heart to know what to do, my Savior comforted me by letting me know that He would lead me. I did not have to face alone the uncertainty of what was going to take place in the future. I knew, because of this promise, that God would take me by the hand and lead me through those trials, as well as other trials that would be ahead. My wisdom doesn't compare with God's wisdom.

January 30

BILL BRIGHT, president, Campus Crusade for Christ International, which he and his wife, Vonette, founded in 1951; from a campus ministry, it has grown to more than forty special thrusts, to groups such as executives, families, athletes, inner-city residents, prisoners, women, and men; 1996 winner of the Templeton Prize for Progress in Religion; author of numerous books and booklets, including *The Coming Revival: America's Call to Fast, Pray, and "Seek God's Face"* and *The Four Spiritual Laws,* now with more than 1.5 billion copies distributed in most major languages of the world.

> *He told his disciples, "I have been given all authority in heaven and earth. Therefore go and make disciples in all the nations, baptizing them into the name of the Father and of the Son and of the Holy Spirit, and then teach these new disciples to obey all the commands I have given you; and be sure of this—that I am with you always, even to the end of the world." (Matthew 28:18–20, TLB)*

I try to evaluate everything I do every day in light of the Great Commission—the way I spend my time, my speaking engagements, the books and articles I write, and the people with whom I meet. Everything else—all the achievements of life, such as fame, fortune, praise, applause of men, and power—is relatively unimportant. Jesus came to seek and save the lost, and in His Great Commission He gives His followers the privilege of continuing what He came to this world 2,000 years ago to do. The movement with which I am associated as founder and president, with a staff of more than 13,000 and trained volunteers and associates numbering more than 100,000, has had the privilege of helping present the gospel to more than 1.5 billion people, counting presentations of the film we produced in the late 1970s titled *Jesus.* That film has now been viewed by more than 600 million people, in more than 300 languages, and in 216 countries. Tens of millions have indicated salvation decisions as a result. For me, the Great Commission is the greatest challenge ever given by the greatest Person who ever lived.

Linked to this Great Commission is another passage, John 14:12–14, where our Lord says, "In solemn truth I tell you, anyone believing in me shall do the same miracles I have done, and even greater ones, because I am going to be with the Father. You can ask him for anything, using my name, and I will do it, for this will bring praise to the Father because of what I, the Son, will do for you. Yes, ask anything, using my name, and I will do it!" (TLB). The Lord Jesus Christ, in whom dwells all the fullness of the Godhead bodily (Colossians 2:9), the visible expression of the invisible God (Colossians 1:15), the One to whom God has given all authority in heaven and earth (Matthew 28:18), has promised that He will enable us, through His indwelling presence in our bodies as His temples, to accomplish in and through our lives more than He accomplished while here on earth (John 14:12). That is the reason I am so confident the Great Commission will be fulfilled, because it is not our responsibility but His. All He wants of His followers is that we love Him with all our heart, soul, mind, and strength and that we trust His promises and obey His commands. He will then give us wisdom, grace, favor, manpower, finances—everything we need—to accomplish all that He has called us to do.

January 31

VONETTE BRIGHT, cofounder with husband Bill, Campus Crusade for Christ International in 1951, now with more than 13,500 full-time staff members and 90,000-plus trained volunteers ministering in 165 countries; she chaired the National Day of Prayer Task Force nine years and led efforts for congressional legislation in 1988 designating the first Thursday in May as the National Day of Prayer each year; author and editor of several books, including two prayer manuals and *The Greatest Lesson I've Ever Learned* compilation of reflections by two dozen prominent women.

*Casting the whole of your care—all your anxieties, all
your worries, all of your concerns, once and for all—on
Him; for He cares for you affectionately, and cares about
you watchfully. (1 Peter 5:7, amplified)*

One of my dearest friends and mentors, the late Henrietta Mears
(whose biography, *Dream Big*, 1990, was compiled by Earl
Roe), gave me this verse at a time when I was expressing something of concern to her. I had heard her share it as one of her favorite verses when she was teaching the college department at
Hollywood Presbyterian Church. But when she shared it with
me personally, it took on new meaning. She explained that being
heavily burdened with our cares robs us of our joy, our assurance, our confidence; it is as if we carry our burdens in our right
hand. She explained that Jesus asked us to hand over our burdens to Him, to cast them upon Him. She graphically took me
through casting the burdens in my right hand to the Lord, as if
He were my left hand. She helped me realize that as I turn loose
of those burdens, Jesus is carrying them. No longer am I burdened, overly concerned, unhappy, without joy and assurance.
The problem now belongs to the Lord.

I realize that it's not handing burdens over visually from one
hand to the other that is the solution to my problems, but it
does help to illustrate the principle. The Lord will carry my burden, that I might be free and creative and prayerful, rejoicing
and praising and giving thanks that the problem or concern is
not mine—it now belongs to God. Henrietta Mears said that as
you have given the gift to the Lord, "stop stealing His property." I have carried that illustration a step further in suggesting
to people that we put all our burdens, cares, worries, anxieties,
and concerns into a box, tie it with a ribbon, and consider it as a
gift to God. It now belongs to Him and He carries all our concerns. As it belongs to Him, we do not take it back. I have been

reminded many times when facing difficulty, cares, and anxieties that I am not handing my burdens over quickly enough so Jesus can carry them. He accomplishes the solution. He gives me wisdom and enables me to cope. Praise God for His Word that gives us solutions and does not leave us with problems.

FEBRUARY

February 1

BOB BRINER, president, ProServe Television, since 1979; producer of various sports series and one-time specials, including *A Hard Road to Glory*, with Arthur Ashe and Bryan Polivka, which won an Emmy in 1987; former positions include chairman, Men's International Professional Tennis Council, worldwide Grand Prix circuit governing body; executive director, Association of Tennis Professionals; and cofounder and first executive director, World Championship Tennis; author, *Roaring Lambs, Squeeze Play: Caught Between Business and Home, Lambs Among Wolves,* and *The Management Methods of Jesus.*

> *Do everything without complaining or arguing, so that you may become blameless and pure, children of God without fault in a crooked and depraved generation, in which you shine like stars in the universe, as you hold out the word of life....* (Philippians 2:14–16, NIV)

As a guy in sports, I am impressed by this passage's phrase *shine like stars.* What that means to me is to do everything we do as excellently as possible so that we may reflect the excellence of the Savior and draw people to Him. It's not that we need to be at the top of the ladder. Sometimes as Christians we're tempted to use the fact that we're Christians as an excuse not to do things in a first-class way, and that's a mistake. Through the years it's become more and more evident in my life that we need to make a commitment to put forth an extra effort to do and be the best that we individually can.

February 2

BILL BROOKS, wide receiver, Washington Redskins; with the Buffalo Bills from 1993 to 1995, he caught seven passes in Super Bowl XXVIII; with the Indianapolis Colts from 1986 to 1992, he became the second-leading receiver in team history behind Raymond Berry; 1986 National Football League Players Association Offensive Rookie of the Year.

Trust in the LORD with all your heart
and lean not on your own understanding;
in all your ways acknowledge him,
and he will make your paths straight.
(Proverbs 3:5–6, NIV)

Even though a lot of things go on in your life—things you worry about or things that concern you—if you trust in the Lord and put Him first, He will take care of them, because He knows what's going on long before you do. A lot of times you get caught up in everyday life and get swamped with trying to figure out things for yourself. I do. And I usually end up messing them up. But once I put things in the Lord's hands, He takes care of them.

As a free agent after the 1992 football season, for example, I was having a hard time deciding whether to stay in Indianapolis or play for another team. My wife, Holly, said we needed to pray about it, leave it in the Lord's hands, and He would open doors for us and close doors to show us where He wanted us to go. It was during that time that I read anew Proverbs 3:5–6. I had been leaning on my own understanding, trying to do it myself, and getting more and more confused. But when I prayed about it and put it in the Lord's hands, He indeed opened doors and closed doors and made my decision: that Buffalo was the team for me.

And I was very happy about being in Buffalo. I had the opportunity to play in the Super Bowl, but most of all, I grew spiritually by being up there with the other believers on the team, guys like Frank Reich, Pete Metzelaars, Don Beebe, Steve Tasker, Mark Pike, and others. It's been great being around other believers. So, that Scripture has meant a lot to me, not just football-wise but in my spiritual growth as well.

February 3

JAMES "J. B." BROWN, cohost with Terry Bradshaw of *Fox NFL Sunday* network pregame telecast; anchor for Fox's National Hockey League telecasts; previously with CBS Sports ten years, his assignments included cohost of the NCAA basketball championship, host of the 1992 Winter Olympics weekday program, and reporting during the NBA Finals; former sportscaster in Washington, D.C., and analyst for Washington Bullets TV broadcasts; three-time All–Ivy League basketball player at Harvard University.

He that dwelleth in the secret place of the most High shall abide under the shadow of the Almighty. I will say of the LORD, He is my refuge and my fortress: my God; in him will I trust. (Psalm 91:1–2, KJV)

These verses, and all of Psalm 91, have played an integral part in helping me lay a foundation with the Lord, and I meditate on these verses frequently. I seek to be diligent in keeping my appointment time with the Lord every morning. In the midst of the busy travel schedule that I keep, even if I'm on an airplane, I try to make time to be quiet and in prayer, just to make certain I am being recharged and energized, giving Him the thanks for another day of life, and being mindful of keeping my mind focused on Him. I can see the difference when I don't. With the daily press of activities, it's easy not to be in control of oneself, to get rushed and stressed out and not walk in love. In the business I'm in—which, like many others, is very competitive—it's easy for some people to misinterpret my kindness for weakness, when I clearly know that any success I enjoy comes from the Lord. I have a very serious work ethic, and I certainly look to be accomplished and successful—but to His praise and glory.

February 4

SHERRY BLOCK BRYANT, 1992 U.S. national champion in women's archery (outdoors); member of the 1992 U.S. Olympic Team; 1990 Olympic Festival gold medalist.

. . . Not by might, nor by power, but by my Spirit, says the Lord of Hosts. . . . (Zechariah 4:6, TLB)

My friend Marie wrote this verse and a few others on index cards and gave them to me before I went to my Olympic Trials in May 1992. During the trials, this verse kept coming to mind over and over again. Continuously I was reminded not to rely on my own ability but to rely on the power of the Holy Spirit working through me. The whole tournament was in His hands and He knew what the outcome would be. I just had to trust in Him and use the talent He had given me to His glory.

February 5

LORRAINE BUCKLEY, professional registered parliamentarian since 1961, Independence, Missouri; president, National Association of Parliamentarians, 1975–77; president, Missouri State Association of Parliamentarians, 1965–66; mother of eight children now with sixteen grandchildren; she served on the Independence (Missouri) Public Schools Board of Education nearly twelve years.

But they that wait upon the LORD *shall renew their*
strength; they shall mount up with wings as eagles; they
shall run, and not be weary; and they shall walk, and not
faint. (Isaiah 40:31, KJV)

The first time I read this Scripture, I had just returned from a
morning at vacation Bible school. It was toward the end of the
second week, the weather had been extremely hot, and I came
home with three hungry children to be fed and put down for
naps. That accomplished, my thoughts turned to some rest for
myself and, before I lay down, I took my Bible and let the pages
fall open to a Scripture I had asked the Lord to reveal to me—
a promise I needed to meet the needs of the day. Isaiah 40:31
was the Scripture. There have been times since then, with eight
children, that I needed the assurance of that verse. I have found
that if I wait on the Lord and turn my thoughts upward to Him,
that promise is truly mine.

February 6

TIM BURKE, relief pitcher who left baseball in 1992, ex-
plaining at the time, "I'm the only father my children have. I'm
the only husband my wife has. And they need me a lot more
than baseball does"; he and Christine had adopted four special-
needs children from abroad, since adding a fifth; author, with
Christine, of *Major League Dad*; highlights from his eight years
in the majors, with the Montreal Expos and New York Yankees
and Mets, included 1989 All-Star appearance (two scoreless in-
nings), all-time record for most games by a rookie pitcher, and
career 2.72 ERA.

Cast all your anxiety on him because he cares for you.
(1 Peter 5:7, NIV)

I've always hung on to 1 Peter 5:7, the verse that, basically,
brought me to the Lord. Back in 1982, Christine and I went to

our first Bible study, which a couple was leading for players and their wives. We both knew we weren't Christians, but I just didn't want to give up running my life. For three months I kept running from the Lord. Then I came across this verse, 1 Peter 5:7. What hit it home to me was that if He loved me—if He loved me with my drinking problem and wanted my drinking problem, and if He wanted my marriage problems and my pitching problems (I was in AA and having a terrible year)— then I figured, man, He must really love me a lot. That's when I became a Christian, August 25, 1982. And so did my wife, right along with me that day.

February 7

LARRY BURKETT, founder and president, Christian Financial Concepts, Inc., teaching biblical principles of money management through various printed resources, a monthly newsletter, and a national network of 1,000 volunteer financial counselors; author of numerous books, including *The Coming Economic Earthquake, What Ever Happened to the American Dream,* and two novels, *The Illuminati* and *The THOR Conspiracy;* featured on daily radio broadcasts *Money Matters* and *How to Manage Your Money* on more than 1,000 stations; former positions include supervisor of a NASA experiments test facility in the Mercury, Gemini, and Apollo programs, vice president of an electronics manufacturing firm, and financial counselor with Campus Crusade for Christ.

> *And He said to them, "Beware, and be on your guard against every form of greed; for not even when one has an abundance does his life consist of his possessions."*
> *(Luke 12:15, NASB)*

A number of years ago, as a financial counselor I began to realize that people's financial problems were often symptoms of deeper, spiritual problems in their lives. Treating the symptoms would help them temporarily. But then the next crisis would hit, and once again they would find themselves struggling under the weight of financial pressures. That's why I believe the concept of "financial freedom" is so important for us to grasp. When we surrender every area of our lives—including our finances—to God, then we are free to trust Him to meet our needs. But if we would rather hold tightly to those things that we possess, then we find ourselves in bondage to those very things.

February 8

MARGARET E. BURKS, at age eighty-one, oldest master of divinity graduate in New Orleans Baptist Theological Seminary's nearly eighty-year history, receiving her degree in May 1996; head auditor, Internal Revenue Service Appellate Division, Atlanta, 1950–62, who joined the IRS as an agent in 1935; youth camp director, Chattahoochee Baptist Association, the past twenty-three years.

Faithful is he that calleth you, who also will do it.
(1 Thessalonians 5:24, KJV)

1 Thessalonians 5:24 is the verse God gave me as I flew to Monrovia, Liberia, West Africa, on the first of ten mission trips there. After my husband Jesse's death in 1985, the Lord began to open doors for me to go on mission trips around the world. Having never flown much, I asked God for a Bible verse of my very own. He said to me: "Faithful is He who calls you, who also will do it!" I have carried this verse with me on the ten trips to Liberia; five to Panama; two to Peru; and one each to Singapore, Hong Kong, China, and Ecuador. God never asks us to do anything for which He has not already prepared us, and He makes the way of doing it easy! The first thing they asked me in Liberia was, "Mother,"—they don't call you mother unless you are over fifty—"how old are you?" I replied, "I'm seventeen—backward!" God waited until I was seventy-one to send me out in His

vineyard to gather His harvest. In Liberia, I was known as "Mud Mother," as I mixed the mortar for building churches there. One day, one of the men on our construction team became ill and I was promoted to "block layer"! From that day on, I laid the blocks for the pulpit end of the eight churches we built there. Now, at age eighty-one, I have received my master of divinity degree at New Orleans Baptist Theological Seminary. God has some wonderful things out there for me to do—and all I have to say, like Isaiah, is, "Here am I; send me." Truly, God is faithful, and He who calls you will do it!

February 9

TERESA YINGLING BURNS, director, National Association of Senior Friends, Columbia/HCA Healthcare Corporation, Nashville, Tennessee; conference speaker, church choir director, and author, *I Planned for Life and Look What Happened: Keeping the Faith in Times of Change.*

> *Trust in the LORD with all your heart,*
> *And lean not on your own understanding;*
> *In all your ways acknowledge Him,*
> *And He shall direct your paths. (Proverbs 3:5–6, NKJV)*

I remember falling into God's trustworthy arms when the "Critter Ridder" caught six possums living in the ventilation system of my abode, when my parents lost their home in Hurricane Andrew, and when returning home from a funeral I discovered fire and smoke coming from my apartment building. I believe trust frees faith during life's surprises and humor during life's ironies.

February 10

EVA BURROWS, retired Thirteenth General, The Salvation Army, 1986–93, only the second woman to hold the post as salvationist world leader; commissioned as a Salvation Army officer in 1951, her assignments included territorial commander, first in Sri Lanka and subsequently in Scotland and southern Australia; leader of Women's Social Services, Great Britain and Ireland; vice-principal and then principal, International College for Officers, London; principal, Usher Institute for girls in Rhodesia (now Zimbabwe); officer teacher and, later, vice-principal and head of the Teachers' College, Howard Institute, Rhodesia.

> *. . . that in all things he [Jesus Christ] might have the preeminence. (Colossians 1:18, KJV)*

Whether as a young missionary educator in Africa or a Salvation Army commander in Asia, whether among the homeless street people in London or the hopeful unemployed youths in our programs in Australia, whether preaching to crowds in the open air or administering in the position of worldwide responsibility as General, I have found that this verse never ceases to express my total ambition—to lift up Jesus Christ as the light of the world and the brightness of my own life.

February 11

BRETT BUTLER, Los Angeles Dodgers outfielder whose 1996 season was disrupted by throat cancer surgery in May and subsequent radiation treatments; 1991 All-Star, setting National League season record for most games without an error by an outfielder, 161; recorded 307-game errorless streak and, in fourteen major-league seasons, committed just thirty-eight errors; one of only twenty-six players in baseball history to record more than 2,000 hits and 500 stolen bases; first player in National League history to lead the league in singles four straight seasons, 1990–93; International League most valuable player, 1979.

Behold, I stand at the door, and knock: if any man hear my voice, and open the door, I will come in to him, and will sup with him, and he with me. (Revelation 3:20, KJV)

While in college I had a dream that my father died. I went home and asked him, "Dad, I had a dream that you died, and I have to ask you if you were to die tonight, would you go to heaven?" That's probably why Revelation 3:20 sticks out in my mind, because he quoted that verse to me and said, "Son, I have opened the door of my heart and have asked Christ into my heart. If I were to die, I know I would have a place in heaven."

February 12

CALVIN O. BUTTS III, pastor and, previously, executive minister, Abyssinian Baptist Church, Harlem; during his twenty-five years with the church, he has initiated various community development projects; a former president of the Organization of African American Clergy, he led a campaign against police brutality and, more recently, campaigns against rap music lyrics that condone violence or demean women and against exploitative billboard advertising in Harlem.

One thing have I desired of the LORD, that will I seek after; that I may dwell in the house of the LORD all the days of my life, to behold the beauty of the LORD, and to inquire in his temple. (Psalm 27:4, KJV)

This Scripture keeps me centered in my faith and my calling as a minister. Whenever I think that my life will be consumed by politics or other civic and social activity, this verse helps me to realize what God has called me to do.

February 13

RICHARD G. CAPEN, JR., U.S. ambassador to Spain, 1992–93; vice chairman, Knight-Ridder, Inc., newspaper chain/

communications company, 1987–92; chairman and publisher, *The Miami Herald*, 1983–89; previous positions include senior vice president for operations, Knight-Ridder; senior vice president, Copley Newspapers; and assistant to Secretary of Defense Melvin Laird, 1968–71; author of *Finish Strong.*

> *For we are God's workmanship, created in Christ Jesus to do good works, which God prepared in advance for us to do. (Ephesians 2:10, NIV)*

This verse has been a powerful motivator in my life and career. Over the years, as a newspaper publisher and as a diplomat, I have been blessed with hundreds of opportunities to offer hope to others. In the process, I have tried to uplift the lives of good people. I believe it has been the Lord's calling for me.

February 14

BEN CARSON, M.D., director, pediatric neurosurgery, Johns Hopkins University Medical Center, Baltimore; he also holds the titles of associate professor of neurological surgery, associate professor of oncology, assistant professor of pediatrics, and associate professor of plastic surgery; coauthor of two books, *Think Big* and *Gifted Hands,* his autobiography, both with Cecil Murphey.

> *Trust in the LORD with all thine heart; and lean not unto thine own understanding. In all thy ways acknowledge him, and he shall direct thy paths. (Proverbs 3:5–6, KJV)*

This passage is particularly meaningful to me and has guided my professional career. I feel that the power of God in my life is what has led to my success and will continue to provide success as long as I realize it is God, and not I, who is responsible for the many wonderful achievements. The verse says, "In all thy ways acknowledge him." I believe that means being willing to take a public stand for God, and I will continue to do so. At first, this caused some people to regard me as strange, but in recent years many colleagues have asked me how to develop a relationship with God and how to pray. I believe that is what witnessing is all about.

February 15

GARY CARTER, Hall of Fame–bound eleven-time National League All-Star catcher, twice winning the game's Most Valuable Player award, 1981, 1984; third on all-time major league list for games caught, 2,056; three-time Gold Glove winner for fielding; 1975 *Sporting News* Rookie of the Year; currently, broadcaster for the Florida Marlins.

> *Jesus answered, "I am the way and the truth and the life. No one comes to the Father except through me."*
> *(John 14:6, NIV)*

Knowing Jesus Christ on a personal basis—inviting Jesus into your life, to be able to know God and go to heaven—is the most important thing for me to understand in one day being able to see my mom again. I lost my mom to leukemia back in 1966 when I was twelve years old. In my mind and heart, heaven is where I believe she is because of how much God and being in church every week meant to her. The guy who led me to the Lord was John Boccabella. He was my roommate and a fellow catcher with the Montreal Expos back in 1973. I was just a young eighteen-year-old who was searching and trying to understand what life was all about. John would take me to mass and different things like that, and he was the one who initially gave me John 14:6 in spring training. March 22, 1973, is when I asked Christ into my life. This Scripture has stayed with me throughout my career and my adult life in seeking to be the best husband I can be to my wife, Sandy, and father to our two daughters, Christy and Kimmy, and son, D.J.

February 16

JIMMY CARTER, thirty-ninth U.S. president whose term included the Camp David Accords between Egypt and Israel and championing of human rights; governor of Georgia, 1971–75; author of *Talking Peace: A Vision for the Next Generation,* a book of poetry, *Always a Reckoning,* and nine other books; regular volunteer for Habitat for Humanity nonprofit organization to build homes for the needy worldwide.

> *And be ye kind one to another, tender-hearted, forgiving one another, even as God for Christ's sake hath forgiven you. (Ephesians 4:32, KJV)*

This verse expresses the importance of forgiving love, reciprocating in human terms what God through Christ has given us.

February 17

STEPHEN L. CARTER, professor of law, Yale Law School, where he has taught since 1982; author of four books, *Integrity, The Confirmation Mess: Cleaning Up the Federal Appointment Process, The Culture of Disbelief: How American Law and Politics Trivialize Religious Devotion,* and *Reflections of an Affirmative Action Baby;* law clerk under Supreme Court Justice Thurgood Marshall, 1980–81.

> *He has showed you, O man, what is good;*
> *and what does the LORD require of you*
> *but to do justice, and to love kindness,*
> *and to walk humbly with your God? (Micah 6:8, RSV)*

This verse captures the link between the Old and New Testaments and, for me as a Christian lawyer and writer, helps to remind me of my obligations, imposed by God, to be just and merciful. I believe that the law must balance the two and that humility, which we learn from Christ's example, helps us understand how to strike the balance.

February 18

JOHNNY CASH, featured on more than twenty-five country albums, from his 1956 release of *Folsom Prison Blues* to his 1996 *Unchained;* member of the Country Music Hall of Fame, Songwriters Hall of Fame, and Rock and Roll Hall of Fame; recipient of 1991 Grammy "Living Legend Award"; author of 1975 autobiography, *Man in Black.*

For if you live according to the sinful nature, you will die; but if by the Spirit you put to death the misdeeds of the body, you will live. . . . (Romans 8:13, NIV)

Years ago I claimed this Scripture as my own promise, and I feel there were many times a lifesaving situation was realized by turning to this Scripture for counsel. In other words, the Scriptures, or God speaking through them, have saved my life. This Scripture, especially.

February 19

JUNE CARTER CASH, singer-songwriter, with two Grammy Awards among her musical credits; wife of Johnny Cash, mother of seven, and author of *From the Heart,* a book of personal vignettes; she also has appeared in various film and network TV dramatic roles; her musical career began at age ten as a member of the famed Carter Family.

For he shall give his angels charge over thee, to keep thee in all thy ways. They shall bear thee up in their hands, lest thou dash thy foot against a stone. (Psalm 91:11–12, KJV)

Sometimes I don't really feel like I can make it without the wings of the angels, so I claim that promise and it's easy for me to fly.

February 20

KELLYE CASH, Miss America 1987.

Your beauty should not come from outward adornment,
such as braided hair and the wearing of gold jewelry and
fine clothes. Instead, it should be that of your inner self,
the unfading beauty of a gentle and quiet spirit, which is
of great worth in God's sight. (1 Peter 3:3–4, NIV)

When I find myself caught up in the "world's standard" of beauty and success (an easy thing to do when you're a former Miss America), I remember this verse. It has helped me in every area of my life as I remember to have a "gentle and quiet spirit" and surrender to what God wants in my life rather than what Kellye wants.

February 21

TRUETT CATHY, founder, president of Chick-fil-A, No. 3 chicken fast-food chain with more than 690 stores in thirty-three states; named by *Business Atlanta Magazine* as Most Admired CEO, 1990, and Entrepreneur of the Year, 1987; author of *It's Easier to Succeed Than to Fail.*

A good name is rather to be chosen than great riches.
(Proverbs 22:1, KJV)

When I was in grammar school, the teacher would select from one of the students a Scripture reference for the week. One morning my verse, chosen with the help of my mother, was the week's verse: Proverbs 22:1. That made an impression on me. Making correct choices is the way to build a reputation and the way to learn how to handle problems.

February 22

CHANDRA CHEESEBOROUGH, women's track coach, Tennessee State University, Nashville; 1984 Olympic gold medalist in the 400-meter and 1,600-meter relays, silver medalist in the 400 meters.

> *Who shall separate us from the love of God? Shall tribulation, or distress, or persecution, or famine, or nakedness, or peril, or sword? As it is written: "For Your sake we are killed all day long; / We are accounted as sheep for the slaughter." Yet in all things we are more than conquerors through Him who loved us. For I am persuaded that neither death nor life, nor angels nor principalities nor powers, nor things present nor things to come, nor height nor depth, nor any other created thing, shall be able to separate us from the love of God which is in Christ Jesus our Lord. (Romans 8:35–39, NKJV)*

This Scripture lets me know that nothing should separate me from the love of God; regardless of what comes up, I've got to be steadfast. I've been through a lot of trials and tribulations, but by being steadfast in the Word and knowing that these things are going to come—tribulation is going to come, stress is going to come—after I've done all I can do to stand, this Scripture lets me know I'm more than a conqueror. And I like that because a conqueror is someone who's already won. All I've got to do is be faithful.

February 23

JOEL CHERNOFF, general secretary, Messianic Jewish Alliance of America, a key organization in the Messianic movement since its founding in 1915; lead singer and songwriter for the musical group Lamb for twenty years, pioneers in Messianic music whose twelve albums have sold more than a half-million copies.

Shew me thy ways, O LORD; teach me thy paths. Lead me in thy truth, and teach me: for thou art the God of my salvation; on thee do I wait all the day. (Psalm 25:4–5, KJV)

In 1970, when I was twenty years old, these two verses became my life verses. I was experiencing a radical spiritual transformation from being a nominal believer in Yeshua (Jesus) to becoming one who could not get enough from God. This, by the way, was during the heat and passion of the revival called the Jesus Revolution. When I read these words written by King David, I knew he was describing the longing for God that was in my heart. I knew that I wanted God to be my personal life tutor, and I desired to follow His instruction the rest of my life.

February 24

ALLEN CLARK, veterans liaison, Dallas Veteran Affairs Medical Center; director, National Cemetery System, 1991–93, assistant secretary for Veterans Liaison and Program Coor-dination, 1989–91, Department of Veteran Affairs; West Point graduate, Green Beret officer in Vietnam who lost both legs in combat; author of autobiography, *Oh, God, I'm Dead.*

For our struggle is not against flesh and blood, but against the rulers, against the authorities, against the powers of this dark world and against the spiritual forces of evil in the heavenly realms. (Ephesians 6:12, NIV)

Having lost both legs in a mortar attack at my Army Special Forces camp at Dak To, South Vietnam, in 1967, I have experienced firsthand the horrors of war. Even after my born-again experience in 1973, I agonized and pondered, "Why me?" to attempt to understand my misfortune. But the mysteries of horror and heartache and hatred among humankind since the Garden of Eden became unveiled only in 1990 when I grasped Ephesians 6:12 and joined in the fight as a warrior on the battlefields of spiritual warfare. I had been among the POWs (prisoners of the world system), but no longer would I be MIA (missing in action).

February 25

ROY CLARK, host of *Hee Haw* during its twenty-five-year syndicated run on TV; featured at the Roy Clark Celebrity Theater, Branson, Missouri; Country Music Association Entertainer of the Year, 1973, Instrumentalist of the Year, 1977, 1978, 1980; Grammy winner, Best Country Instrumental Performance, 1982; recipient of a star on Hollywood's Walk of Fame; member of the Grand Ole Opry.

For God so loved the world, that he gave his only begotten Son, that whosoever believeth in him should not perish, but have everlasting life. (John 3:16, KJV)

My favorite Bible verse is John 3:16 because it says everything. It's the whole message of the Bible in one verse.

February 26

VAN CLIBURN, classical pianist; winner of the first Tchaikovsky International Piano Competition in Moscow, 1958, at age twenty-three; subject of the 1993 Van Cliburn biography by Howard Reich; featured on numerous classical recordings. Named in his honor by its founders, the Van Cliburn International Piano Competition is held every four years in Fort Worth, Texas.

Trust in the LORD *with all thine heart; and lean not unto thine own understanding. In all thy ways acknowledge him, and he shall direct thy paths. (Proverbs 3:5–6, KJV)*

My parents had me memorize these verses of Scripture when I was three years old. I have lived with them all my life. King Solomon, the writer of Proverbs, expresses it all so eloquently and much better than I could.

February 27

JERRY CLOWER, named country comic of the year by various music industry publications, 1973–81; featured on more than twenty albums; author of four books of humor; member of the Grand Ole Opry; cohost of *Country Crossroads* with deejay Bill Mack, heard weekly on more than 1,000 radio stations and now in video syndication; cohost of the former syndicated show *Nashville on the Road;* president, Agricultural Missions Foundation; fertilizer salesman, later director of field services during eighteen years with Mississippi Chemical Corp., Yazoo City, Mississippi.

He must increase, but I must decrease. (John 3:30, KJV)

I have the honor to know Jesus and am a forerunner, an introducer and supporter for Him. In show business you have advance people who make all the plans and preparation. John the Baptist was such a person. His main objective was to point people to the Lamb of God. In all things if you conduct yourself to make sure Jesus increases and you decrease, you will always be doing what will honor God. If you live this verse, you will know the will of God. And the greatest achievement in life is to do the will of God.

February 28

DAN COATS, U.S. senator from Indiana since 1988; member of U.S. House of Representatives, 1981–88.

He has showed you, O man, what is good.
And what does the LORD require of you?
To act justly and to love mercy
and to walk humbly with your God. (Micah 6:8, NIV)

Many years ago, Fort Wayne Bible College gave me a marble piece inscribed with Micah 6:8. The piece now sits on my desk, a daily reminder of what it means to live a faithful life. Each time I consider this verse, I am encouraged to be a servant:

- of my Lord, with submission to His will and trust in His wisdom and strength, and
- of others, with the same mercy God has shown me and with a commitment to justice in my relationships that makes personal integrity and a kind spirit the cornerstones of how I deal with family, friends, colleagues, and constituents.

February 29

FRANCIS S. COLLINS, M.D., Ph.D., director, National Center for Human Genome Research, a fifteen-year National Institutes of Health project to map and sequence the human body's 100,000 genes; professor of internal medicine and human genetics, University of Michigan, 1991–93, and faculty member there beginning in 1984; research by Collins and his colleagues identified the cystic fibrosis gene in 1989; named "Michiganian of the Year" by *The Detroit News,* 1990; member, National Academy of Sciences.

If any of you lacks wisdom, let him ask God, who gives to all men generously and without reproaching, and it will be given him. (James 1:5, RSV)

As a scientist devoted to uncovering the intricacies of God's creation in the field of genetics, I am many times stumped and frustrated by my inabilities to see the truth. This verse from James hangs on my wall, elegantly illustrated by my daughter's calligraphy, and I often glance up at it when I am looking for inspiration. It reminds me of the true Source of all wisdom.

MARCH

March 1

CHARLES W. COLSON, founder, Prison Fellowship, which has grown to more than 50,000 volunteers nationally since 1976, in ministries to prisoners, juvenile offenders, their families, and crime victims; special counsel to President Nixon who spent six months in jail in the Watergate aftermath; 1993 winner, Templeton Prize for Progress in Religion; author or coauthor of fifteen books, beginning with *Born Again* in 1976; *Christianity Today* columnist and contributing editor; daily commentator on *BreakPoint* weekday radio broadcast.

> *. . . I have learned to be content whatever the circumstances. I know what it is to be in need, and I know what it is to have plenty. I have learned the secret of being content in any and every situation, whether well fed or hungry, whether living in plenty or in want. I can do everything through him who gives me strength.*
> *(Philippians 4:11–13, NIV)*

These verses have given me strength no matter what the situation in which I find myself. In a real sense they are the story of my life. I have been at the top, sitting in the office next to the president of the United States; I've been at the bottom, in a prison cell. And I know exactly what the apostle Paul means, that we can live in abundance or we can live with humble means. But in every circumstance the secret is to know that we can do all things through Christ who strengthens us. Our human circumstances do not determine the course of our lives;

our relationship with Christ does. Sometimes people are more distant from God when they are in the midst of prosperity than when they are in the midst of want. Paul reminds us that in both good and bad circumstances there is but one thing that matters. This passage is God's ultimate comforting assurance that we can handle all of life, the triumphs and the tragedies, through Jesus Christ our Lord.

March 2

ANDREW J. COOPER, member of the USS *Alabama* Battleship Commission in Mobile, 1988–95; national vice commander, The American Legion, 1989–90, and Alabama commander, 1968–69; World War II veteran, European theater of operations; retired bank president and CEO who also served four years in the Alabama House of Representatives.

> The LORD is my shepherd; I shall not want. He maketh
> me to lie down in green pastures: he leadeth me beside the
> still waters. He restoreth my soul: he leadeth me in the
> paths of righteousness for his name's sake. Yea, though I
> walk through the valley of the shadow of death, I will fear
> no evil: for thou art with me; thy rod and thy staff they
> comfort me. Thou preparest a table before me in the pres-
> ence of mine enemies: thou anointest my head with oil;
> my cup runneth over. Surely goodness and mercy shall fol-
> low me all the days of my life: and I will dwell in the
> house of the LORD for ever. (Psalm 23, KJV)

Psalm 23 has been a source of comfort and has undergirded me many times in my life, especially during my World War II combat experience. Once, on a combat patrol mission during battle, another soldier and I were cut off from the main force by a heavy enemy artillery and mortar barrage in an open area with no protection. The shells were falling and exploding all around us. Our bodies were being lifted off the ground by the impact of shells bursting. I lay flat on my stomach with my face buried in the ground and continued to repeat the only prayer I could think of at the time—the Twenty-third Psalm. After the shelling ceased, litter bearers from my infantry company came out to pick up our bodies or what was left of them. They were speechless when my buddy and I stood up and walked. God surely led us "through the valley of the shadow of death," and after several months of combat as an infantry soldier with the Third Army, commanded by General George S. Patton, I came back home alive but not without battle wounds for which I was awarded the Purple Heart and Oak Leaf Cluster.

Another experience that will always be strong in my memory from the winter months of 1944–45 is that my mother died on December 15, 1944, at her home in Alabama. I received the message of her death on or about January 20, 1945, in Bastogne, Belgium. My faith and strong belief in prayer undergirded me at this time. When my commanding officer asked if I wanted to remain in a rest area awhile, my answer was, "No, I will go back with my company to the front lines." I knew the Lord had answered a very special prayer. The last few hours I spent with my mother before leaving for overseas duty in World War II, we knelt beside her bed and prayed that God would bring me back home safely. God answered that prayer—I came back home and my mother had moved on to her eternal home that God had prepared for her in His heavenly kingdom.

March 3

KENNETH H. COOPER, M.D., who fueled the international physical fitness movement, with his books selling more than 20 million copies in forty-one languages and Braille; most recent of his thirteen books: *It's Better to Believe*, 1995, and *Antioxidant Revolution*, 1994; founder of The Aerobics Center, a clinic, aerobics health club, exercise research institute, and guest lodge in Dallas.

*Bodily exercise is all right, but spiritual exercise is much
more important and is a tonic for all you do. So exercise
yourself spiritually and practice being a better Christian,
because that will help you not only now in this life, but in
the next life too. (1 Timothy 4:8, TLB)*

I have used this verse both in my books and in my lectures. It is
amazing the number of people who have commented that they
know I must be a Christian because of the way I use Bible verses
in my writings. Perhaps that is a subtle but, I hope, effective way
of witnessing.

March 4

ADOLPH COORS IV, investment adviser; founder, Adco
Enterprises, Inc., marketing company; in 1979, he left the family
business, Adolph Coors Company, founded in 1873 by his
great-grandfather, which had become one of the world's largest
breweries.

*What good will it be for a man if he gains the whole
world, yet forfeits his soul? Or what can a man give in exchange for his soul? (Matthew 16:26, NIV)*

Before I became a Christian about twenty years ago, I was
caught up in the frantic world of business. I was climbing the
corporate ladder of success in my family brewing business. I was
so busy and caught up in what "the world" defines as success
that, in the process, I was destroying those who were the closest
to me—my wife, B.J., and my son, Adolph Coors V. I was about
to learn the very painful lesson that money and possessions are a
universal passport to almost everything *but* happiness and a universal passport to anyplace *but* heaven. Yes, I was succeeding in
the eyes of man, but I was a total failure in the eyes of my Lord.
A tragic mistake.

March 5

EMMITTE CORNELIUS, pastor, Grace Bible Baptist Church, Jackson, Mississippi, since 1962; founder, Macedonian Call Missionary Fellowship, supporting missionaries in six African countries.

And we know that God causes all things to work together for good to those who love God, to those who are called according to His purpose. (Romans 8:28, NASB)

During the early years of my spiritual pilgrimage, I misunderstood the nature of both the "all things" and the "good." I envisioned a heavenly Father who made the "all things" always good things, and the "good" my satisfaction and happiness according to my own interests and desires. I truly believed that if I strove to please God, I would be exempted from the heart-wrenching trials experienced by those who were not His own. I viewed my heavenly Father through the eyes of my childhood experiences with my earthly father. My dad was a gentle and kind man who devoted his life to giving my sister and me all that he thought would make us happy. Surely, my heavenly Father would do no less, and even more for His children, I reasoned. I honestly believed that if painful difficulties beset a believer, they must have been the result of some grievous sin. I remember those times when I experienced painful circumstances, I searched for the offense I must have committed against God. When I saw other believers suffering, I immediately concluded that they were being chastened for some sin. Of course, there were kernels of truth in my thinking—sins we commit can bring great suffering upon us.

In September 1974, a new day began to dawn upon my thinking; in my first two years of studies at Reformed Theological Seminary in Jackson, Mississippi, I was puzzled by what I perceived to be a disproportionate amount of suffering within the student body, such as spousal desertion, terminal illness, and tragic accidents. These were godly young men and women. Many had made great sacrifices to attend seminary. Their hearts burned to go forth and serve the Lord with gladness, yet they were going through such bitter experiences. I recoiled from the thought that God, in His sovereign providence, would allow such bitter afflictions to come upon those who sincerely wanted to serve Him. As I began a reading of church history and the history of world missions, the scales began to fall from my eyes. I was faced with the historical record that down through the ages many of God's choice servants—even youth in the flower of life—walked through the fiery trials of persecution and suffering, some unto death. They did not complain that God had allowed bad things to happen to them; rather, they counted it an honor to suffer for Christ's sake. Those experiences of suffering were not mere isolated cases; they were all too common. A life-changing truth began to unfold and continues to do so in my heart. It was there all the time in the Scriptures. The "all things" of Romans 8:28 are not merely the sweet things of life, but the bitter mixed with the sweet—oftentimes more bitter than sweet. And the good I desired in the earlier years of my spiritual journey was not the good God purposed for His children. I have come to see that God's plan for those who love Him is something far greater than our self-seeking happiness, something ultimate and more glorious than the passing satisfactions of earth.

Four years ago, God brought this truth home to me in heart-wrenching personal experience. Our church was attacked with factions and division that almost devastated me as a pastor. At first I was numb with disbelief. Despondency came over me like the darkest night. Indeed, it was a bitter thing unmixed with sweetness. I blamed myself, I blamed others, I blamed God. I asked God why. What was the purpose behind it all? In the numbness of my emotions, I somehow knew that divine purpose was being worked out. But what? Today, the billows of that crisis have long subsided. Romans 8:28 best describes what has happened, and what is happening. God was weaving all the heart-wrenching things of that experience into a glorious tapestry of divine purpose. I was able to see, at least in part, what He was working out in me and my brothers and sisters in Christ. He began to purge my heart of sinful attitudes I had never acknowledged. I confessed that those were things unlike the character of His Son. I began to see that I had placed my trust in man, and what man can do, and that my dependence should be in Him and Him only. He revealed His jealousy for His holiness and the purity of His church. He was beckoning me and my congregation to come and be filled and fulfilled at the table of His sweet grace. I know now that the "all things" of Romans 8:28 is a bittersweet cup. But as I drink of it—and I must—it constrains me to affirm that only the Lord is good and worthy of my trust. He alone is sufficient to fill the deepest longings of my soul from here throughout eternity. This verse has become the capstone of my faith. I have confidence that whatever things happen in my life—bitter and sweet, and the admixture of all circumstances between—they are perfectly and beautifully woven into the fabric of God's gracious purpose to bring me to the ultimate goal to be conformed to the glorious image of His Son wherein there is fullness of joy and pleasures forevermore— to the praise and glory of His grace.

March 6

MARGARET COURT, member of the International Tennis Hall of Fame, Newport, Rhode Island; all-time Grand Slam leader, with sixty-four titles including three Wimbledon singles championships (1970, 1965, 1963), five at the U.S. Open, five at the French Open, and eleven at the Australian Open, along with twenty-one doubles and nineteen mixed doubles championships; several years after retiring from competition in 1975, she was diagnosed with a torn valve in her heart; founder, Margaret Court Ministries, based in Perth, Australia, engaging in evangelism, discipleship, family ministry, missions, and ministry to the poor; featured in the biography, *A Winning Faith*, by Barbara Oldfield.

> *I can do all things through Christ who strengthens me.*
> *(Philippians 4:13, NKJV)*

Back in 1980, when I was in a mess from a torn valve in my heart, I could not take too many Scriptures into my life, for I was not capable of doing so. I simply found two Scriptures and wrote them down and concentrated on just those two until I found I could handle more. I found other Scriptures that talked about healing and wrote them down, too, and when I rested on my bed, I spoke out the Scriptures, and I went over and over them all day long. I was desperate and, if you are desperate, you need to do the same. I didn't know back then just how powerful my words were and that my body and my circumstances were changing according to the words I was speaking. Philippians 4:13 gave me great confidence and strength as I faithfully repeated over and over again that the Word of God says, "I can do all things through Christ who strengthens me."

Before I started to say this Scripture, it seemed that I was always tired and fearful, and certainly not strong enough to play tennis even though I was just thirty-nine. My body felt like it was eighty, for the tear in my heart valve seemed to cut the circulation to my head. But I kept on saying that "I can do all things through Christ who strengthens me." My close friend Anne, who is a Christian, walked in one day some months later and said to me that I looked tired. Immediately, without thinking, I turned to her and said, "No, 'I can do all things through Christ who strengthens me.'" The power of God hit me and for the very first time those words "became flesh" to me. I knew I had my healing, because I had allowed those words to drop deep down into my spirit so that my flesh was going to be strong and healed just as I was saying. This one incident more than any other taught me the reality of the Word of God, for I was not brought up with the Scriptures and so I knew almost none. I had to keep saying what God's Word says, to remind myself it was God speaking to me.

The day after Anne's visit, I went down onto the tennis court and I truly felt like an eighteen-year-old. I remembered the Scripture that talks about those "that wait upon the LORD shall renew their strength; they shall mount up with wings as eagles; they shall run, and not be weary; and they shall walk, and not faint" (Isaiah 40:31). That day I became an eagle, and ever since I have walked in this strength that comes from being in Christ and trusting His Word to do what it promises to do.

March 7

NICKY CRUZ, former gang leader whose conversion is chronicled in the book and film *The Cross and the Switchblade;* founder, Nicky Cruz Outreach ministry to youth and gang members; author of an autobiography, *Run Baby Run,* and twelve other books.

Therefore, there is now no condemnation for those who are in Christ Jesus, because through Christ Jesus the law of the Spirit of life set me free from the law of sin and death. (Romans 8:1–2, NIV)

Coming from an abusive background in Puerto Rico with my parents heavily involved in witchcraft, I grew up feeling unloved and unworthy. My mother, for example, in a spiritualistic trance called me the "son of Satan" and hurled curses at me when I was eight years old. Then, in New York City, with my involvement in the gangs, the negative feelings increased. It was not until I met Christ that I was healed of these feelings and my soul was made clean by the blood of Jesus. No more sin, guilt, shame, or despair.

March 8

RAYMOND DAMADIAN, inventor, MRI (magnetic resonance imaging) medical technology; president and chairman, FONAR Corp., the first manufacturer of MRI scanners; National Inventors Hall of Fame inductee, 1989; National Medal of Technology recipient from President Reagan, 1988.

He shall not be afraid of evil tidings: his heart is fixed, trusting in the LORD. (Psalm 112:7, KJV)

We as a people have drifted away from the legacy of grace left us by our Puritan forebears. We have so long profited mightily from the legacy of their self-discipline and devotion to the Almighty and from the Great Awakenings that restored us when we wandered away over the centuries that we have permitted our vanity to let us dare believe that we have done it by ourselves and that our stunning string of successes in technology, free government, war, individual freedom, and finances came to us by dint of some superior effort or intelligence. Americans must come to recognize that America runs off its spiritual batteries, not off its bank accounts, and that when its spiritual batteries are drained, its bank accounts will be empty.

March 9

JOHN DANFORTH, U.S. senator from Missouri, 1976–95; an ordained Episcopal priest; Missouri attorney general, 1967–76; author of 1994 book, *Resurrection: The Confirmation of Clarence Thomas.*

Therefore if any man be in Christ, he is a new creature: old things are passed away; behold, all things are become new. And all things are of God, who hath reconciled us to

himself by Jesus Christ, and hath given to us the ministry of reconciliation; To wit, that God was in Christ, reconciling the world unto himself, not imputing their trespasses unto them; and hath committed unto us the word of reconciliation. Now then we are ambassadors for Christ, as though God did beseech you by us: we pray you in Christ's stead, be ye reconciled to God. For he hath made him to be sin for us, who knew no sin; that we might be made the righteousness of God in him.
(2 Corinthians 5:17–21, KJV)

This passage is about the reconciling work of God in Christ and the duty of Christians to do the work of reconciliation. It is a good message to people in political life in a fragmented world.

March 10

MARIA DAOUD, physical therapist, Beirut, Lebanon, employed in a Baptist ministry to patients who are homebound or in nursing homes and unable to afford other physical therapy services for injuries sustained during Lebanon's 1975–91 civil war or disabilities from birth defects, strokes, or other ailments.

And my God shall supply all your needs according to His riches in glory in Christ Jesus. (Philippians 4:19, NASB)

As a physical therapist to the poor and disabled in Lebanon, I have to drive a lot. Driving in Lebanon is a nightmare in times of peace—and I can't describe what it was like during the war. In fact, living in Lebanon, where nothing works properly, and keeping sane could be an accomplishment or a miracle. On top of all this, I worry a lot. I struggled for years to have peace in the Lord. This verse has helped me let the Lord supply my needs as He promised. Now, wherever I want to go or whatever I need, I let the Lord supply it: the time, the safety, the road, and the place to park. Sometimes, I take it away from Him, but I have peace only when I let God supply my every need.

March 11

MARY LEE DAUGHERTY, executive director, Appalachian Ministries Educational Resource Center, Berea, Kentucky, since the 1985 founding of the nonprofit organization for rural/small town community ministry training; former missionary to Brazil.

> . . . you shall love the Lord your God with all your heart, and with all your soul, and with all your mind, and with all your strength. . . . You shall love your neighbor as yourself. . . . (Mark 12:30–31, NASB)

Verse 30 requires us to focus on God, who must be above all others and above all else in our lives, but verse 31 calls us to care for others as we would like to be cared for ourselves. I believe we must see God in every human face and be Spirit-drawn to a ministry of selflessness and servanthood.

March 12

BILLY DAVIS, JR., rhythm-and-blues performer whose credits include nearly a decade with The Fifth Dimension, winning six Grammys and honored with a star on Hollywood's Walk of Fame, and a Grammy for rhythm-and-blues duo with wife Marilyn McCoo, "You Don't Have to Be a Star (To Be in My Show)"; active in such causes as the Children's Miracle Network Telethon and Lou Rawls's Parade of Stars telethon for the United Negro College Fund.

> This is my commandment, That ye love one another, as I have loved you. . . . Ye have not chosen me, but I have chosen you, and ordained you, that ye should go and bring forth fruit, and that your fruit should remain: that whatsoever ye shall ask of the Father in my name, he may

give it you. These things I command you, that ye love one another. (John 15:12, 16–17, KJV)

That's the Scripture I really lean on, about the unconditional love Jesus tells us to give one another. You can't let anything get in the way of your love for a person—for a human being. You don't even have to know people to love them. We're to love them just because they're human and God said to love them. I lean on that all the time. We see so many acts of wrongdoing in today's world, people doing stuff that's just unexplainable. We know the devil is behind all of that. He's doing his job and doing it well. And in order for me not to turn into that type of beast—or for anyone not to turn into that—we have to lean on this kind of love. If you have love in your heart, you can't have hate in there. You can't put both love and hate in there together; it doesn't work.

I've always been the type of person who could love others. But I never really understood it until I was born again about fifteen years ago—when I started getting deeper into what Jesus did for us and what God wants from us, scripturally digging into it. So many things change when it really starts to mean something in your life. Years ago, for example, we used to have a bunch of fun singing "When the Saints Go Marching In." But since I've been born again, it's a whole different ball game. I mean, it just means so much more; I'm not just singing it—I truly want to be in the number when all the saints go marching into heaven. Now that I have it coming from the heart, I've added it to my shows because I think I can deliver the message of the song to where it's supposed to go—to another heart. Now I can sing that song the way I know it should be sung.

March 13

CLIFTON DAVIS, actor who has starred in TV's *Amen, That's My Mama,* and *Love, American Style* and in numerous film and stage roles.

Trust in the LORD with all thine heart; and lean not unto thine own understanding. In all thy ways acknowledge him, and he shall direct thy paths. (Proverbs 3:5–6, KJV)

At critical times in my life, when I found myself confused as to which direction to go in terms of important life decisions, I found this Scripture to be encouraging. While seeking guidance in secular terms, we tend to overlook the spiritual. Sometimes I find myself looking at a decision through worldly eyes while blindly moving forward in the Spirit. Then when I am confronted with impenetrable obstacles, this Scripture helps me to open my eyes and see that with God there is always a way. But His help is conditioned upon our trusting in Him. Over the years I have found that He indeed will direct our paths.

March 14

GLENN DAVIS, former Houston Astros first baseman; in seven seasons became team's second all-time home run hitter; runner-up as National League MVP, 1986; founder with wife Teresa of Carpenter's Way Ranch in Georgia, home for children who have suffered abuse and neglect.

In thee, O LORD, do I put my trust; let me never be ashamed: deliver me in thy righteousness. Bow down thine ear to me; deliver me speedily: be thou my strong rock, for a house of defence to save me. For thou art my rock and my fortress; therefore for thy name's sake lead me, and guide me. . . . O love the LORD, all ye his saints: for the LORD preserveth the faithful, and

*plentifully rewardeth the proud doer. Be of good courage,
and he shall strengthen your heart, all ye that hope in the
LORD. (Psalm 31:1–3, 23–24, KJV)*

This psalm is the cry of my heart today. When I cannot find the
right words to say or express my innermost thoughts to God, I
turn to Psalm 31 and read it as if it's my own personal prayer.

March 15

ROBYN DAVIS, student at Hardin-Simmons University,
Abilene, Texas; 1994 Young American Medal for Service recipient from President Clinton for school and community efforts,
such as successful advocacy of an alcohol-free day at the New
Mexico State Fair; as a student at Albuquerque (New Mexico)
High School, she was the only teenager among twenty members
of a U.S. Department of Health and Human Services commission
for drug abuse prevention policies for the twenty-first century.

> *"O Lord God," I said, "I can't do that! I'm far too young!
> I'm only a youth!" Then he touched my mouth and said,
> "See, I have put my words in your mouth! Today your
> work begins, to warn the nations and the kingdoms of the
> world. In accord with my words spoken through your
> mouth I will tear down some and destroy them, and plant
> others and nurture them and make them strong and
> great." (Jeremiah 1:6, 9–10, TLB)*

Being a youth in today's society is hard. Standing up for something you believe is even harder, especially when you do it alone
and in the name of Jesus Christ. Many times I was doubtful of
my witness to others through my public service. God has revealed to me through these verses that I am doing this for a reason, and that reason is God.

March 16

PAT DAY, leading jockey in career wins at Churchill Downs (some 1,100); member of racing's Hall of Fame; 1992 Kentucky Derby winner; five-time Preakness winner, including 1994–96 streak; four-time winner of annual Eclipse Award as best jockey in North America.

For God so loved the world, that he gave his only begotten Son, that whosoever believeth in him should not perish, but have everlasting life. (John 3:16, KJV)

This verse expresses the magnitude of God's love as well as we can perceive it in our finite minds. Being a father myself, I find it almost inconceivable that you would have a love so great that you would be willing to sacrifice your only son.

March 17

SHARON ALLRED DECKER, vice president and executive director, Duke Power Company Foundation, Charlotte, North Carolina, overseeing corporate relations and more than $8 million in corporate contributions to community initiatives across the Carolinas; she joined the company in 1979 and, among other positions, has been vice president of communications and community relations, vice president of customer services, and manager of marketing program development.

Don't worry about anything; instead, pray about everything; tell God your needs and don't forget to thank him for his answers. If you do this you will experience God's peace, which is far more wonderful than the human mind can understand. His peace will keep your thoughts and your hearts quiet and at rest as you trust in Christ Jesus. (Philippians 4:6–7, TLB)

Life can become very chaotic when you are a wife, a mother of three small children, and a career person! This verse comes to mind often and, by following the guidance given here, I can find *peace even amid the chaos!* What a joy to know I don't have to worry about all the responsibilities I carry or all the needs I feel I have to meet. God is in control of it all. My primary job is to stay in touch with Him!

March 18

TRESSA DECKER, first-grade teacher in Mishawaka, Indiana; Indiana winner of the Sallie Mae Outstanding First Year Teacher Award, 1988–89, sponsored by the federal Student Loan Marketing Association.

. . . Freely you have received, freely give.
(Matthew 10:8, NIV)

As a first-grade teacher, I pray that every day I will give love, forgiveness, mercy, joy, and peace to my students as freely as Christ has given those things to me.

March 19

RICK DEES, radio and TV personality; host of *Rick Dees Weekly Top 40* each weekend on more than 350 radio stations across the United States and in some sixty other countries; named *Billboard* magazine's No. 1 radio personality thirteen of the last fourteen years; recipient of a star on the Hollywood Walk of Fame.

> *Love is patient, love is kind, and is not jealous; love does not brag and is not arrogant, does not act unbecomingly; it does not seek its own, is not provoked, does not take into account a wrong suffered, does not rejoice in unrighteousness, but rejoices with the truth; bears all things, believes all things, hopes all things, endures all things.*
> *(1 Corinthians 13:4–7, NASB)*

These are explicit words, directly from God's lips, about how to treat people. This passage is fascinating to me because it's the Lord's own definition of love—His personal answer to our age-old question: What is love?

March 20

CALVIN B. DeWITT, professor of environmental studies, University of Wisconsin, Madison, and director of the Au Sable Institute of Environmental Studies, Mancelona, Michigan, serving eighty Christian colleges and universities with courses in ecology and environmental stewardship; chair, Christian Environmental Council; author of *Earth-Wise: Biblical Principles for Environmental Stewardship* and author or editor of several other books on the environment.

The LORD God took the man and put him in the garden of Eden to till it and keep it. (Genesis 2:15, RSV)

What should our response be to environmental issues today? This verse, more than any other in the Bible, helps answer this pressing question of our time. Its importance is that it tells much about what God expects of us in Creation. We see that God put Adam in the garden to "till" and "keep" it. Investigation of the Hebrew here shows that the word for "till" literally means "serve," as it does in Joshua 24:15, ". . . choose you this day whom ye will *serve* . . . " (KJV). The Hebrew word for "keep" here also is used in Aaron's blessing (Numbers 6:24), "The Lord bless you and *keep* you . . . " (RSV). Adam is expected to serve and keep the garden. This is a critically important verse for our time because it tells us that we are appointed God's stewards of Creation, servants who should *keep* Creation and God's creatures. It tells us that we should be reflecting God's love for the world by serving it, nurturing it, and keeping it with all its wholeness and integrity, with all its God-given relationships intact. Taking the form of a servant (Philippians 2:7), we should be imaging the love of the Creator, Sustainer, and Reconciler of all things (John 1:1–5, 3:16; Colossians 1:15–20). The Scriptures expect us to be *earthkeepers*—God's stewards of Creation.

March 21

NELSON A. DIAZ, general counsel, U.S. Department of Housing and Urban Development; Philadelphia judge, Court of Common Pleas, First Judicial District of Pennsylvania, 1981–93.

I can do all things through Him who strengthens me.
(Philippians 4:13, NASB)

Born to an unwed young mother without a roof over her head and very little to eat in cold New York City is not a good start for anyone, especially one of Puerto Rican ancestry. Through Christ I found strength to deal with the prejudice and discrimination so visible in my world. And now, as a judge who needs to speak the truth to all situations, I can think of no better verse. God gives me His strength as I try to do His will. He holds me firm in my conviction of faith in Him, for I do all things as unto Him. If it were not so, my human imperfections would botch up terribly the decisions and actions I make and take. When I am told that something cannot be done, or that I cannot do it owing to political circumstances or the power of evil in a given situation, I cling to this verse and God shows His great mercy to me and strengthens me to overcome.

March 22

RUTH GRAHAM DIENERT, consultant to Samaritan's Purse, international relief organization led by her brother, Franklin Graham; she and Franklin are two of Billy and Ruth Graham's five children.

Because of the LORD's great love we are not consumed,
for his compassions never fail.

They are new every morning;
great is your faithfulness. (Lamentations 3:22–23, NIV)

In times of anxiety or failure, I have turned to this promise and assurance. It comforts and quiets my heart. It gets my focus off my problems and onto the greatness and love of my God. As well, it assures me that each day is new, yesterday is gone, and God is the God of a second chance. Though others may fail and disappoint, He never will. I also love the hymn taken from this verse, "Great Is Thy Faithfulness."

March 23

DION DiMUCCI, member of the Rock and Roll Hall of Fame for such hits as "A Teenager in Love," "The Wanderer," "Runaround Sue," and "Abraham, Martin, and John"; author, with Davin Seay, of *The Wanderer: Dion's Story* autobiography.

I am the vine; you are the branches. If a man remains in
me and I in him, he will bear much fruit; apart from me
you can do nothing. (John 15:5, NIV)

We can build castles on sand all day long. People do it every day without God in their lives. But what happens to those castles? They disappear. Jesus said if you own the world and lose your soul, it profits you nothing. This verse is so important because it tells us that Jesus gives us the strength, the power, the wisdom, the insight, the ability to make an eternal difference in people's lives. If a man becomes sensitive to what God is saying and changes, he can make a difference in the lives of his wife, his kids, his friends, his business—it just goes on and on. It's amazing to touch one life, the eternal impact it makes.

March 24

JAMES C. DOBSON, founder and president, Focus on the Family; radio host and speaker whose daily broadcasts are aired on more than 2,900 stations in North America and in more than sixty countries; author of fifteen books, beginning with *Dare to Discipline*, 1970, now with more than 3 million in print and revised and updated as *The New Dare to Discipline*, 1992; member of various government panels on child and family welfare, juvenile delinquency, missing and exploited children, teen pregnancy, and pornography; former associate clinical professor of pediatrics, University of Southern California, for fourteen years, and on the attending staff of Childrens Hospital of Los Angeles, division of child development and medical genetics, seventeen years; named Layman of the Year by the National Association of Evangelicals, 1982.

> *I know what it is to be in need, and I know what it is to have plenty. I have learned the secret of being content in any and every situation, whether well fed or hungry, whether living in plenty or in want.*
> *(Philippians 4:12, NIV)*

Have you ever wondered where one finds the ability to remain poised under pressure? It can't come from circumstances or our emotional reactions to them. And it doesn't simply "happen" automatically, even for Spirit-filled believers. The answer, I think, is so plain and practical that some of us might prefer not to hear it. It's really a matter of discipline, training, and practice. Consider the apostle Paul. Here is a man whose Christian life was marked by "afflictions, hardships, distresses, beatings, imprisonments, tumults, labors, sleeplessness, and hunger." He knew what it was like to be shipwrecked, incarcerated, pelted with stones, left for dead. And yet in the midst of a terrifying storm on the Adriatic Sea, being advised by a heavenly messenger that the ship on which he was a passenger would surely run aground, he was able to cheer his guards and fellow travelers with the word that all would survive the impending disaster. It seems fitting somehow that he should have summed up the meaning of these experiences in his epistle to the Philippians—a letter he wrote from prison. In Philippians 4:12, he says this about the peace and poise that had become so characteristic of his life under trial: "I have learned the secret of being content in any and every situation, whether well fed or hungry, whether living in plenty or in want." That attitude doesn't come naturally. It is an acquired serenity.

March 25

SHIRLEY DOBSON, chairwoman, National Day of Prayer Task Force, since 1992; coauthor, with Gloria Gaither, of *Let's Make a Memory* and *Let's Hide the Word;* active in numerous Christian women's ministries over the years; wife of James Dobson, Focus on the Family founder; her and her husband's film series, *Turn Your Heart Toward Home,* has been viewed by more than 30 million people.

. . . we walk by faith, not by sight: . . .
(2 Corinthians 5:7, KJV)

In our modern day, we like to see instant, tangible results. Drive-through windows, fax machines, electronic mail—everything is right at our fingertips. While these conveniences may be valuable time-savers in our day-to-day dealings, the "instant" mentality can become dangerous if applied to our prayer lives. Often, when we pray about a problem or for a loved one, we don't "see" any evidence that God is hearing our prayers, much less acting upon them. In such cases, we must constantly remind ourselves that we're not walking by "sight," but by faith. God values faith infinitely more than quick fixes and streamlined schedules. Above all, He prizes the development of our hearts.

And He promises to complete the work He began in us when we accepted Him as Lord (Philippians 1:6). When we keep this perspective in mind and trust Him for the timely and perfect growth of our relationship with Him, then we don't *have* to see results. God is faithful to the prayers of His children and when "nothing is happening, something is happening with God." As 1 Thessalonians 5:17 encourages us: Never, never give up!

March 26

DAVID DOCKERY, director of Surface Geology Division, Mississippi Office of Geology.

> *The earth is the LORD's, and all it contains,*
> *The world, and those who dwell in it. (Psalm 24:1, NASB)*

As a geologist, paleontologist, and naturalist, I find this verse appealing because it is an exultant declaration of God's ownership over the material world. It is the details of this world that so fascinate me. This declaration places a goodness and value on the rocks, hills, and creatures (fossil and living) that make up the earth, a value based not merely upon human interest but upon their Owner.

March 27

PHIL DOWNER, president, Christian Business Men's Committee of USA evangelism and discipleship outreach to the business and professional communities; formerly a senior managing partner in an Atlanta law firm.

> *. . . men of Issachar, who understood the times and knew*
> *what Israel should do. . . . (1 Chronicles 12:32, NIV)*

For the United States and the world, these are times of unprecedented and unrelenting change. For the Christian community, the challenges and obstacles to carrying out Christ's Great Commission of Matthew 28:10, 20 are greater than ever. Secularization, pluralism, and privatization, just to name a few, are among the incredible forces dramatically remolding the face of our nation. People need to know Jesus Christ as much as they ever did, but because secularized thinking has virtually pushed God and biblical views off center stage, people today are less responsive to the Good News. Pluralism and the hodgepodge of religions that has accompanied it have muddled humankind's pursuit of God. And owing in part to privatization, many people view it as "politically incorrect" to advocate a particular faith or belief system. Therefore, like the men of Issachar, we in the waning years of the twentieth century also must understand our times and discern what we must do to communicate the gospel of Christ in relevant, meaningful ways. This calls for innovation and creativity, merging still-useful and time-tested strategies with novel approaches for communicating an unchanging message in an ever-changing environment. This challenge might seem overwhelming were it not for our all-knowing God, the author of creativity, who is fully able to give us the necessary insight and discernment to minister effectively to "make disciples of all nations" through the remainder of the 1990s and beyond, if He so wills.

March 28

SUSAN DRAKE, environmentalist currently in Ph.D. studies, University of Wisconsin, Madison; foreign affairs officer, U.S. Department of State's Bureau of Oceans, Environmental and Scientific Affairs, 1992–95, who worked as United Nations program manager in preparations for the 1992 U.N. Conference on Environment and Development (Earth Summit) in Rio de Janeiro and as a U.S. delegation negotiator; former Environmental Protection Agency U.N. representative and project manager, Office of Wetlands Protection.

He has shown you, O man, what is good;
And what does the LORD require of you
But to do justly,
To love mercy,
And to walk humbly with your God? (Micah 6:8, NKJV)

I memorized this Scripture in song soon after accepting Jesus Christ as my Lord and Savior. It has meant more to me in my daily walk with Christ than any other in the Bible, particularly as a public servant and policy maker in the U.S. government. I awake each morning and submit my*self*—ambition, striving to meet deadlines and demands with perfection, and so on—before a holy and righteous God, seeking the Lord's guidance and wisdom to serve Him in a manner pleasing to Him: not by (my) might nor by (my) power but by *His* Spirit. It is knowing that we can do nothing of ourselves without Christ who keeps us at the foot of the cross. Only by submitting to the power of the Holy Spirit—"not my will but Yours be done"—can a believer hope to develop policies or make judgments that are just and merciful to both His people and His creation. We are created from the dust of the earth and have been given the mandate by God to "tend and keep his garden." For the earth is full of the goodness of the Lord. Let us serve all the Lord's creation in a state of complete surrender and humility and with a heart full of justice and mercy! May all the glory resulting from our lives be directed to the Father of all living things—the Creator of the universe!

March 29

DAVE DRAVECKY, professional speaker; major league pitcher, 1982–89, whose career included National League playoff appearances with the San Diego Padres and San Francisco Giants but was ended by cancer that, in 1991, required amputation of his left arm and shoulder blade; author, with Tim Stafford, of *Comeback*; with his wife, Jan, and Ken Gire, *When*

You Can't Come Back; and with C. W. Neal, *The Worth of a Man.*

> *Not that I have already attained all this, or have already been made perfect, but I press on to take hold of that for which Christ Jesus took hold of me. Brothers, I do not consider myself yet to have taken hold of it. But one thing I do: Forgetting what is behind and straining toward what is ahead, I press on toward the goal to win the prize for which God has called me heavenward in Christ Jesus.*
> *(Philippians 3:12–14, NIV)*

The encouragement that comes from these verses is to not give up. Perfection is not something that comes overnight; it is a life-long journey.

March 30

CHARLES DUKE, former NASA astronaut; Apollo 16 lunar module pilot, 1972, tenth man to walk on the moon; now U.S. Air Force Reserve brigadier general.

> *Trust in the LORD with all thine heart; and lean not unto thine own understanding. In all thy ways acknowledge him, and he shall direct thy paths. Be not wise in thine own eyes: fear the LORD, and depart from evil. It shall be health to thy navel, and marrow to thy bones.*
> *(Proverbs 3:5–8, KJV)*

In my life there have been many situations where I have had to trust in the Lord and gain His understanding. It has, at times, been difficult to follow God because His ways are not our ways and we seem to be going opposite to how we feel. I can testify, however, that when I trust Him in spite of my feelings, I experience the peace of God and this fills me with joy. Walking on the moon was exciting, but it lasted three days. Walking with Jesus lasts forever.

March 31

DIANA DWELLE, missionary bush pilot in Africa, working in tandem with the Assemblies of God and Mission Aviation Fellowship; her husband, Terry, talked her into taking an introductory flying lesson in 1977—"and I knew this was God's direction for my life."

Just as each of us has one body with many members, and these members do not all have the same function, so in Christ we who are many form one body, and each member belongs to all the others. We have different gifts, according to the grace given us. . . . (Romans 12:4–6, NIV)

As I read these verses, I began to realize that God's call was not just for pastors or evangelists, but to *all* of us who are Christians. And one calling is not higher or more important than any other; we all have a responsibility to be faithful not only in what we do but in how we do it. This is a constant challenge and also a great joy when I see God take the ordinary things in my life and combine them with the work of fellow Christians all over the world and use them to be a blessing and accomplish His purpose.

APRIL

April 1

MARK EATON, twelve-season center with the Utah Jazz, finishing second in NBA history in blocked shots, 3,064, just 125 behind Kareem Abdul Jabbar; NBA Defensive Player of the Year, 1989, 1985, and 1989 All-Star; first player in NBA history to block more than 400 shots in a season—456 in 1984–85, a record that still stands; Jazz all-time leader in games played, 875.

Finally, brothers, we instructed you how to live in order to please God. . . . Make it your ambition to lead a quiet life, to mind your own business and to work with your hands, just as we told you, so that your daily life may win the respect of outsiders and so that you will not be dependent on anybody. (1 Thessalonians 4:1, 11–12, NIV)

I have spent the last year in deep thought and prayer as my life has changed from professional athlete to businessman. As I investigate new challenges, I must make sure that whatever I choose to do falls within the will of our Father as well as passing the test of self-examination. Ultimately, we are all accountable to God, and whatever we do must glorify Him. The verses that are most appropriate at this turning point in my life are 1 Thessalonians 4:1, 11–12. I want people to see Christ's impact in my daily life.

April 2

JACK ECKERD, retired founder, Jack Eckerd Corp., with more than 1,700 drugstores in fifteen states; chairman, Eckerd Family Youth Alternatives, Inc., foundation operating wilderness camps in seven states, assisting nearly 30,000 youth with emotional problems since 1968; administrator, General Services Administration under President Ford; Republican candidate in Florida for U.S. Senate in 1974 and governor in 1978; author, with Paul Conn, *Eckerd: Finding the Right Prescription* autobiography and, with Charles Colson, *Why America Doesn't Work.*

> . . . then choose for yourselves this day whom you will serve. . . . But as for me and my household, we will serve the LORD. *(Joshua 24:15, NIV)*

In all aspects of my life, whether it be in business dealings, relationships with family and friends, or day-to-day events, one truth helps hold me on course: when you honor God and put Him first, He leads you to what is truly right and honorable.

April 3

JERRY L. EISLEY, founder and director, Washington Arts Group, sponsor of performances, workshops, multidiscipline conferences, and Bible studies for professionals in the visual and performing arts, entertainment, and journalism; owner of Foxhall Gallery, Washington, D.C.

> *In the beginning God created the heavens and the earth. The earth was without form, and void; and darkness was on the face of the deep. And the Spirit of God was hovering over the face of the waters. Then God said, "Let there be light"; and there was light. (Genesis 1:1–3, NKJV)*

It occurred to me in thinking about this account of creation:

- that God created first and then spoke. Before God did anything else, He acted, bringing order out of chaos. He didn't do that because He "wanted to" but because it was His nature to do so. Over the years, it has been my experience with artists that their gift is something compulsive, something so deeply ingrained that it cannot be denied. And if it is denied, great psychic damage can occur. The urge also can be skewed and become self-serving. The difference between God and us is that, unlike God, who formed many things out of *no* thing, we can create only out of preexisting matter.

- to recall the story of Michelangelo, who, looking at a mere slab of stone, saw his *David* and commenced to call it forth with his hands. Seeing with the eyes of the Holy Spirit, the artist/Christian not only calls forth the perceived image but names it for the kingdom.

- to recall a friend's observation that goodness, truth, and beauty are like a tree: the trunk of goodness and truth is straight while the wild branches, leaves, and blooms exhibit the randomness of beauty as well as of order. Like God, whose infinite variety is a basic characteristic of His being, the artist also can find loveliness and magnificence in the erratic and asymmetric.

- that when God had finished His work, He looked it over and found it good. Most artists, on the other hand, rarely feel that a product of their hands is totally satisfactory. Indeed, the imperfectness of a work is a goad to further creation by the artist, who seeks that one masterpiece that God Himself could sign—which is only another way of saying that the artist's search is for God Himself, for the complete harmony and union with which Adam once walked in the Garden with his maker.

- that when a work has been finished, it is an entity in itself and, although it may become the property of someone else, it belongs only to itself. However closely the artist identified with it during its creation, he or she can never again find himself or herself totally in it. God, on the other hand, can reenter His work and continually involve Himself in it. Having made the earth and separated it from the heavens, He left the heavens and went to live in and among His creatures. The artist cannot do that.

April 4

ELISABETH ELLIOT, author of more than two dozen books, including *Through Gates of Splendor, Shadow of the Almighty,* and *Let Me Be a Woman;* wife of Jim Elliot, one of five missionaries killed in making initial contact with the Auca tribe of Ecuador in 1956; she remained a missionary after his death and later worked two years among the Aucas; featured on *Gateway to Joy* weekday radio broadcast aired on more than 250 stations.

> *When thou passeth through the waters, I will be with thee; and through the rivers, they shall not overflow thee: when thou walkest through the fire, thou shalt not be burned; neither shall the flame kindle upon thee. For I am the LORD thy God.... (Isaiah 43:2–3, KJV)*

When I received word that my husband, Jim Elliot, was missing in Auca territory back in 1956, the Lord immediately brought this verse to my mind. God faithfully kept His promise—He always does.

April 5

DIET EMAN, author, *Things We Couldn't Say,* with James Schaap, recounting the risks she and her fiancé, Hein Sietsma, took during World War II as part of the Dutch underground shielding Jews from Nazi arrest in occupied Holland—and their own imprisonment by the Nazis; now a retired nurse in Grand Rapids, Michigan.

The LORD is my light and my salvation;
whom shall I fear?
The LORD is the stronghold of my life;
of whom shall I be afraid?
When evildoers assail me,
uttering slanders against me,
my adversaries and foes,
they shall stumble and fall.
Though a host encamp against me,
my heart shall not fear;
though war arise against me,
yet I will be confident.
One thing have I asked of the LORD,
that will I seek after;
that I may dwell in the house of the LORD
all the days of my life,
to behold the beauty of the LORD,
and to inquire in his temple.
For he will hide me in his shelter
in the day of trouble;
he will conceal me under the cover of his tent,
he will set me high upon a rock.
And now my head shall be lifted up
above my enemies round about me;
and I will offer in his tent
sacrifices with shouts of joy;
I will sing and make melody to the LORD.
(Psalm 27:1–6, RSV)

I can never read Psalm 27 without tears of gratefulness streaming down my cheeks. Evil men did advance against me, and the Lord kept me safe during all those years, in prison and in the concentration camp. I love all the psalms because during the two years the Gestapo (German secret police) was looking to arrest me, my life was a bit like that of King David, who had to hide from King Saul. Many of the psalms were written during that time in David's life, and I could identify with so many of them.

And, of course, there were the words of Jesus, "Lo, I am with you always," in Matthew 28 that I engraved with a bobby pin on the brick walls of my prison cell. I would not have known how to get through that time—not knowing what they would do to my parents; knowing that Hein also was arrested but not knowing what they would do to him whom I loved; knowing I would get a hearing with my captors and being very scared whether I would be strong enough not to betray anything if they were to torture me; knowing I was human and weak—I think I would have gone stark crazy with all these worries if I had not had this wonderful promise. And Jesus said this just before He returned to heaven. If you think about how people on their deathbeds say important things to the loved ones who surround them, this was Jesus' important message to us, the last thing He promised. And I can truly say He kept His promise and was always there.

Everybody in life at some point gets a cross to bear. There is not one life that from cradle to grave never has a cross. But when that happens, He is there with us and helps us to carry it and then His yoke is light. During these times, it is so important *how* we carry our cross—grudgingly, because we cannot escape it, or in His strength, joyfully. It is in these times that we can be the best witnesses to people who have no faith—to make them desirous of what we have. Heavy burdens are not punishment from God, as Job's friends tried to imply. Sometimes, as in Job's case, they can be a special honor.

April 6

IRENE M. ENDICOTT, special consultant on grandparenting issues, Southern Baptist Sunday School Board; author of *Grandparenting by Grace,* a book and a twelve-week church study, and two other books, *Grandparenting Redefined: Guidance for Today's Changing Family* and *Out of the Mouths of Grandchildren,* sayings and prayers of grandchildren; former radio talk-show host in Seattle for eleven years; mother of four, stepmother of three, grandmother of fifteen.

> *Only be careful, and watch yourselves closely so that you do not forget the things your eyes have seen or let them slip from your heart as long as you live. Teach them to your children and to their children after them.*
> *(Deuteronomy 4:9, NIV)*

We are in a battle for the souls of our grandchildren. Society, their peers, even their parents may fail them. Grandparents have a unique opportunity to teach children that God never fails. Deuteronomy 4:9 is God's job description for grandparents. It is a scriptural mandate to pass on to the generations the truth of His love and faithfulness as manifested in our lives; it is our task for as long as God gives life and breath.

April 7

CARL ERSKINE, Brooklyn/Los Angeles Dodgers pitcher, 1948–59; pitched in five World Series—ranked tenth in number of Series pitching appearances; career highlights included two no-hitters and fourteen strikeouts in a 1953 World Series victory over the Yankees; vice chairman of the board, Star Financial Bank, Anderson, Indiana.

> *My grace is sufficient for thee: for my strength is made perfect in weakness. (2 Corinthians 12:9, KJV)*

A serious arm injury threatened to end my career in 1956. I was taking my regular pitching turn but struggling. I was scheduled to start against the Giants at Ebbets Field on Saturday, May 12, but was very despondent over my circumstance. Fearing a total failure was in store for me against a strong Giant team led by Willie Mays, I asked God to help me and I would trust Him for the outcome. Result: a no-hit, no-run 3–0 win. Yet the win wasn't as important as experiencing the truth of this Scripture.

April 8

CAROL EVERETT, founder of Life Network, Dallas, pro-life educational and post-abortion counseling organization; twenty-year businesswoman who became director of four abortion clinics, co-owner of two; she had an abortion in 1973 and was in the abortion industry from 1977 until a preacher's words of faith in 1983 led to her conversion.

". . . I took you from the ends of the earth,
from its farthest corners I called you.
I said, 'You are my servant';
I have chosen you and have not rejected you.
So do not fear, for I am with you;
do not be dismayed, for I am your God.
I will strengthen you and help you;
I will uphold you with my righteous right hand.
All who rage against you
will surely be ashamed and disgraced;
those who oppose you
will be as nothing and perish.
Though you search for your enemies,
you will not find them.
Those who wage war against you
will be as nothing at all.
For I am the LORD, *your God,*

who takes hold of your right hand
and says to you, Do not fear;
I will help you.
Do not be afraid, O worm Jacob,
O little Israel,
for I myself will help you," declares the LORD,
your Redeemer, the Holy One of Israel.
"See, I will make you into a threshing sledge,
new and sharp, with many teeth.
You will thresh the mountains and crush them,
and reduce the hills to chaff.
You will winnow them, the wind will pick them up,
and a gale will blow them away.
But you will rejoice in the LORD
and glory in the Holy One of Israel. . . .
(Isaiah 41:9–16, NIV)

I was asked to testify about the abortion industry before the Texas Legislature in 1985. I didn't want to—it would be the first time I had ever stepped out in public on the pro-life issue—but we kept praying and it became clear I was to go. I flew down to Austin expecting great change. I thought they would say, "You're Carol Everett? Weren't you pro-choice?" And I'd say, "Yes, but I'm now pro-life, and we're killing babies, and that's wrong," and I'd go home and abortion would be changed. But that's not what happened. I walked inside the capitol and ran right into my old friends, the pro-choicers. And they were fighting, not with us but among themselves as to who was going to speak first. When I came near, my spirit felt that anger and that oppression for the first time in the two years since I had become a Christian. And I ran. As I sat on one of those rocks by our state capitol, I tried to make deals with God: "Lord, why don't you zap these abortion clinics and let me go on with my life?" But at that point in my Christian walk, I didn't read the

Old Testament. My Bible was so "trained" it never fell open to the Old Testament. I didn't like all that law and legalism. I wanted the grace in the New Testament. But the dog had chewed that Bible, and I had picked up a new, "untrained" Bible that opened to Isaiah 41, starting with verses 9 and 10: ". . . I took you from the ends of the earth, from its farthest corners I called you. I said, 'You are my servant'; I have chosen you and have not rejected you. So do not fear, for I am with you; do not be dismayed, for I am your God. I will strengthen you and help you; I will uphold you with my righteous right hand. . . ." When I read those verses, for the first time in my life I knew God had a plan for my life, though I didn't have the spiritual maturity to understand what God was going to do. But I did know He was going to protect me and my family as long as He had a purpose.

Verses 11 through 14 continue: "All who rage against you will surely be ashamed and disgraced; those who oppose you will be as nothing and perish. Though you search for your enemies, you will not find them. Those who wage war against you will be as nothing at all. For I am the Lord, your God, who takes hold of your right hand and says to you, Do not fear; I will help you. Do not be afraid, O worm Jacob. . . ." I see myself as that worm. Worms can't walk, can't talk; they are toothless and spineless. When you come out of an abortion clinic like I did, you think you're so bad nobody could use you, certainly not God. In my mind, the abortion clinic was the "farthest corner of the earth." But I began to see that God wanted to use the worst experiences in my life for good—and if I didn't tell these experiences, God couldn't possibly use them for good.

Then in verses 15 and 16, it says, "See, I will make you into a threshing sledge, new and sharp, with many teeth. You will thresh the mountains and crush them, and reduce the hills to chaff. You will winnow them, the wind will pick them up, and a gale will blow them away. But you will rejoice in the Lord and glory in the Holy One of Israel. . . ." My prayer is that He will make us all into that threshing sledge. The body of Christ can be the teeth that will stand up and stop the killing of the unborn, the killing of the elderly, all the ungodly things that are going on in our nation. The church is the answer. The church needs to know what's happening in the abortion clinics. We're the only ones with the morals stored up. We let the world do it too long, and look where we are. I feel my job is to tell the church, so they can go from there and ask God what He's called them to do.

April 9

BOB FENN, founder, former executive director, Lay Renewal Ministries, St. Louis, which organizes laity teams for renewal events in more than one hundred churches of various denominations across the United States and Canada each year, as well as providing workshops and printed resources for laypeople to become more effective in their churches; currently, he is the ministry's director of resourcing.

And my God shall supply all your need according to His riches in glory by Christ Jesus. (Philippians 4:19, NKJV)

When I was a new Christian, I struggled with God really being concerned about individuals enough that He would supply our needs financially, emotionally, and relationally, and yet I knew He could supply my spiritual needs. During my more than forty years of being a Christian, I have experienced in specific ways how God provided the money I needed at the right time from resources that were a total and complete surprise. He has given me emotional stability that is supernatural; without His concern, I would have been a "basket case." Coming from a broken family, I experienced no solid relationships until I met Him. When I learned this verse, my life turned around as I relied on its truth.

April 10

FRED FETTEROLF, retired president and chief operating officer, Aluminum Company of America (ALCOA), who joined the company in 1952 as a sales trainee and filled numerous managerial positions during his thirty-nine-year career; chairman of the 1993 Greater Pittsburgh Billy Graham Crusade.

> *Ye are the light of the world. A city that is set on an hill cannot be hid. Neither do men light a candle, and put it under a bushel, but on a candlestick; and it giveth light unto all that are in the house. (Matthew 5:14–15, KJV)*

This passage has energized me to be a visible Christian in the marketplace. It simply doesn't square that you can be a Christian and keep it quiet from peers in any walk of life. For too many years, I was a closet Christian.

April 11

THOMAS A. FLEMING, special assistant to the provost, Eastern Michigan University, Ypsilanti; 1992 National Teacher of the Year, 1991 Michigan Teacher of the Year as teaching coordinator for the Washtenaw County (Michigan) Juvenile Detention Center, where he worked from 1972 to 1993.

> *I want to know Christ and the power of his resurrection and the fellowship of sharing in his sufferings, becoming like him in his death, and so, somehow, to attain to the resurrection from the dead. (Philippians 3:10–11, NIV)*

It has been my privilege for more than twenty years to provide instruction to young people attending public schools in Michigan. My personal understanding of this privilege is based on the importance of developing and encouraging creativity while the brain is young. During my college days I selected this verse as my life's verse, and it has continued to challenge both my public and my personal behavior. Like the great apostle Paul, I too must say, "Not that I have already obtained all this ... I press on toward the goal ... " (Philippians 3:12–14).

April 12

TED FLETCHER, founder, president emeritus, Pioneers, international missions agency based in Orlando, Florida; national sales manager of *The Wall Street Journal*, 1963–74.

Ask of me,
and I will make the nations your inheritance,
the ends of the earth your possession. (Psalm 2:8, NIV)

The greatest day of my life was December 8, 1952, while I was serving with the First Marine Division in Korea. It was there that I came to know Jesus Christ as my personal Savior. During that time I began thinking about God's concern for all peoples. I wanted everyone in the world to know the joy and peace I found in Christ. I began to pray that someday the Lord would give me a part in reaching peoples of other cultures with the gospel. While I was reading my Bible one day, the Lord spoke to me from a verse that in later years led me to launch a new mission agency called Pioneers aimed at the unreached people of the world. That verse was Psalm 2:8. The words came with terrific authority and I knew it was God speaking. Today, after more than fifteen years, God has answered prayer and blessed Pioneers with more than 550 missionaries and 150 national workers in thirty-nine countries.

April 13

CHERI FULLER, Oklahoma City; mother of three, educator, and author of fourteen books, including *A Mother's Book of Wit and Wisdom, Unlocking Your Child's Learning Potential, 365 Ways to Develop Your Child's Values, 365 Ways to Build Your Child's Self-Esteem,* and *How to Grow a Young Music Lover.*

As each of you has received a gift (a particular spiritual
talent, a gracious divine endowment), employ it for one
another as (befits) good trustees of God's many-sided
grace—faithful stewards of the extremely diverse (powers
and gifts granted to Christians by) unmerited favor.
(1 Peter 4:10, amplified)

How unique God has made each of us—with a one-of-a-kind
brain and different gifts and talents! This verse reminds me how
each child is "gifted" in some way. We need to be looking for
those gifts, just as a treasure hunter would search for them—
whether they are artistic gifts, spiritual gifts, intelligence, or musical talents—then help young people develop their talents and
skills and use them for God's glory. Nothing builds a sense of
purpose and mission like sensing God's smile when we serve
Him with the special abilities He has given us. As Eric Little,
Scottish missionary and Olympic runner, said, "God made me
fast. And when I run I feel His pleasure."

April 14

LINDA CALDWELL FULLER, cofounder with her husband,
Millard, of Habitat for Humanity International, Christian organization based in Americus, Georgia, nation's largest nonprofit
builder, providing housing for low-income families in more than
1,250 U.S. cities and nearly fifty countries; with their four children, she and her husband piloted a ministry to build low-cost
housing in Zaire, Africa, from 1973 to 1976; coauthor with
her husband of the 1990 Habitat history, *The Excitement Is*
Building, and editor of the organization's fund-raising cookbook, *Partners in the Kitchen: From Our House to Yours.*

. . . Ask and it will be given to you; seek and you will find;
knock and the door will be opened to you. For everyone
who asks receives; he who seeks finds; and to him who
knocks, the door will be opened. (Luke 11:9–10, NIV)

Life can be so fulfilling when we seek God's will. Sometimes, however, puzzling things happen. When things happen that I don't understand, Luke 11:9–10 gives me hope and encouragement that answers and help will come. It's so easy to get "off track" in life and lose sight of what is really important in God's eyes. Millard and I, during the first five years of our marriage, were focused on getting rich to the detriment of our relationships with each other, family members, and God. When we realized we were on the wrong track, God cleansed us from our sins, restored and even deepened relationships, and gave us a whole new focus, this time on Christian missions. Working in partnership with God, Habitat for Humanity International, which was started nearly twenty years ago, is building thousands of houses for needy families all over the world.

On a personal level, one of my most recent puzzlements was a series of frightening health symptoms. For more than eight months I suffered from depression, insomnia, loss of appetite, anxiety attacks, backache, and difficulty with concentration. Having always considered myself healthy both mentally and physically, I couldn't understand why, all of a sudden at age fifty-one, I was literally falling apart. My faith in God and trusting in Scriptures such as this one in Luke assured me I would eventually find out the reason I was feeling so poorly. Sure enough, I found a friend who had had similar symptoms five years previously. Hormone replacement therapy returned her and me to a normal state of health. This Scripture calls us to action. We cannot allow ourselves to sit around and think that God or anyone else will solve our problems. When we actively seek and ask, the answers will come. It helps to have patience, too.

April 15

MILLARD FULLER, president, Habitat for Humanity International, Christian organization he and his wife, Linda, founded in 1976; marketing millionaire at age twenty-nine who, with his wife, later sold their possessions and, from 1973 to 1976, directed a pilot project for low-income family housing in Zaire, Africa; author or coauthor of five books, most recently, *The Theology of the Hammer.*

> *For God so loved the world, that He gave His only begotten Son, that whoever believes in Him should not perish, but have eternal life. . . . (John 3:16, NASB)*

This Scripture is important to me personally and to the ministry of Habitat for Humanity for two reasons. First, of course, there is the awesome assurance of salvation through Christ because of God's great love for us. The second reason is, I think, missed by many people. The Scripture clearly states that God so loved *the world!* His love does not stop at any national boundary. Think about that! God loves a man in India just as much as He loves an American man. God's love penetrates to the heart of Iran and China and Africa and extends to the poorest of the village people or those huddled in teeming slums, as well as to the wealthy of those lands, just as it goes out to every man, woman, and child in the United States. This theological understanding is why, in Habitat for Humanity, we expect our affiliates in the United States and in other countries to tithe the contributions they receive locally, to be used to build houses in developing countries while they are building houses in their own hometowns, cities, and counties. God *gave* and so should we. And our loving and our giving should have no limiting boundaries, just as God's love has none.

April 16

GEORGE GALLUP, JR., chairman, The George H. Gallup International Institute, Princeton, New Jersey; cochairman, The Gallup Organization, Inc.; executive director, Princeton Religion Research Center; coauthor of twelve books, most recently,

Growing Up Scared in America, with Wendy Plump, and *The Saints Among Us*, with Timothy Jones.

> *... encourage one another and build one another up. ...*
> *(1 Thessalonians 5:11, RSV)*

This passage relates to one of the numerous occasions when the apostle Paul exhorted the followers of Christ to come together and meet on a deep level in the name of Jesus Christ. Small groups of Christians joining together for Bible study, prayer, caring, and sharing in fellowship are, many believe, a vital way in which to grow up in the Lord. It has been well said that "Faith grows best in the presence of faith." Many believe that such small groups are a particular blessing in our present-day fragmented and impersonal society.

April 17

EVELYN GANDY, first woman to hold the elected offices of Mississippi lieutenant governor, 1976–80, and state treasurer, 1960–64, 1968–72; also commissioner of insurance, 1972–76; also the first woman to be appointed Mississippi commissioner of public welfare and assistant attorney general; currently director of legal services for Central Euro TeleKom, Inc., an international telecommunications corporation with offices in Mississippi and Hungary.

> *And the King shall answer and say unto them, Verily I say*
> *unto you, Inasmuch as ye have done it unto one of the*
> *least of these my brethren, ye have done it unto me.*
> *(Matthew 25:40, KJV)*

Our Lord and Savior, Jesus Christ, the greatest teacher of all time, left us a powerful message that we are to help others. Our responsibilities as Christians include seeking to understand the needs of others, giving witness of our Christian faith, offering our help and encouragement, and striving to improve the quality of life for every person in the communities where we live.

April 18

LARRY GATLIN, Grammy-winning country music performer and songwriter featured on numerous albums and No. 1 country hits; featured in *The Will Rogers Follies* lead role on Broadway, 1993, and on tour, 1994; Larry Gatlin and the Gatlin Brothers (Steve and Rudy) perform thirty-five weeks each year at the Gatlin Brothers Theatre, Myrtle Beach, South Carolina; songwriting credits include music recorded by Johnny Cash, Dottie West, and others and a 1994 musical, *Alive and Well;* made film debut in *The Legend of O. B. Taggart*, 1994.

By this shall all men know that ye are my disciples, if ye have love one to another. (John 13:35, KJV)

For long periods of my life, I didn't love anybody—myself or other people. The challenge to love was the hardest job I ever had. But Christ said the way of the transgressor is hard, while His yoke is easy, and I believe that by loving your neighbor, you make your load a lot lighter.

April 19

JOHN GARCIA GENSEL, retired pastor, Saint Peter's (Lutheran) Church, New York City, who became known as the "Pastor to the Jazz Community" for his longtime ministry to jazz performers.

Wherefore let him that thinketh he standeth take heed lest he fall. (1 Corinthians 10:12, KJV)

This was back in 1932, if you can imagine that, more than sixty years ago: I was a freshman in high school in Catawissa, Pennsylvania, and had already made the varsity team. I started my first game against Mainville, which was just up the road about seven miles. I was pretty cocky, because here I was only a freshman and I was on the varsity baseball team and starting a game. And they scored five runs off me in the first inning and knocked me out of the game. Well, every night I was reading the Bible, and that night I read 1 Corinthians 10:12. I've always remembered that I thought, "Boy, how appropriate that was." So I learned a great lesson there: don't be cocky, be humble, and if you're going to stand, stand with the Lord. There are other great passages of Scripture that have meant a great deal to me, of course, but I don't know of any that have stuck with me for sixty-some years.

April 20

JEANNETTE CLIFT GEORGE, founder and artistic director, A.D. Players, Houston-based Christian theater company; her acting credits include the film *The Hiding Place,* in the role of Dutchwoman Corrie ten Boom who saved scores of Jews' lives during the Nazi occupation, plus Off-Broadway and touring productions with the New York Shakespeare Company; author of two books, *Some Run with Feet of Clay* and *Travel Tips from a Reluctant Traveler.*

> *There is therefore now no condemnation for those who are in Christ Jesus. (Romans 8:1, RSV)*

To me this has been a liberating verse. The fear of condemnation can paralyze us. Strangely enough, it is as threatening in seasons of success as it is in times of failure. I have sensed my creative impulses, my appetite for growth, and even my intention to obey God halting at the thought of error resulting in condemnation. God's message of grace to the believer frees us from such fear, and in that freedom we can respond to the convicting direction of the Holy Spirit. We can learn and grow within the certain security of His grace.

April 21

HEIDI GILLINGHAM, center, Vanderbilt University women's basketball team, 1990–94; 1992–93 season honors included NCAA Final Four All-Tournament Team and Kodak All-American; 1993–94 season honors included first team, All-SEC (Southeastern Conference); elected 1993 Vanderbilt homecoming queen; current member of the Athletes in Action national team.

I will praise thee; for I am fearfully and wonderfully
made: marvellous are thy works. . . . (Psalm 139:14, KJV)

Experiencing God's abundant love and personal interest in my life has given me a complete satisfaction with who I am and a strong desire to serve the Lord with all my heart. My accolades in basketball have given me a small amount of esteem, but nothing compared to the knowledge that God knew me before I was born and has a purpose in mind for my life. For that reason, at six-feet-eight-inches there's no height I'd rather be, no person I'd rather be. Respecting ourselves as God's beautiful, unique creations can do that for all of us.

April 22

OWEN GINGERICH, senior astronomer, Smithsonian Astrophysical Observatory, and professor of astronomy and professor of the history of science, Harvard University; chairman of Harvard's history of science department, 1992–93; author and/or editor of numerous works, including author of *Album of Science: The Physical Sciences in the Twentieth Century* and editor of the twentieth-century section of the International Astronomical Union's *General History of Astronomy.*

*So God created man in his own image, in the image of
God created he him; male and female created he them.
(Genesis 1:27, KJV)*

The first chapter of Genesis is not a scientific textbook but a
magnificent, universal statement of God's creative powers. It
rises to a climax in this verse, which tells us there is a divine
spark in each of us, including those godly attributes of con-
sciousness, creativity, and conscience.

April 23

FRITZ GLAUS, former tennis teaching pro who founded
and led a chaplaincy ministry on pro tennis tour for ten years,
subsequently serving as director of ministry development,
Patrick Morley Ministries' outreach to the nation's cities.

*But by the grace of God I am what I am, and his grace to
me was not without effect. No, I worked harder than all
of them—yet not I, but the grace of God that was with
me. (1 Corinthians 15:10, NIV)*

My identity and motivation come as a result of God's grace. In
spite of Paul's past, he found his identity in God's grace and was
motivated to work harder by the grace of God within him. An
athlete should not find his identity in his accomplishments or be
motivated solely by his desire to win. We will find our true
selves in His grace and we will find no greater motivation than
His grace.

April 24

JOYCE GLEAVE, elementary school art teacher, Mustang,
Oklahoma, nearly twenty-five years; after school officials discouraged her from distributing to her students during school
hours olive-wood crosses she had purchased on a trip to the

Holy Land, she delivered the crosses and a Christian tract in personal visits to her 600 students' homes.

> *. . . I will never leave thee, nor forsake thee.*
> *(Hebrews 13:5, KJV)*

This precious promise that God has repeated various times in His Word has meant so much to me throughout my life. In times of distress, I have turned to run to Jesus only to bump into Him, because He is always so very near. Even as I turn, I find myself already in the safety of His arms. That's how it was after thirty-two years of marriage, when my husband went home to our Lord. God did not leave me alone. He stayed right there with me and took such good care of me. When I have decisions to make, I do not have to make them alone. The Holy Spirit is my counselor. When there is something on my heart that I really need to talk to someone about, I write to the Lord. He is a wonderful listener. I can be perfectly honest with Him because He already knows my heart; He never judges me; He is ready and able to give me help; and He gives me peace. One thing I talk to the Lord about—a lot—is my students. It never fails, He is always there at school to guide me, help me, and encourage me. My faith is renewed as I go back and read my files from these visits with the Lord. I am made to remember how faithful God has always been. There are two things I know for sure: my place is in the classroom with my students; and God, who always keeps His promises, truly never will leave me nor forsake me.

April 25

CHRIS GODFREY, starting right guard for Super Bowl XXI champion New York Giants and, earlier, the Michigan Panthers championship team in the United States Football League; starting defensive tackle for three University of Michigan Rose Bowl teams; currently an attorney in South Bend, Indiana, and president, Pro-Life Athletes, Inc., a fellowship of current and former professional athletes fostering respect for human life among youth and assisting maternity care centers.

> *But strive first for the kingdom of God and his righteousness, and all these things will be given to you as well.*
> *(Matthew 6:33, NRSV)*

I had a strong love for God when I was young, but in high school and college, while I never fully denied God, I started doing things my way—my ambition, my pleasure, my sense of morality. I wasn't drafted out of college in 1980; I was kind of undersized for a defensive lineman and had had mononucleosis for six months. But I did sign as a free agent with Washington. Nobody really gave me a chance to make the team, but I never wanted anything as bad as I wanted a spot with the Redskins. So I put on twenty pounds, got in the best shape of my life, went to camp, and was the coach's dream, giving 100 percent every play of every practice. By the end of the 1980 preseason, the local media and my teammates were talking about how I was going to make the team. And I remember just letting go and deciding to enjoy the good life to the fullest.

Well, the next day I got cut. A couple of weeks later I was picked up by the New York Jets and spent the year backing up Joe Klecko and Mark Gastineau. The day before I came out to training camp the next year, I injured my knee, came to Jets camp, but got cut. I drove home and a message was waiting that Green Bay wanted to sign me. So I flew there the next morning. When I was told I had made the team, I had all my things brought up and was really excited about playing. But I got a phone call in my hotel room the next morning telling me I had been cut. It was then that I just fell to my knees and said, "Lord, I give up. I've got nothing left. Whatever You want me to do. Wherever You want me to go. You're the boss now." I was heading out the door after cleaning out my locker when Bart Starr, then the head coach, waved me back into the office, apologized that a mistake had been made, and asked if I'd stay. I just knew God had a hand in the whole thing—and He had gotten my attention.

A week or two later I was invited to the team Bible study, and the Bible just started coming alive in a way it never had before. One passage in particular jumped off the page at me, and that was Matthew 6:33: to seek first His kingdom and His righteousness and all the things I was concerned about—the car, the money, getting married—would fall in place. But I had to get my priorities straight. I really held onto that promise of God, even when things didn't start off so well. The next summer, I separated my shoulder and the whole league went on strike. I was out of a job. But I signed with the new United States Football League that year, moved from defense to offense, and we won the championship. I also got married. The next year, I signed a million-dollar contract with the New York Giants, won a starting spot, went to the Super Bowl a couple of years later, and on and on. God has kept His promise in giving me all those other things. Even so, the most important thing I have now is my identity as God's son. Nothing else matters nearly as much.

April 26

SAM GONZALES, chief of police, Oklahoma City Police Department, since 1991; former first executive assistant chief of police, Dallas Police Department, who joined the Dallas force as a patrol officer in 1963.

> Trust in the LORD with all your heart,
> And do not lean on your own understanding.
> In all your ways acknowledge Him,
> and He will make your paths straight.
> (Proverbs 3:5–6, NASB)

I picked these verses up from Bob Vernon (then Los Angeles assistant police chief) a number of years ago. I was a deputy chief in Dallas, and he was in Dallas to address the fellowship of Christian law enforcement people. Bob talked about Proverbs 3:5–6 and trusting in the Lord. He used an example I have since used on numerous occasions when I speak, and I'm always careful to quote it as coming from Bob. It's an example people in law enforcement can relate to. He said, "Belief is me taking a bulletproof vest, bringing it up on the stage, and firing at it with my service revolver—and you can see that the bullets will not penetrate the vest. That's belief. Trust is when you put the vest on and say, 'Now shoot.'" It was a real good example for me of the difference between believing what the Lord says for me to do and trusting in what the Lord wants me to do. It was a big step in my obedience, my commitment, to actually go beyond believing—to doing.

April 27

W. WILSON GOODE, regional representative, U.S. Department of Education, six-state Region III; mayor of Philadelphia, 1984–92, the first black elected to the post; former positions include managing director, Philadelphia, the city's number-two position; chairman, Pennsylvania Public Utility Commission; president and chief executive officer, Philadelphia Council for Community Advancement, nonprofit corporation to assist nonprofit housing corporations; with Joann Stevens, author of *In Goode Faith* autobiography.

The fear of the LORD is the beginning of knowledge: but fools despise wisdom and instruction. (Proverbs 1:7, KJV)

I learned early in life that knowledge is the key to success. Further, all real knowledge comes from God. My success in life is directly tied to my faith in Him. Through Him, impossibilities become possible. Those who deny Him do so at their own peril. From sharecropper to mayor is evidence of His miracles.

April 28

AL GORE, U.S. vice president; U.S. senator from Tennessee, 1984–93; U.S. congressman, 1976–84; chairman, U.S. Senate Delegation to the 1992 Earth Summit, Rio de Janeiro, Brazil, and author, *Earth in the Balance: Ecology and the Human Spirit*, 1992; 1988 candidate for the Democratic presidential nomination, winning primaries in seven states.

> *Therefore all things whatsoever ye would that men should do to you, do ye even so to them: for this is the law and the prophets. (Matthew 7:12, KJV)*

I regularly find great inspiration and strength from the Scriptures, and this is a passage I have turned to at many different points in my life.

April 29

MILTON GOSSETT, national chairman, Religion in American Life, 1990–96; chairman emeritus, Saatchi & Saatchi Advertising Worldwide, New York City, world's largest advertising company, with offices across the United States and associate agencies in sixty-four countries and such clients as IBM, Toyota, Johnson & Johnson, Procter & Gamble, and General Mills; he joined the former Compton Advertising agency in 1949, rising to chief executive officer and chairman, remaining in those positions when Compton merged with Saatchi & Saatchi.

> *Trust in the LORD with all your heart,*
> *And do not lean on your own understanding.*
> *In all your ways acknowledge Him,*
> *and He will make your paths straight.*
> *(Proverbs 3:5–6, NASB)*

I have found that these verses comfort me when I run up against situations that seem impossible to solve. They remind me that things that seem impossible are only impossible from my own perspective and from my own understanding. Over the years, I've slowly begun to realize the power of faith in the Lord. Now if I can just learn to listen for His directions more often and follow His path, I will save myself from sleepless nights of trying to solve my problems my way.

April 30

BILLY GRAHAM, who has preached the gospel to more people in live audiences than anyone else in history—more than 210 million in 180-plus countries and territories; worldwide media efforts highlighted by April 14, 1996, *World Television Series* aired by satellite to 2.5 billion people in more than 160 countries; *Hour of Decision* preacher on more than 1,000 radio stations worldwide weekly; author of seventeen books; "My Answer" columnist in newspapers with circulation of more than 7 million; listed in *Who's Who in America* since 1954 and in Gallup poll of world's ten most admired men since 1955; 1982 winner, Templeton Prize for Progress in Religion; 1996 recipient with wife Ruth, Congressional Gold Medal, Congress's highest civilian honor.

> *For God so loved the world, that he gave his only begotten Son, that whosoever believeth in him should not perish, but have everlasting life. (John 3:16, KJV)*

My favorite verse of Scripture was taught to me by my mother when I was just a little boy. John 3:16 is the one Scripture I always preach on in a crusade, usually on the opening night. I suppose it is the most familiar passage in the Bible. It has only twenty-five words in the English translation of it, but it is the gospel in a nutshell. Someone has called it a miniature Bible.

The word *whosoever* in this verse means the whole world. Whatever the color of a person's skin, whatever language he or she speaks, God loves that person and is willing to save him or her. To me, that is marvelous. This Scripture also says that life doesn't begin when you die; it begins here and now.

MAY

May 1

MAURICE GRAHAM, associate pastor, Bon Air Baptist Church, Richmond, Virginia; Baptist worker among Americans held hostage at U.S. Embassy in Kuwait after Iraqi invasion in 1990; director of pastoral care, Saint Jude Children's Research Hospital, Memphis, Tennessee, 1980–86.

If you have any encouragement from being united in Christ, if any comfort from his love, if any fellowship with the Spirit, if any tenderness and compassion, then make my joy complete by being like-minded, having the same love, being one in spirit and purpose. Do nothing out of selfish ambition or vain conceit, but in humility consider others better than yourselves. Each of you should look not only to your own interests, but also to the interests of others. Your attitude should be the same as that of Christ Jesus. (Philippians 2:1–5, NIV)

I call this passage my attitude checklist. I remind myself to have the same attitude Christ would have in a situation. Normally that keeps me out of trouble. It keeps me close to the Lord. If we have the attitude of Christ, we're not going to go wrong.

May 2

HOWARD D. GRAVES, retired U.S. Army lieutenant general; superintendent of the United States Military Academy, West Point, 1991–96; Rhodes Scholar who earned advanced degrees at Oxford University in England in international relations and modern history from 1961 to 1964; among his military assignments: assistant to the Chairman of the Joint Chiefs of Staff; vice-director, Joint Staff; and military assistant to the Secretary of Defense.

> *For since the world began no one has seen or heard of such a God as ours, who works for those who wait for him! (Isaiah 64:4, TLB)*

I have enjoyed the way this verse describes God's sovereignty, and His unique relationship with humanity, in that He is glorified by providing for all we need. Our role is to walk with Him and enjoy His glory in and through us.

May 3

DARRELL GREEN, cornerback on the Washington Redskins' Super Bowl XXVI and XXII champion teams and all-time Redskins interception leader; three-time winner of the "NFL Fastest Man" competition, five-time Pro Bowl selection; Redskins' first-round draft choice in 1983 and Lone Star Conference Defensive Player of the Year, 1982, at Texas A & I; founder, Darrell Green Youth Life Foundation, Washington, D.C., with inner-city efforts including a state-of-the-art learning center for youth, offering computer learning programs that teach technical skills and character development.

> *But Jesus called them to Himself and said, "You know that the rulers of the Gentiles lord it over them, and those who are great exercise authority over them. Yet it shall not be so among you; but whoever desires to become great among you, let him be your servant. . . ."*
> *(Matthew 20:25–26, NKJV)*

The world perceives athletes as great, but God calls us to be servants like Him.

May 4

ERIC GREGORY, doctoral candidate in religious studies, Yale University; Rhodes Scholar at Trinity College, Oxford, England, 1992–95, earning master's degrees in philosophy and in New Testament and systematic theology; bachelor of arts graduate cum laude, Harvard University, 1992.

> *Be still, and know that I am God;*
> *I will be exalted among the nations,*
> *I will be exalted in the earth. (Psalm 46:10, NIV)*

This verse about God's majesty has spoken to me in times of sorrow, anxiety, and frustration. God reveals that in our stillness, we come to realize not only His existence but also His loving presence and His ultimate victory. In stillness before God, we know truly about peace—a kind of knowing that is vastly more real and total than any other kind. Surely, our God reigns! This is the knowledge that the whole world needs.

May 5

ARCHIE GRIFFIN, college football's only two-time Heisman Trophy winner; NCAA Top Five Award winner for athletic, academic, and leadership excellence; Ohio State's career rushing leader who led OSU to a 40–5–1 record during his four years as starting tailback; three-time first-team All-American, holder of NCAA records for most consecutive 100-yard games, thirty-one, and most yards per carry average, 6.1; current associate director of athletics at Ohio State.

> *Delight yourself in the LORD*
> *and he will give you the desires of your heart.*
> *(Psalm 37:4, NIV)*

After winning the Heisman my junior year, I felt that I was carrying a heavy load. People were always asking me if I thought I could win in my senior year, and deep down inside I did want to win the trophy again. When I read this verse, I felt the load was lifted. To me, the verse meant to find joy in serving God. If I did that, He would take away the desire to win the Heisman my senior year. And, if I did win, it would be a gift.

May 6

DON HABERER, American Falls, Idaho, western artist and photographer.

> *I will instruct you and teach you in the way which you should go. I will counsel you with My eye upon you. (Psalm 32:8, NASB)*

As I continue to seek the Lord's guidance and will in the development of my artwork, the subject matter has gone through various changes, as has my personal growth. These periods of development have come when the objective is no longer to see how well I can paint a landscape or a horse, though I still strive for accuracy, but when I seek for the pieces I produce to give the viewer an awareness that all things are created by God and a yearning for the godly values this country once held.

May 7

THOMAS S. HAGGAI, chairman since 1976, and chief executive officer since 1986, IGA (Independent Grocers Alliance), third-largest supermarket group in North America; public speaker who averaged 250 speeches a year for fifteen years; author of three books; speaker on *One Minute, Please* daily radio program.

> *I will lift up mine eyes to the hills, from whence cometh my help. My help cometh from the LORD, which made heaven and earth. (Psalm 121:1–2, KJV)*

I was raised by godly parents on the premise that, as someone said many, many years ago, "We pray like it all depends on God and then we work like it all depends on us." It was very important to me as an undergirding to know that I had the omniscient and omnipotent God; therefore, I've been able in most instances to leave the tomorrows to Him as well as leaving the strength to Him.

May 8

FRANK HALEY, news director, KOB-AM, Albuquerque, New Mexico, who joined the station as morning news anchor and reporter in 1977.

> *For unto us a child is born, unto us a son is given: and the government shall be upon his shoulder: and his name shall be called Wonderful, Counsellor, The mighty God, The everlasting Father, The Prince of Peace.*
> *(Isaiah 9:6, KJV)*

For years I read this verse at Christmastime and just skipped over the part about "everlasting Father." I had known since I was saved in vacation Bible school at age twelve that Jesus was the Son of God, but not until I was thirty-six did the "light" come on to the fact that that little baby in the manger was God Almighty, the Father, the Creator of everything, come down in the flesh to be with humanity. When I finally understood that, it made the love I felt from God so much more precious and real. Praise the Lord for a God who loves us so much that He'll not only send His only Son, but He'll come Himself.

May 9

RICHARD C. HALVERSON, chaplain, U.S. Senate, 1981–95; pastor of Fourth Presbyterian Church, Bethesda, Maryland, 1958–81; chairman of the board, World Vision—U.S., 1966–83;

author of seven books. (He died November 28, 1995, at age seventy-nine.)

> *And lest I should be exalted above measure through the abundance of the revelations, there was given to me a thorn in the flesh, the messenger of Satan to buffet me, lest I should be exalted above measure. For this thing I besought the Lord thrice, that it might depart from me. And he said unto me, My grace is sufficient for thee: for my strength is made perfect in weakness. Most gladly therefore will I gather glory in my infirmities, that the power of Christ may rest upon me. Therefore I take pleasure in infirmities, in reproaches, in necessities, in persecutions, in distresses for Christ's sake: for when I am weak, then am I strong. (2 Corinthians 12:7–10, KJV)*

For many reasons, I grew up with a low self-image. At twenty years of age, I discovered I was protecting my low self-esteem in many false ways. When God led me to this passage, it slowly captured my attention, and for at least two-thirds of my ministry of more than fifty years, I have been able to rejoice in my weakness, that the strength of Christ might be manifest in me.

To me, Christ is the only real issue the human race faces. Ignoring that, nothing can be resolved. Taking it seriously opens the door to every human need.

May 10

GEORGE HAMILTON IV, twenty-five-year Grand Ole Opry member featured on more than fifty albums; named by *Billboard* magazine as "International Ambassador of Country Music" in 1974 after being the first country music star to perform in Russia and Czechoslovakia; was master of ceremonies at the first international country music festival in Sweden in 1976 and subsequently in Finland, Holland, Norway, and Germany.

I beseech you therefore, brethren, by the mercies of God,
that ye present your bodies a living sacrifice, holy, accept-
able unto God, which is your reasonable service. And be
not conformed to this world: but be ye transformed by the
renewing of your mind, that ye may prove what is that
good, and acceptable, and perfect, will of God.
(Romans 12:1–2, KJV)

I grew up in a Christian home but took it all for granted and coasted along for much of my youth. After going to Eastern Europe in the early seventies and meeting young people who not only carried the cross but literally laid their lives on the line for their faith, I went through a time of awakening and recommitment in my own walk with the Lord. These verses became especially meaningful for me then and have been ever since.

May 11

VALERIE HANCOCK, copy editor, Baptist Sunday School Board, Nashville, Tennessee; lifestyle editor, *Register-News,* Mount Vernon, Illinois, after graduating from Eastern Illinois University, Charleston, in 1992, where she was president of the Baptist Student Union.

". . . For I know the plans I have for you," declares the
LORD, "plans to prosper you and not to harm you, plans
to give you hope and a future. . . ." (Jeremiah 29:11, NIV)

In the summer of 1992 when I graduated from a four-year university, I, along with many other graduates my age, thought a college degree was my ticket to the perfect job. But when that perfect job didn't come after I had sent hundreds of résumés and received almost as many rejection letters, I knew the task was going to be harder than I had expected. But I found comfort in these words—God's words—knowing that even though I am not where I thought I would be at this point in my life, God has a plan for me, and He is teaching me through the job I now have. In His time He will direct me to where He wants me to be and to the job He wants me to have—not where I want to be or the job I want to have. Even now, I am still unsure of the path God has chosen for me, but I know it will be much more rewarding than any I could have chosen myself. It is a plan that gives me a hope and a future.

May 12

BRIAN HARPER, catcher for the Minnesota Twins World Series champions, 1991, batting .381 in seven games; one of only four catchers in forty years to hit .300 three consecutive seasons, 1991–93; other Twins marks include American League record for longest hitting streak by a catcher, 25 in 1990, and top defensive American League catcher, just 11 errors in 1989; also appeared in the World Series with St. Louis in 1985 and has played with three other teams during fifteen years in the majors.

> *Delight thyself also in the LORD; and he shall give thee the desires of thine heart. Commit thy way unto him; and he shall bring it to pass. (Psalm 37:4–5, KJV)*

My success has come from trusting in the Lord! He has done it!

May 13

DONALD HARRIS, pastor of Timberlake Baptist Church, Timberlake, North Carolina; at age forty-six, he became the one hundredth successful heart transplant patient at Duke University Medical Center, Durham, North Carolina.

> *And the prayer of faith will save the sick, and the Lord will raise him up. . . . (James 5:15, NKJV)*

For three years, folks prayed for me, that a heart would become available and I could continue my ministry if it be God's will.

Folks were praying from as far west as Texas, as far south as Florida, as far north as Maine, and all through the East Coast. Praying just for me, Donald Harris. And the Lord saw fit to answer those prayers with the heart of a sixteen-year-old boy who unfortunately had taken his life by a self-inflicted gunshot. As I and others prayed, I don't know whether you would call it a sensation or not, but I had confidence that God was going to intervene and do what needed to be done. Although my condition was weakening, I just felt the power of the Lord within me, giving me the faith to know He was in charge and everything was going to be all right. And when the heart came on June 9, 1994, that absolutely confirmed it. I had very little fear, if any at all, when I went into surgery that afternoon. I knew that God had provided for me and had everything in hand. It was one of the quickest surgeries (four hours) that they've had and one of the most complete—the heart started on its own. You could see the pattern of God's work in it.

Doctors told me in June 1991 that I needed a heart, that mine could stop functioning at any time. It was devastating; it was a shock to be facing the reality of looking at death itself, of leaving my family at any time. During those three years of waiting, the meaning of life's relationships became so much more pure than it was before. I'm closer to the Lord than I've ever been before; I'm closer to my wife, my children, my friends, and fellow Christians. When we reach the point where death may soon come into our presence, we begin to realize that the relationships we have with others are the most precious things on earth. They're priceless—so much more important than any material possessions in life. We learn to appreciate the family values God intends for us and the love and care we're to have for each other. We want to give ourselves to others, to live out fully the love based on our Lord Jesus Christ and what He's done for us through the blood of Calvary.

May 14

LONNIE HARRIS, pastor of Bethel House of Prayer, thirty-five-member congregation in Clover, South Carolina, and a $5 million *Reader's Digest* 1994 sweepstakes winner; married, with four children, he told the media he would use the winnings to buy a van for his gospel music group and to help the needy.

> ... *Repent, and be baptized every one of you in the name of Jesus Christ, for the remission of sins, and ye shall receive the gift of the Holy Ghost. (Acts 2:38, KJV)*

As an Apostolic minister, I believe the keys to the kingdom that Jesus gave to the apostle Peter were used in Acts, chapter 2, verse 38. To open the door to the kingdom of God, regardless of what faith a person is, one should obey Acts 2:38.

May 15

MARK HATFIELD, U.S. senator from Oregon, 1967–96; chairman, Senate Appropriations Committee; former chairman, Congressional Arms Control and Foreign Policy Caucus; Oregon governor, 1959–67; Oregon secretary of state, 1957–59, and earlier, member of the state's senate and house of representatives; author of three books, coauthor of four others.

> *And thou shalt love the Lord thy God with all thy heart, and with all thy soul, and with all thy mind, and with all thy strength. . . . Thou shalt love thy neighbour as thyself. There is none other commandment greater than these. (Mark 12:30–31, KJV)*

These words from Mark have guided my thinking through the course of my life. They drive my work in public service and shape my thoughts as a husband, a father, and a man. The passage forms a foundation for establishing a peace within ourselves and a peace throughout our planet. I hope others can draw from it what I have through the years.

May 16

FINLEY HAYS, founder, with wife Jean, of *Loggers World* magazine in 1964 and three subsequent logging-related magazines, *Timber Cutter, Log Trucker,* and *Christian Logger;* founding member, Christian Loggers and Truckers Association; author of four logging books, most recently *Saginaw Timber Company;* logger from 1935 to 1964.

> *Therefore, my dear brothers, stand firm. Let nothing move you. Always give yourselves fully to the work of the Lord, because you know that your labor in the Lord is not in vain. (1 Corinthians 15:58, NIV)*

In 1978 as I was traveling and showing little progress in setting up chapters of the Christian Loggers and Truckers Association, I was overtaken by the three-day flu in Coeur D'Alene, Idaho, while staying at a Holiday Inn. I was sick, disgusted, and ready to turn about and discard the idea of Christian loggers banding together. The Lord led me to this verse, and since then I've come back to it time and again. It is as strengthening, as fresh, and as new now as it was then—"your labor in the Lord is not in vain."

May 17

BOBBY HEBERT, quarterback, Atlanta Falcons; tenth most accurate passer in NFL history; in the 1993 Pro Bowl, he led the NFC to a come-from-behind victory; with the New Orleans Saints seven seasons, he led the team in 1987 to its first-ever playoff game and best-ever record, 12–3; as a rookie in the former United States Football League, he helped the Michigan Panthers win the 1983 championship.

Trust in the LORD *with all your heart*
and lean not on your own understanding;
in all your ways acknowledge him,
and he will make your paths straight.
Do not be wise in your own eyes;
fear the LORD *and shun evil. (Proverbs 3:5–7, NIV)*

When I first became a Christian, it finally gave me a destiny in life. Jesus gives you the peace of God that passes all understanding, as well as joy unspeakable. God said, "Never will I leave you; never will I forsake you" (Hebrews 13:5). What great assurance that gives all Christians. We must always have faith in Jesus, that He will always guide us in everything we do, whether in sports, school, or everyday life. Just trust in Jesus.

May 18

FRANKEE HELLINGER, Orlando city commissioner, 1988–96; former chair, Central Florida Regional Transit Authority and the East Central Florida Regional Planning Council and its Affordable Housing Task Force and Transportation Disadvantaged Local Coordinating Board; she and her husband, Richard, were missionaries in India seven years, and she served terms as president of the American Woman's Club and Baptist Women of India.

I have been crucified with Christ; it is no longer I who
live, but Christ who lives in me; and the life I now live in
the flesh I live by faith in the Son of God, who loved me
and gave himself for me. (Galatians 2:20, RSV)

This verse has been the anchor of my life for many years, as a wife, mother of six children, missionary to India, and elected official. It clearly states my qualification and my mandate for serving—I have been spiritually crucified with Christ, which results in a completely new orientation in my life's goals and priorities. It is He who defines my purpose and gives me the strength and courage to deal with my fears of failure and personal incompetence. It tells me that to the extent I live my life by faith and in obedience to Jesus Christ, there is an eternal perspective to my actions, and the very strong and infallible resources of Jesus Christ Himself reside in me to enable me to become all that is needed to effect the very will of God in the circumstance at hand. Does this make my decisions easier and less of a struggle? No, but it surely provides the proper perspective for me as a struggling Christian and the reassurance needed to face the next challenge!

May 19

MAX HELTON, founder, president, Motor Racing Outreach, with ministries to NASCAR and other racing sports; chaplain for NASCAR's Winston Cup division.

This book shall not depart from your mouth, but you shall meditate on it day and night, so that you may be careful to do according to all that is written in it; for then you will make your way prosperous, and then you will have success. . . . (Joshua 1:8, NASB)

Here was Joshua in troublesome times—Moses had died and Joshua had assumed the leadership of Israel—and God gave him the keys to a successful life—not success in material things but for a contented and joyful life. Three things are noted in the verse: one, to know the Word of God; second, to meditate on it; and third, to do it. I believe these will produce a successful life for anyone, and this is why Bible study is so important. In our country, it's interesting that so many people have a copy of the Bible; they would probably fight for it and maybe even die for it. And yet, so many people don't know what's in it.

May 20

CARL F. H. HENRY, theologian; founding editor of *Christianity Today* in 1956 who led the periodical for twelve years; previously professor of theology and Christian philosophy, Fuller Theological Seminary, Pasadena, California; author of more than thirty-five books, including the six-volume *God, Revelation and Authority* from 1976 to 1986, and *Has Democracy Had Its Day?*

> *Now thanks be unto God, who always leads us forth to triumph in the Anointed One, and who diffuses by us the fragrance of the knowledge of Him in every place.*
> *(2 Corinthians 2:14, trans. unknown)*

The text focuses on the triumphant victory of our sovereign Lord, on God's work advanced in us and through us by His messianic Son, and how we to the perishing and putrefying world around us become the fragrant aroma of salvation. What profounder reason for thanksgiving and gratitude than this, that He leads us ever and always on this mission of mercy, in which we in turn bring glory to our great Redeemer.

May 21

THOMAS H. HERLONG, cofounder of the Fellowship of Christian Farmers International in 1985 and president from 1985 to 1993 of the organization, which now has more than 13,000 members; cattle farmer in South Carolina; U.S. Department of Agriculture staff member in South Carolina, 1991–93.

> *Trust in the LORD with all your heart*
> *and lean not on your own understanding;*
> *in all your ways acknowledge him,*
> *and he will make your paths straight.*
> *(Proverbs 3:5–6, NIV)*

After starting the Fellowship of Christian Farmers, Wilson Lippy (who is now FCF president) and I were traveling together in the western United States to meet with several groups of people to help organize the FCF in their states. Those first years in the organizational effort were very trying at times. While we were traveling and listening to a tape on Proverbs, verses 5 and 6 of the third chapter took on a powerful meaning in my walk with the Lord. I have a terrible weakness in my faith of trying to direct my own path. It is so important for me to keep reminding myself of what faith is all about. We worship a God who has shown His love beyond our comprehension. How much better we are when we allow Him to direct our paths.

May 22

ROBERTA HESTENES, president of Eastern College, St. Davids, Pennsylvania, 1987–96; chairperson, World Vision International board of directors, 1985–92; associate professor and director of Christian formation and discipleship, Fuller Theological Seminary, Pasadena, California, 1975–87; author of two books, coauthor of two others.

Therefore, since through God's mercy we have this ministry, we do not lose heart. (2 Corinthians 4:1, NIV)

This is my favorite verse (and chapter) in the Bible because it reminds me that the work or ministry I do and the burdens that come with that work for the cause of Christ are not a burden but a blessing, not a duty but a privilege, not something I do for God but something significant that God has given me as part of His love and mercy. Serving God and people gives my life significance and meaning. The problems of caring for the world's poor or the challenges of running a Christian college would be overwhelming without this knowledge that ministry is a gift, a calling, an opportunity rooted in God's mercy.

May 23

BOBBY HILLIN, JR., NASCAR driver who won the 1986 Talladega 500; youngest driver ever to run 200 miles per hour, at age twenty in Winston Cup qualifying at Talladega; he and his wife, Kim, and two other NASCAR couples founded Motor Racing Outreach in 1988, offering worship services before each NASCAR race and Bible studies in numerous shops where Winston Cup teams build and repair their race cars.

> *Trust in the LORD with all your heart*
> *and lean not on your own understanding. . . .*
> *(Proverbs 3:5, NIV)*

Proverbs is the most useful book in the Bible for anyone to read and receive day-to-day living instructions. Proverbs 3:5 is my reminder that God's wisdom is much greater than mine; therefore I will lean on Him always.

May 24

KIM HILLIN, wife of NASCAR driver Bobby Hillin, Jr., and one of the founders of Motor Racing Outreach, NASCAR ministry based in Charlotte, North Carolina.

> *And we know that God causes all things to work together*
> *for good to those who love God, to those who are called*
> *according to His purpose. (Romans 8:28, NASB)*

In May 1990, Bobby was running fourth in the Charlotte race and catching the cars in front of him. It looked as though he was going to have a great finish, which he really needed, when he blew a tire and hit the wall. He broke his shoulder in the crash. On the way to the hospital, our friends Nancy and John "Bull" Bramlett were riding with us and Bull said, "Remember Romans 8:28, Bobby," and quoted it to us. Bull is an ex–pro football player and an evangelist. His words meant so much that day, and the verse has stuck in my head ever since. I think of it and apply it in many situations, especially during difficult times when things are hard to understand.

May 25

MELISSA HIMES, twenty-four-year-old Food for the Hungry worker taken captive by Cambodian rebels in March 1994, along with two Cambodian co-workers; all three were released unharmed six weeks later; within a few weeks she resumed her work in Cambodia with Food for the Hungry, based in Scottsdale, Arizona.

The LORD is my light and my salvation—
whom shall I fear?
The LORD is the stronghold of my life—
of whom shall I be afraid?
When evil men advance against me
to devour my flesh,
when my enemies and my foes attack me,
they will stumble and fall.
Though an army besiege me,
my heart will not fear;
though war break out against me,
even then will I be confident.
One thing I ask of the LORD,
this is what I seek:
that I may dwell in the house of the LORD
all the days of my life,
to gaze upon the beauty of the LORD
and to seek him in his temple.
For in the day of trouble
he will keep me safe in his dwelling;
he will hide me in the shelter of his tabernacle
and set me high upon a rock.

Then my head will be exalted
above the enemies who surround me;
at his tabernacle will I sacrifice with shouts of joy;
I will sing and make music to the LORD.
(Psalm 27:1–6, NIV)

The psalms have often been a source of comfort, yet never before did David's songs speak to me as this one. Working for a relief and development organization in Cambodia, two Cambodian colleagues and I were taken hostage by Khmer Rouge guerrillas. During our six weeks as captives, there were times when we thought we were going to be killed, or worse. We did not know what plans our captors held for us. Yet this psalm gave me a tremendous peace through it all. With the Creator of the universe protecting us, what did I have to fear from these mere men? He gave me the strength to be strong and take heart and wait on Him. Praise God for His never-failing love and protection. He is faithful!

May 26

JEROME HINES, bass singer with most consecutive seasons, forty-one, and performances, 830, in the history of the Metropolitan Opera; guest performer with the world's major symphonies and opera companies; founder, Opera Music Theatre International for aspiring performers.

And this is life eternal, that they might know thee the only
true God, and Jesus Christ, whom thou hast sent.
(John 17:3, KJV)

I came to Christ not through any human agency but by reading the Scriptures, particularly the Gospel of John. Mine has since been a very experiential Christianity; the Lord dealt with me in miraculous ways and convinced me that I could know Him. At the time, I didn't know anything about evangelicals, but then I found this community of people all over the world who say, "Do you know the Lord?"—and I found my family. I've leaned so heavily upon that fact of knowing God. Not believing as much as knowing, and then believing.

May 27

DON HODEL, secretary of the interior, 1985–89; secretary of energy, 1982–85; currently, managing director, Summit Group International, Ltd., energy and natural resources consulting firm based in Silverthorne, Colorado.

> . . . The Lord is my Helper and I am not afraid of anything that mere man can do to me. (Hebrews 13:6, TLB)

I was in Washington, D.C., during the eight years of the Reagan administration, for six of those years in the cabinet. There was a continual sense of being embattled, because the Washington establishment, Congress, and the media were all determined to keep President Reagan from succeeding. This verse was one of two I kept taped to my mirror during those years. The other was Proverbs 29:25: "The fear of man brings a snare, But he who trusts in the Lord will be exalted" (NASB).

May 28

JIM HODGES, founder and general director, Hard Hats for Christ, a ministry of Construction Workers Christian Fellowship, based in Kelso, Washington, that does evangelism in industrial settings and has coordinated volunteers for construction projects in the United States and twenty-one countries.

> . . . but in the multitude of counsellors there is safety. (Proverbs 11:14, KJV)

In the early days of Hard Hats for Christ, I got very discouraged. Was I really where God wanted me? But I could not get rid of the responsibility of the ministry. Not only was there an increasing interest in Hard Hats from various people, but we had sent our second man to the mission field. Yet the funds and time to keep up with administration were not there. On the basis of Jesus' parable in Luke 13:6–9, about giving a vineyard one more year to bear fruit, my wife, Jean, and I poured ourselves into Hard Hats. We then carried out the intent of Proverbs 11:14 by taking a three-month trip to meet face-to-face with the counselors God had given us. These were men of spiritual maturity, successful in their fields of service, who had been an encouragement to me in the past. Each was then serving on Hard Hats' advisory council and board of reference.

Our trip took us into Illinois, Michigan, Georgia, Florida, Texas, and Kansas. I had to pick up construction work on the way because we traveled with limited funds. Our old Ford pickup broke down. We had to rebuild the engine and transmission. But each of the men I visited with gave us confirmation that we were where we were supposed to be. At the end of the trip, I knew I should persevere. No turning back out of discouragement. I would give up the ministry only if God gave a very clear directive, such as most of our supporters dropping us, the board asking us to leave, or my becoming too disabled to function as director. It would need to be unmistakable and not based on "feelings" or the "greener grass" syndrome.

The result of sticking by Proverbs 11:14 has ordered my life and the life of my family for more than twenty-five years. My goal is to be reproductive in the lives of people who may not otherwise realize they can really know God or understand that they can serve Him with their talents.

May 29

J. DOUGLAS HOLLADAY, chairman, The Thornton Group, merchant bank with offices in New York and Washington, D.C., aiding new and established businesses; founding president, former chairman of the board, One to One Partnership, Inc., an effort by the New York financial community to address urban youth problems; former senior officer with Goldman, Sachs & Company investment banking firm, New York City; U.S. ambassador under President Reagan coordinating U.S. response to challenges related to South Africa; earlier, Reagan White House official under chief of staff James A. Baker III.

> *. . . Love the Lord your God with all your heart and with all your soul and with all your mind.*
> *(Matthew 22:37, NIV)*

Americans are taught to focus almost exclusively upon production and tangible results. By contrast, our Lord challenges us to define our worth by our relationship with Him alone. What results from an intimate love bond with our living God is fruit that is solid and lasting—a real contribution to furthering God's kingdom.

May 30

BOB HOLMES, the "One-Man Volleyball Team" featured in *USA Today* and in TV interviews across the country who plays conventional six-member teams in school assemblies and church-sponsored events, amassing 8,000-plus wins, with fewer than 160 losses, against more than 100,000 opponents since 1986; his wins include games against players from the Washington Redskins, Pittsburgh Steelers, Miami Dolphins, and Buffalo Bills.

> *I can do all things through Christ which strengtheneth me. (Philippians 4:13, KJV)*

When I go on the road, I play sixty to eighty games a week. And the Lord has given me supernatural strength, as well as the opportunity to speak to about a million people now. I had been an evangelist for five years preaching church revivals, and I'd see five or ten or more unsaved people come to Christ. Then it struck me that Jesus went to the woman at the well. Today He probably would go into a gym or wherever the people are. I began praying for a way that God would get me into the public schools, not even knowing volleyball would be the answer.

After every revival meeting, I'd play a few volleyball games in the churches. I was getting out of shape and I liked the workout it gave me. I'd take on two or three guys and then began taking on six, or as many as they wanted to put up against me. I kept playing teams everywhere I went. Then the Lord laid it on my heart to call up some public schools to challenge girls' teams, boys' teams, faculty teams. They'd say, "You're going to take on the whole team? I want to see that." So they booked me. I was never on a volleyball team in high school or college. The talent just developed as I went along. I've said many times, "It's not a one-man volleyball team. Christ has been my partner all through the years." And in every public school, I close the exhibition by saying, "I'm not ashamed to tell you that I'm a Christian and Christ is a solid rock for my life, and if He can be a curse word in the halls all week, there's nothing wrong with somebody saying something good about Him for a change."

I've been asked to try out for the Olympics or for beach volleyball teams, but I feel there is more to life than trophies, medals, and money. There are just too many lives that are empty and lost and need the hope Jesus has to offer. As long as God gives me strength to do this, my goal is to reach the kids in the schools and the whole community.

May 31

LAUREN B. HOMER, attorney and chairwoman, International Law Group, P.C., Annandale, Virginia, law firm assisting Christian mission and humanitarian organizations in legal compliance in former Soviet republics and other parts of the world; founder and president, Law and Liberty Trust, a nonprofit organization supporting restoration of the rule of law and religious liberty.

> *But one who looks intently at the perfect law, the law of liberty, and abides by it, not having become a forgetful hearer but an effectual doer, this man shall be blessed in what he does.* (James 1:25, NASB)

James 1:25 has become the keynote verse for my activities in bringing the rule of law to Russia and other former Soviet republics. The Bible is replete with verses that state that God's law and adherence to it will provide every form of material and spiritual blessing, while departure from it will bring only defeat and disorder.

JUNE

June 1

RACHELLE HOOD-PHILLIPS, president, Inclusive Business Strategies, Inc., diversity consulting firm based in Greenville, South Carolina; Burger King vice president for corporate human resources and diversity affairs, 1991–93, who joined the corporation's staff as director of advertising and promotion in 1984; former advertising agency account supervisor in Chicago.

But small is the gate and narrow the road that leads to life, and only a few find it. (Matthew 7:14, NIV)

I had read the verse often. I had even given a speech from this text the week before. But this time, on my way to our Sunday evening worship service, as I heard the radio commentator speak from this passage, something gripped my heart and stirred deep within my soul. I *had* to talk to God. I raced to church, found an empty room, turned out the lights, and fell prostrate on the floor. I wept profusely. Gratitude washed over me. How precious, fine, and costly was my salvation, a rare gift that most people will not experience. "Father, You created and regenerated me for a purpose. Don't let me come before Your throne and discover I have not used the talents, gifts, and resources You have lavished on me," I prayed. "Help me discover and fulfill my reason for being—for Your glory." Many glorious and wondrous things have happened since that November evening several years ago. God often leads me into deep stormy places, far away from safe harbor. He gently reminds me, "Beloved, I'm here. I am answering your November prayer."

June 2

REX M. HORNE, JR., pastor, Immanuel Baptist Church, Little Rock, Arkansas, home church of President Bill Clinton; weekly columnist for the *Arkansas Democrat-Gazette*.

Call unto me, and I will answer thee, and shew thee great and mighty things, which thou knowest not.
(Jeremiah 33:3, KJV)

This verse has been special all my life because it was my dad's favorite. In our testimonial meetings at First Baptist Church in Cullendale, Arkansas, I remember Dad standing and quoting this verse. It has been a double blessing as a challenge from my heavenly Father and as lived by my dad, who now is in heaven.

June 3

SUSAN HOWARD, actress whose roles have included Donna Culver Krebbs on the CBS series *Dallas*, Maggie Petrocelli on *Petrocelli*, and a homeless mother with three children in the 1994 film *Come the Morning*.

Now faith is the substance of things hoped for, the evidence of things not seen. (Hebrews 11:1, NKJV)

In the day and age we live in, there is the expectancy of getting it all now—as soon as we can, as fast as we can, because we deserve it. I'm not sure how all this came about over the years, but that's the human wisdom that surrounds us. Only faith in Jesus Christ can give you the peace to know and understand that life is more than just getting. There are so many things I hope for in this life, so many promises I would hope to see come to pass, but if they never do, my hope is beyond this world and I can trust that God will fulfill all His promises by His riches in glory. My pastor, Jack Hayford in Van Nuys, California, said on Good Friday several years ago, "It is not the exercise of faith that causes the release, but the exercise of faith to receive what has already been done." My salvation and eternity are a done deal—that is substantive enough for this sinner.

June 4

JACK HOWELL, third baseman, Tokyo Giants; Tokyo League's most valuable player, 1992, with the Yakult Swallows, finishing with highest batting average and most home runs; member of the Swallows' 1993 Japan World Series championship team; set season "Sayonara" record (game-winning home runs), with five in 1993; California Angels third baseman, 1985–90, finishing the '89 season as the major leagues' top fielding third baseman, with .974 percentage.

> *But seek ye first the kingdom of God, and his righteousness; and all these things shall be added unto you. Take therefore no thought for the morrow: for the morrow shall take thought for the things of itself. Sufficient unto the day is the evil thereof. (Matthew 6:33–34, KJV)*

I feel these are key verses to everyone, but especially to professional athletes. In my eleven years in pro baseball, I have witnessed many athletes—including myself—trying to find peace from fame, money, and recognition, only to realize when they achieve more of these things that they still are not happy or satisfied. The only way to find peace is to seek first the kingdom of God and his righteousness rather than the kingdom of money, fame, and recognition. Most athletes' careers are relatively short-lived. And we don't always know where we will be tomorrow (traded?) or if a career-ending injury will cut us short. Many times when in a hitting slump, I have thought my career was ending or my skills were fading, or have heard rumors that I was being traded or released. I have reminded myself of Matthew 6, verse 34 and realized that God already has blessed me in so many ways and will surely take care of not only today but tomorrow.

June 5

DONNA RICE HUGHES, director of communications and marketing, "Enough Is Enough!" campaign to reduce sexual violence and prevent children, women, men, and families from becoming victims by combating child pornography and hardcore pornography; featured in "Donna Rice: My Faith Gave Me Strength," three-page article in *People* magazine's twentieth-anniversary issue, recounting God's healing after national publicity derailing the presidential campaign of Gary Hart in 1987.

> *And we know that all things work together for good to them that love God, to them who are the called according to his purpose. For whom he did foreknow, he also did predestinate to be conformed to the image of his Son, that he might be the firstborn among many brethren.*
> *(Romans 8:28–29, KJV)*

I was brought up in a Christian family and gave my life to the Lord in the ninth grade and was blessed in all areas of my life. I had always heard the first part of this passage, verse 28, and in my mind it meant that everything would work to the good the way I interpreted "good." Later, in my twenties, I strayed from my faith and eventually hit rock bottom and lost everything. I rededicated my life to the Lord, and I came to realize what God was saying in that verse. His good for me, His purpose in my life—as it says in the next verse—is to conform me to the image of His Son. That is what is "good"—God's definition of good. I had always translated my "good" as success, health, vitality, happiness, joy, peace, which are all wonderful. But as I was going through the years of deep, dark valleys of pain and suffering from public humiliation, slander, and disgrace, I began to understand that if I could yield those tough places to God, He could smooth out the rough edges to begin to conform me to His image. That helped me go through the trials and the valleys. I began to see those hard, fiery times as opportunities for growth—for God to mold me into the image of His Son. If I had looked at "good" as good circumstances in human terms, I don't think I could have gotten through it. Even then, I still needed to feel that there was a future, that brighter days would be ahead. And that's where Jeremiah 29:11 came in: "'. . . For I know the plans I have for you,' declares the LORD, 'plans to prosper you and not to harm you, plans to give you hope and a future . . .'" (NIV). Even though God oftentimes may use tough circumstances and trying times to mold me and get me to where He wants me to be, He still has plans for me. There were times that I didn't know if I could get through another day, so I would always remind myself that God was conforming me to the image of His Son and He knew the plans He had for me, plans to give me a future and a hope, not for evil, but for good.

June 6

EARL HUTTO, U.S. congressman, Florida's First District (Pensacola area), 1978–95; former chairman, Subcommittee on Readiness of the House Armed Services Committee and Subcommittee on Coast Guard and Navigation of the House Merchant Marine and Fisheries Committee; prior to his election to Congress, he had been a member of the Florida House of Representatives, an advertising agency owner, and sports director at TV stations in Pensacola and Panama City, Florida, and Montgomery, Alabama.

I can do all things through Christ who strengthens me.
(Philippians 4:13, NKJV)

There are many verses in the Bible that guide me, but this one took on special meaning when I went to Congress in 1978. At that time, my brother-in-law, Albert Myers, gave me a plaque with Philippians 4:13 inscribed on it. It was placed on the door to my inner office and served as a constant reminder that I needed the Lord's involvement in all the decisions I had to make.

June 7

BILL HYBELS, senior pastor, Willow Creek Community Church in Chicago suburb of South Barrington, second-largest Protestant church in the country, with more than 16,000 attending services each week, a staff of more than 300, and a 127-acre campus; he began the church in 1975 in a rented movie theater when he was twenty-three; former Chicago Bears chaplain; author or coauthor of more than ten books, including *Becoming a Contagious Christian* and, with wife Lynne, *Fit to Be Tied: Making Marriage Last a Lifetime*.

> *Now when Jesus had entered Capernaum, a centurion came to Him, pleading with Him, saying, "Lord, my servant is lying at home paralyzed, dreadfully tormented." And Jesus said to him, "I will come and heal him." The centurion answered and said, "Lord, I am not worthy that You should come under my roof. But only speak a word, and my servant will be healed. For I also am a man under authority, having soldiers under me. And I say to this one, 'Go,' and he goes; and to another, 'Come,' and he comes; and to my servant, 'Do this,' and he does it." When Jesus heard it, He marveled, and said to those who followed, "Assuredly, I say to you, I have not found such great faith, not even in Israel!" (Matthew 8:5–10, NKJV)*

I think this is the only time in the Bible where Jesus marveled at the faith of a man or a woman. I was studying this text about twenty years ago, trying to apply it to my life, and I remember saying to myself, "I want to be a just-say-the-word follower of Christ. I want to have a faith Jesus would marvel at. I want to learn the discipline of follower-ship." And this passage has become a life text to me with regard to commitment.

There was something in my spirit wanting to honor the sovereignty, the kingship, the rulership of Christ in the world and in my life. I wanted to be completely surrendered, a fully devoted follower of His. I wanted His influence to affect my whole life— my values, my relationships, my vocabulary, my money management, how I control and treat my body, my decision making, my political ideology. I wanted His way in my life across-the-board. That dynamic swept over me spiritually when I really locked into this passage. I found myself saying, "More than anything else, I want to be totally committed to Jesus Christ and His purposes in this world. To the best of my ability and with regular help from the Holy Spirit between now and the grave, I want to be a just-say-the-word follower of Christ. Say it, I'll do it. Say it, I'll follow it. Say it, I'll obey it."

I haven't always lived up to that commitment. When I've failed, I've tried to confess it, to say it was sin and it was off track. Then I've tried to get back up and have Christ pick me up and dust me off and go back to this text and say, "Okay, for the next leg of the race, I want to be a just-say-the-word follower of Christ." Sometimes I feel like nothing is going right in my life. There are times when I know that my leadership isn't as effective as it ought to be, or I don't feel like I'm hitting home runs as a dad or as a husband. There are times when I'm not proud of how I'm relating to people. And I get into a discouragement phase and, as I'm falling into that, sometimes God catches me before I fall too far. And by His Spirit, He says, "You're right. Things are kind of a mess right now in most places in your life. But don't forget, you have the most important, most fundamental commitment of all. You've got it focused in the right place. And I honor that. And you can hold on to that. If you can feel great about nothing else, you can feel great about the fact that

you're a just-say-the-word follower of mine. Hold on to it."
And in a strange kind of way, that has lifted me out of the funk
many, many times. I feel like I have a private follower-ship pact
with God. And nobody can mess with that. Nobody can take
that away from me. I mean business and God knows it. And it's
a treasured part of my Christian experience.

June 8

RODNEY D. ICE, principal research scientist and manager,
Office of Radiation Safety, Georgia Institute of Technology;
former vice president, Eagle-Picher Industries, and director of
Eagle-Picher Research Laboratory with studies in environmental
sciences; former professor at the University of Oklahoma,
University of Michigan, and Temple University.

> *But as we have been approved by God to be entrusted*
> *with the gospel, even so we speak, not as pleasing men,*
> *but God who tests our hearts. (1 Thessalonians 2:4, NKJV)*

Why is this verse meaningful to me? (1) God has entrusted me
with the Word (John 1:1) as a reference standard with which to
assess every step of my daily walk (establishing an ethical, non-
cultural, nonsituational basis for daily decisions, defining truth
per se); as a testimony of a living Christ in support of daily decisions; and as encouragement to espouse those daily decisions
knowing that God is my assessor—not people. (2) New scientific discoveries challenge people's ethics and decisions. Without
a reference standard for comparison, such discoveries are meaningless. The unchanging, always illuminating gospel, entrusted
to believers, provides that reference for me.

June 9

BILL IRWIN, public speaker whose book *Blind Courage* recounts his hike of the Appalachian Trail with his Seeing Eye dog

Orient from March to November 1990; a family Christian counselor, he entered private practice after twenty-five years in corporate management.

> *For we walk by faith, not by sight: . . .*
> *(2 Corinthians 5:7, KJV)*

I began my through-hike of the Appalachian Trail in the middle of the worst flood Georgia had experienced in seventy years. I picked up Orient's harness and said, "Orient, forward," and we began hiking. I had no idea which direction we were going because there was no sun and the man who had brought us to the area was unable to find the mailbox placed at the beginning of the Appalachian Trail for prospective through-hikers to sign in on a notebook inside the mailbox. Within a few hundred feet God taught me the first lesson that became crucial to the success of our hike. With no warning or prompting from me at all, Orient suddenly turned left off the old woods road on which we were walking and I knew we were on some kind of trail but I had no idea which trail it was. Three days later when we encountered our first people, I learned we were indeed on the Appalachian Trail. Truly God was leading Orient, and Orient was leading me, and that was the way it happened for the 2,168 miles that followed. We had many encounters with wild animals, were exposed to all kinds of bad weather, and traversed the roughest terrain in the eastern part of the United States for eight and one-half months until we reached Mount Katahdin in Maine, fourteen states away. Even though I didn't have the sight to see, God gave me faith to trust Him to guide us every step of the way.

June 10

DAN ISSEL, head coach, NBA's Denver Nuggets, 1992–95, leading the team to the Western Conference semifinals for the

1993–94 season; member of the Naismith Memorial Basketball Hall of Fame; in fifteen pro seasons, he ranked fifth all-time in scoring, with 27,482 points; four-time all-star (three in the former American Basketball Association with the Kentucky Colonels, one in the NBA with the Nuggets); member of the Colonels' 1975 ABA championship team; all-time scoring leader at the University of Kentucky who set twenty-three school records in leading the team to three Southeastern Conference championships.

> *Rejoice in the Lord always: and again I say, Rejoice. Let your moderation be known unto all men. The Lord is at hand. Be careful for nothing; but in every thing by prayer and supplication, with thanksgiving, let your requests be made known unto God. And the peace of God, which passeth all understanding, shall keep your hearts and minds through Christ Jesus. (Philippians 4:4–7, KJV)*

In today's world, there seems to be a ton of anxiety for everybody, and to me, this passage fits the times. More recent Bible translations replace "Be careful for nothing . . ." with something to the effect, "Don't worry about anything; with thanksgiving present your requests to the Lord." It doesn't promise that everything will be taken care of the way you want, but it says you will get a peace. It's a peace you get only when you trust in the Lord and give Him your problems. I think other believers understand it, but it's difficult for people who are nonbelievers to really understand how peaceful that can be. When I first came across these verses at a time of anxiety in my life, I tried it and it worked. It's been a favorite passage of mine ever since. In situations in my life in the past, and I'm sure in the future, when I'm worrying about something I don't have any control over anyway, I've learned to give it to the Lord. And you do get a peace when you're able to let it go and let God handle it.

June 11

JOE IVEY, president and founder, Fellowship of Christian Airline Personnel, Fayetteville, Georgia, which has grown from one fellowship in Atlanta in 1971 to groups in more than eighty cities across the United States and more than twenty-five countries; Delta Air Lines pilot who retired in 1992.

> *But sanctify the Lord God in your hearts, and always be ready to give a defense to everyone who asks you a reason for the hope that is in you, with meekness and fear. . . .*
> *(1 Peter 3:15, NKJV)*

Many verses have meant so much to me, but my life verse is 1 Peter 3:15. This verse was a wonderful guide to me as a pilot for thirty-six years with Delta Air Lines and as leader of the Fellowship of Christian Airline Personnel. It gives the priorities of ministry: (1) Make Christ Lord in your life. (2) Be prepared to give answers to those interested. Know how to present the gospel in an intelligent way. (3) Do it with gentleness and respect. Don't buttonhole people with the message. Let the message do its work through the power of the Holy Spirit.

June 12

KAY COLES JAMES, dean, Regent University's Robertson School of Government; Virginia secretary of health and human resources, 1994–96; former positions include associate director, Office of National Drug Control Policy, responsible for the Bureau of State and Local Affairs; executive vice president and chief operating officer, One to One Partnership national mentoring program; assistant secretary for public affairs, U.S. Department of Health and Human Services; director of public affairs, National Right to Life Committee; author, with David Kuo, of *Transforming America from the Inside Out*, 1995.

And it shall be, when the LORD *your God brings you
into the land of which He swore to your fathers, to
Abraham, Isaac, and Jacob, to give you large and beautiful cities which you did not build, houses full of all good
things, which you did not fill, hewn-out wells which you
did not dig, vineyards and olive trees which you did not
plant—when you have eaten and are full—then beware,
lest you forget the* LORD *who brought you out of the land
of Egypt, from the house of bondage. . . .*
(Deuteronomy 6:10–12, NKJV)

These verses in Deuteronomy served as the theme and title for
my autobiography, *Never Forget,* because I strongly believe we
must remember that it is God who has delivered all of us out of
slavery into the inheritance and freedom that is in Christ. As we
struggle with the difficult public policy issues of today, seeking
solutions for our future, we must remember the God of our fathers who has brought us this far. Whether we have been delivered from poverty, discrimination, addiction, or spiritual death,
God has given us blessings we do not deserve. We must never
forget; we must teach our children not to forget.

June 13

KEVIN J. JENKINS, president and chief executive officer,
PWA Corporation and Canadian Airlines International, Ltd.,
based in Calgary, Alberta, Canada; he joined the company in its
finance department in 1985; member of the International Air
Transport Association's Executive Committee.

*I am the vine; you are the branches. If a man remains in
me and I in him, he will bear much fruit; apart from me
you can do nothing. . . . (John 15:5, NIV)*

As a Christian, I have found that my most important job is to
maintain and nurture my relationship with God. The best way

to accomplish this is to regularly read the Bible and pray. Once I understood my most important job, it changed my life. I realized that a branch not connected to the vine will *never* bear fruit. It is useless. Therefore, for over a year, I have prayed every day. Two things that have helped me are that I choose a different Bible verse to meditate on each day, and at the beginning of the day I ask God to guide me in every meeting, phone call, or other interaction on my calendar for that day.

June 14

DEE JEPSEN, national president, "Enough Is Enough!" campaign to reduce sexual violence and prevent children, women, men, and families from becoming victims by combating child pornography and hard-core pornography; special assistant to President Reagan, 1982–83, as White House liaison to women's organizations; wife of former U.S. Senator Roger Jepsen of Iowa; author of four books; former board of trustees chairperson, Regent University.

> *And to the angel of the church in Philadelphia write; These things saith he that is holy, he that is true, he that hath the key of David, he that openeth, and no man shutteth; and shutteth, and no man openeth; I know thy works: behold, I have set before thee an open door, and no man can shut it: for thou hast a little strength, and hast kept my word, and hast not denied my name.*
> *(Revelation 3:7–8, KJV)*

Revelation 3:7–8 has a special meaning in my life, because the Lord spoke to my heart through these verses in 1978. My husband was campaigning for the U.S. Senate in what was thought to be an unwinnable race, and I was not looking forward to a move to Washington, D.C., even if he were to win. He did win, opening a door that took us to the nation's capital and into many new activities and opportunities. I've recalled that scriptural promise many times as God has opened many doors that were totally unexpected and amazing to me—including one to serve as special assistant to President Reagan at the White House in the early 1980s.

June 15

DAVE JOHNSON, decathlon bronze medalist, 1992 Olympics, despite a broken foot during the two-day, ten-event competition; gold medalist, 1990 Goodwill Games; former four-time national and World University Games champion; featured in popular "Dan vs. Dave" Reebok ad campaign with decathlete competitor Dan O'Brien.

I can do all things through Christ who strengthens me.
(Philippians 4:13, NKJV)

This verse came to have special meaning for me when I broke my foot in the 1992 Olympics in Barcelona. It was by the power of God that I competed to take the bronze medal. I like to say, "My finest day is yet unknown." You may see me at a future Olympics winning the gold medal, running around the track carrying the flag, and say to yourself, That's got to be Dave's finest day! But I'll let you know it's not my finest day. It's just another experience that the Lord has allowed me to have. My finest day will be in heaven, when I've got my arm around Jesus Christ and we're looking at all the things that were unknown to me that I could have only wondered about before.

June 16

DAVID "WOODY" JOHNSON, JR., special agent in charge, FBI, Atlanta, Georgia; an FBI agent since 1969, he has held positions that include chief of the Criminal Investigative Division's Criminal Intelligence Section; chief of the division's Drug Section;

commander of the Hostage Rescue Team; and leader of the SWAT Team for the Washington (D.C.) Metropolitan Field Office.

> *Hast thou not known? hast thou not heard, that the ever-lasting God, the* LORD, *the Creator of the ends of the earth, fainteth not, neither is weary? there is no searching of his understanding. He giveth power to the faint; and to them that have no might he increaseth strength. Even the youths shall faint and be weary, and the young men shall utterly fall: But they that wait upon the* LORD *shall renew their strength; they shall mount up with wings as eagles; they shall run, and not be weary; and they shall walk, and not faint. (Isaiah 40:28–31,* KJV)

I have reached to these verses in a number of situations, especially protracted crisis incidents in which I was the senior (responsible) tactical officer at the scene. These incidents have included several of the major hostage situations the FBI has addressed. I have also used this Scripture passage to advise my sons when the pressure mounted in their lives. I especially recall offering this to my middle son for encouragement as he worked his way through Navy Seal Team training.

June 17

PHILLIP E. JOHNSON, professor of law, University of California, Berkeley, since 1968; author of *Darwin on Trial, Reason in the Balance: The Case Against Naturalism in Science, Law, and Education,* and numerous articles critical of Darwinian evolutionary theory.

> *In the beginning was the Word, and the Word was with God, and the Word was God. He was in the beginning with God. All things came into being by Him; and apart from Him nothing came into being that has come into being. (John 1:1–3,* NASB)

This passage is the most important statement about creation in the Bible. It states the principle of creation, that creation was through the Word and not through some unintelligent, materialistic process.

June 18

BOBBY JONES, four-time NBA All-Star forward and member of the 1983 NBA champion Philadelphia 76ers; the team retired his No. 24 jersey in 1986; fifth pick in the 1974 NBA draft; member of the 1972 U.S. Olympic team; currently, teacher and basketball coach, Charlotte Christian High School, 1992 North Carolina private school basketball champions.

> *Therefore, I urge you, brothers, in view of God's mercy, to offer your bodies as living sacrifices, holy and pleasing to God—which is your spiritual worship. Do not conform any longer to the pattern of this world, but be transformed by the renewing of your mind. Then you will be able to test and approve what God's will is—his good, pleasing and perfect will. (Romans 12:1–2, NIV)*

As the world tries to mold us into its image, we are exhorted to follow God's plan of personal growth to be the people He wants us to be. The first part of the verse also reminds us of our obligation to preserve and use the physical body the Lord has allowed us to use.

June 19

LARRY JONES, founder and president, Feed the Children, nonprofit hunger and disaster relief organization based in Oklahoma City, with assistance programs in all fifty states, the District of Columbia, and more than seventy countries; ranked fifth-largest international relief and development organization by *The Chronicle of Philanthropy* in 1993.

He shall not be afraid of evil tidings: his heart is fixed,
trusting in the LORD. (Psalm 112:7, KJV)

I've been in war zones, I've been in flood areas, I've been in places where they told us it would be impossible to get food in. In places where they're in a time of disaster, that particular area did not have what you would call "disaster training" the week before or the month before. You're going into an unknown situation. I went into Armenia after the earthquake when it was still the Soviet Union. I went in on a cargo plane, with no visa, and everybody said, "You'll never get in. You're crazy to get on that plane, because you'll just come right back out." But they let me stay. I went into Tehran, Iran, and spent a week and we didn't have diplomatic relations with them at the time. It just comes to the point that you just believe God and go, rather than turn around and go back.

In this Scripture, "evil tidings" means bad news, of course. I'm not going to be afraid of bad news. Before I get the bad news, the good news is my heart's already fixed, I know what I'm going to do before the news gets here, and that's trust God in the situation. God has the answer before I have the problem.

June 20

DEE DEE JONROWE, competitor in Alaska's 1,049-mile Iditarod Trail Sled Dog Race since 1980, holding the Iditarod women's speed record and fourth-fastest finish: nine days, eleven hours, and twenty-four minutes in 1995, for fourth place; named "Most Inspirational Musher" for second-place Iditarod finish in 1993; she has finished in the Iditarod top ten since 1988; winner of numerous awards for outstanding treatment of sled dogs.

The LORD gives strength to those who are weary.
Even young people get tired, then stumble and fall.

But those who trust the LORD will find new strength.
They will be strong like eagles soaring upward on wings;
they will walk and run without getting tired.
(Isaiah 40:29–31, CEV)

When I entered the 1993 Iditarod, I had both a broken hand, with a plate and seven screws in it, and a wrenched knee that required a brace the whole time. I shouldn't have been able to compete in the top ten, but at that point in the race, I was racing for first place, seven minutes out. A friend, Liller Cotter, felt the Lord's leading to send me that Scripture as an encouragement at the next-to-last checkpoint, when I was seventy miles from the finish line. She called up the checker, a really sweet Eskimo fellow, and asked if he owned a Bible. He said he did, so she asked him to copy it for me when he got home and have it waiting when I got in. The fellow was all excited and said he would. But Liller was nervous whether he really would, and she also called a pastor there. So I received the Scripture a couple of times when I got to White Mountain. The checker came and said, "Your good friend, Liller, had me write this for you!"

It was truly miraculous to be in the position I was in. I had promised my husband I would scratch from the race if I got in a situation I knew would permanently damage my knee. But that situation never seemed to come. We definitely felt like we were in over our heads, but I was always able to get up and get going again. The Scripture is marked in my Bible "Iditarod '93." I ended up finishing second by twenty minutes, which at that point was my career-best finish and time. I've since beaten my time but haven't yet finished first.

Something I once heard brings to mind how I actually feel racing dogs—that God's bigness is brought out in my smallness; the magnitude of what God can do is shown by the weakness that I have. The competition I compete in isn't anything different than life. It has its hills and its mountains and its valleys and its flats and its boring times and its particularly stressful times. When people look at me in particular, they might say, "Well, she shouldn't be able to be competitive. How in the world can somebody who's five-foot-two-inches, 125 pounds do that?" The mountains are just as high for me as they are for anybody else, and the valleys are just as low, and the obstacles just as difficult. But because I know that I, of myself, can't do this, I rely on God right off the bat.

June 21

DAWN SMITH JORDAN, recording artist; Miss South Carolina and second runner-up in the Miss America Pageant, 1986; the previous year, Dawn's younger sister, Shari, was kidnapped and, in a letter before her murder, urged her family not to let her death ruin their faith; the family's story became the subject of a CBS movie, *Nightmare in Columbia County,* and Dawn's autobiography, *Grace So Amazing.*

> Trust in the LORD with all your heart
> and lean not on your own understanding;
> in all your ways acknowledge him,
> and he will make your paths straight.
> (Proverbs 3:5–6, NIV)

This is my life verse, and became so out of a tragedy in my life. In 1985 my younger sister was kidnapped and brutally murdered, and her murderer began to threaten that I would be his next victim. During a time of utter despair, grief, pain, and fear, God's grace became more real than ever before to me. In that time I began to see that although we may never understand the whys of our lives, we have a heavenly Father who is completely trustworthy in all circumstances. When it seems that all hope is lost and we feel we will never understand, God is one in whom we can completely put our trust.

June 22

JO KADLECEK, New York City–based writer specializing in cross-cultural issues; associate editor, *Inklings,* Denver-based literary magazine with a Christian worldview; author with John Perkins, *Resurrecting Hope: Powerful Stories of How God Is Moving to Reach Our Cities.*

> *Is not this the kind of fasting I have chosen:*
> *to loose the chains of injustice*
> *and untie the cords of the yoke,*
> *to set the oppressed free*
> *and break every yoke?*
> *Is it not to share your food with the hungry*
> *and to provide the poor wanderer with shelter—*
> *when you see the naked, to clothe him,*
> *and not to turn away from your own flesh and blood?*
> *Then your light will break forth like the dawn,*
> *and your healing will quickly appear;*
> *then your righteousness will go before you,*
> *and the glory of the* LORD *will be your rear guard. . . .*
> *(Isaiah 58:6–8, NIV)*

These and other verses from Isaiah 58 have been especially life-changing for me. They discuss our mandate as Christians to "spend" ourselves on behalf of the poor and oppressed; in the process, our own healing will come as our light rises in the darkness. These verses were instrumental in my decision to relocate to Denver's inner city so that I could learn to be a Christian neighbor in the biblical sense, a witness of God's incarnational love in an economically impoverished area. Consequently, I have never experienced a greater joy or sense of community than I have living here.

June 23

RUDY KALIS, sports director and twenty-year sportscaster, WSMV-TV, Channel 4, Nashville, Tennessee.

Let not mercy and truth forsake you;
Bind them around your neck,
Write them on the tablet of your heart,
And so find favor and high esteem
In the sight of God and man. (Proverbs 3:3, NKJV)

This verse has been vitally important to me, especially in light of my work. In everything I do—writing, projecting, talking on television—I am always trying to balance those two: mercy and truth.

June 24

PATRICK KAVANAUGH, executive director, Christian Performing Artists' Fellowship, Washington, D.C., which encompasses more than 700 performers and sponsors performances in the arts in the Washington area; composer of nearly twenty published works and director of the Washington branch of the National Association of Composers; conductor appearing regularly at the Kennedy Center Concert Hall and Terrace Theatre and Constitution Hall and, in 1993, becoming the first American invited to conduct an opera at Moscow's Bolshoi Theatre; author of four books, including *The Spiritual Lives of Great Composers* and *Raising Musical Kids.*

> *. . . Do not let this Book of the Law depart from your*
> *mouth; meditate on it day and night, so that you may be*
> *careful to do everything written in it. Then you will be*
> *prosperous and successful. Have I not commanded you?*
> *Be strong and courageous. Do not be terrified; do not be*
> *discouraged, for the LORD your God will be with you*
> *wherever you go. (Joshua 1:8–9, NIV)*

God's charge to Joshua has in it two basic thoughts that have pulled me through many demanding challenges. It underlines the fundamental importance of God's Word in our lives—reading, studying, memorizing, and meditating. And it portrays our critical need for courage, which comes from relying on God's presence and guidance.

June 25

GLEN KEANE, supervising animator for Walt Disney Pictures' *Pocahontas;* directing animator for *Aladdin* and the "Beast" in *Beauty and the Beast,* the first animated feature ever nominated for an Oscar as Best Picture of the Year. His other Disney credits include *The Little Mermaid* and *Rescuers Down Under.*

I said to the LORD, "You are my Lord;
apart from you I have no good thing." (Psalm 16:2, NIV)

That verse reminds me how everything I have of any value comes from God. It's easy for me to look at what I do as something that comes from me, because I draw and create characters like the Beast and the Little Mermaid. All of that can really start to make you live for your own glory. And I needed to be reminded that everything I have is only from God. If I were separated from Him, there would be nothing in my life worth having. Nothing compares to the beauty of Him.

June 26

LEROY KEITH, chairman and chief executive officer, Carson Products Company, Savannah, Georgia, manufacturer of ethnic hair-care products; president, Morehouse College, Atlanta, 1987–94; previous positions include vice president for policy and planning, University of Maryland; chancellor, Massachusetts Board of Higher Education, the first black to hold such a position in American higher education; executive vice president, University of the District of Columbia; associate vice president for university policy for the University of Massachusetts system; and associate dean and assistant professor of education and urban studies, Dartmouth College.

> For the vision is yet for an appointed time, but at the end it shall speak, and not lie: though it tarry, wait for it; because it will surely come, it will not tarry.
> (Habakkuk 2:3, KJV)

To me, this verse offers certainty that God's plans for us will always manifest themselves, leading us in the right direction at the right time in our lives. This verse gives me hope that prayers are heard while reinforcing the virtues of patience and faith.

June 27

JACK KEMP, Republican party vice presidential nominee, 1996; secretary, Department of Housing and Urban Development, 1989–92; member, U.S. House of Represen-tatives, New York's Thirty-first District, 1971–89; pro quarterback who led the Buffalo Bills to two American Football League championships, 1964, 1965; AFL player of the year, 1965; cofounder, AFL Players Association, and president, 1965–70; father of Jeff Kemp, also a former pro quarterback and now executive director, Washington Family Council.

> Trust in the LORD with all your heart,
> And lean not on your own understanding;
> In all your ways acknowledge Him,
> And He shall direct your paths. (Proverbs 3:5–6, NKJV)

This proverb has always been a source of inspiration, motivation, and encouragement to me and my family as we contemplate those human decisions that impact our lives, our nation, and our future. God's will and direction is the lodestar around which we try to make decisions that can be a blessing to our family and neighbors.

June 28

JEFF KEMP, executive director, Washington Family Council, an organization based in Bellevue, Washington, for encouraging communities to value and nurture family life; former quarterback with the NFL's Los Angeles Rams, San Francisco 49ers, Seattle Seahawks, and Philadelphia Eagles; son of Jack Kemp, former secretary, U.S. Department of Housing and Urban Development.

All things work together for good for those who love Him, who have been called according to His purpose. (paraphrase of Romans 8:28)

The value of memorizing Scripture was proved when this verse came to my mind after I graduated from college. Despite much success, I found myself feeling empty and purposeless after four years of trying to run my own life without a committed relationship with the Lord. This verse echoed in my head late at night for three nights in a row, prompting me to dedicate my life to Jesus Christ and His purpose for my life.

June 29

JOANNE KEMP, wife of Jack Kemp and mother of Jeff Kemp, and another son, James, and two daughters, Jennifer and Judith; involvements include board member, Community Bible Study, interdenominational women's Bible study organization, and Prison Fellowship, national ministry to prisoners and their families.

Do not be anxious about anything, but in everything, by prayer and supplication, with thanksgiving, present your requests to God. And the peace of God, which transcends

all understanding, will guard your hearts and your minds
in Christ Jesus. (Philippians 4:6–7, NIV)

Philippians 4:6–7 has been a very helpful and encouraging teaching from the Bible that has lifted me often from my human tendency to assume responsibility that God didn't intend for me to carry alone. More than twenty-five years ago, I happened to read these verses when I was in the midst of a crisis in pregnancy and felt great anxiety. In prayer and supplication I made my request known to God and immediately I knew the peace that passes all understanding.

June 30

MEL KENYON, owner with brother Don of 3-K Racing, Lebanon, Indiana, building and maintaining race cars; eight-time Indianapolis 500 driver, third in 1968, fourth in 1969 and 1973, fifth in 1966.

> *. . . let us also lay aside every encumbrance, and the sin*
> *which so easily entangles us, and let us run with en-*
> *durance the race that is set before us, fixing our eyes on*
> *Jesus, the author and perfecter of faith. . . .*
> *(Hebrews 12:1–2, NASB)*

There are so many avenues in life and so many sudden stops. A lot of races are just there to be run and aren't of any great value. And even though you run a race, unless you finish it, it doesn't mean anything. I do a lot of speaking before different age groups, from seniors to teens. My racing career is the focal point for them. But I tell them, whatever you do, you have to do it well and reach the goal.

JULY

July 1

GRAHAM KERR, TV chef and international culinary consultant seen on *The Best of Kerr* on public broadcasting stations and *The Graham Kerr Show* on the Discovery Channel, featuring recipes based on nutrition research to reduce fat, cholesterol, sodium, and sugars via herbs and spices for aroma, color, and texture—updating recipes from his popular *Galloping Gourmet* 1969–71 telecasts and since aired in nearly forty countries; also featured on "Take Kerr" four-minute Cable News Network segments during the mid–1970s; author of thirteen cookbooks on healthy cuisine; the son of hoteliers in England; his early career included five years as Royal New Zealand Air Force chief catering adviser.

He must increase, but I must decrease. (John 3:30, KJV)

My experience with this verse began shortly after my wife, Treena, and I became Christians in 1974. For several years we actively shared our testimony in many churches that celebrated celebrities. I asked a noted pastor how he responded when asked to sign someone's Bible, an odd but not unusual request. He replied with the idea that I simply write John 3:30. "Later the recipient will discover that it is necessary for you to decrease and the Lord to increase," he explained. I began to reflect on John 3:30 and have experienced it to be of enormous and enduring value in my often-very-public life. I have found that it is never inappropriate as a personal meditation.

July 2

GRACE KETTERMAN, pediatrician who also completed a residency in child psychiatry, focusing on troubled families for more than forty years; former medical director, Crittenton Center, Kansas City, Missouri, psychiatric hospital for children with emotional problems; author of fourteen books, including *Mothering: The Complete Guide for Mothers of All Ages, Parenting the Difficult Child,* and *Depression Hits All Families.*

> But they that wait upon the LORD shall renew their strength; they shall mount up with wings as eagles; they shall run, and not be weary; and they shall walk, and not faint. (Isaiah 40:31, KJV)

The Bible has a number of symbolic statements about eagles, but this one especially has sustained me. Trying to be a good wife and mother as well as a conscientious physician has resulted in exhaustion many times. But always God's energy has uplifted me, like the parent eagle upholds the young when they falter. The strength, swiftness, and basic functioning of the eagle are the qualities God offers me in Himself.

July 3

RICHARD KIEL, seven-foot–two-inch actor whose credits include the role of villain "Jaws" in the James Bond movie *Moonraker* and appearances in numerous TV series; founder, New Generation Entertainment, family/Christian values company that produced *The Giant of Thunder Mountain* as its first film.

> And so I am giving a new commandment to you now — love each other just as much as I love you. Your strong love for each other will prove to the world that you are my disciples. (John 14:34–35, TLB)

Jesus' new commandment that we love one another is so very important to Christians. We seem to focus more on loving God and Jesus, which is relatively easy by comparison. What's hard is to love your enemies while they are taunting you, beating you with whips, and crucifying you—to love as Jesus did in His prayer on the cross, "Father, forgive them, for they know not what they do." It is even hard for us to forgive a Christian brother or sister who sins against us just once and says, "I'm sorry," let alone seven times in one day or "seventy times seven" as recorded in Matthew 18:22. It is only when we see in the Word of God the perfect, unconditional love that Jesus has for the world that we can even try to be an imitator of Him and try to find that perfect love in ourselves. Then, and only then, are we willing to reach out to a murderer, as Ananias did with Saul (Acts 9:17), or pray with a drug addict or a prostitute. Only when we empty ourselves of all selfish desires, pride, and covetous thoughts, and when we love one another enough to go into all the world preaching the gospel to every creature, will we begin to come even close to hitting the mark. I know I find myself constantly falling short of that mark.

Another area where we fail to love one another as Jesus commanded is pointed out in Galatians 6:1—especially these days in regard to those in the ministry who are "overcome by some sin" (TLB). We forget that we are to "gently and humbly help him back onto the right path, remembering that next time it might be one of you who is in the wrong." I have three "begotten" sons and I cannot imagine seeing one of them go through what Jesus did for all of us "good Christians," let alone all the most terrible sinners in the world. Yet: "God so loved the world, that he gave his only begotten Son, that whosoever believeth in him should not perish, but have everlasting life" (KJV). Is it too much, then, for Him to ask that we love one another?

July 4

DIANE M. KOMP, M.D., pediatric hematologist-oncologist, Yale University School of Medicine, since 1978; member of the University of Virginia faculty the previous nine years; a leading authority on histiocytosis, a rare, sometimes-fatal childhood disease; author of five books, including *Images of Grace: A Pediatrician's Trilogy of Faith, Hope, and Love,* bringing together her three books about the spiritual experiences of children facing serious illness and possible death and of their families, and *Breakfast for the Heart: Meditations to Nourish the Soul.*

> *. . . being confident of this, that he who began a good work in you will carry it on to completion until the day of Christ Jesus. (Philippians 1:6, NIV)*

God gave me a verse in a song during a bout of insomnia. I turned on the radio at 2:00 A.M. and heard, "He who began a good work in you is faithful to complete it." It was a promise that even if I couldn't get all my work done, God could get His work in me done. A year later, I passed the verse along to a young man I met in Germany who was discouraged that his spiritual growth rate wasn't as fast as that of other Christians he knew. His face brightened up. "This isn't the first time God has sent me that verse through someone! The man who led me to Christ gave it to me the last time I got discouraged." Now he's working for a Christian radio station in Germany and passing the verse along to others—sometimes in the song over the airwaves.

July 5

C. EVERETT KOOP, M.D., professor of surgery, Dartmouth Medical School; chairman, "Shape Up America!" national campaign to promote healthy weight and physical activity; surgeon general and deputy assistant secretary for health, U.S. Public Health Service, 1981–89; surgeon-in-chief, Children's Hospital of Philadelphia, 1948–81; author or coauthor of numerous books and articles on medicine, biomedical ethics, and health policy, including *Whatever Happened to the Human Race?* with the late theologian Francis A. Schaeffer and *Sometimes Mountains Move* with wife Elizabeth, about the death of their son; 1991 Emmy winner, news and documentary category, for a five-part series on health care reform.

> *Call unto me, and I will answer thee, and shew thee great and mighty things, which thou knowest not.*
> *(Jeremiah 33:3, KJV)*

Not only will God answer a call but, in His response, He will go far beyond all that we ask or think. Our times are in His hands, and I bask in His sovereignty. This was true in the time of my deepest distress, when our twenty-year-old son, David, was killed when the face of the cliff on which he was rock climbing broke away. I called out to God to show us what He would accomplish by taking our son. He answered and showed us far more than we were able to anticipate. For example, we had wondered whether he had done something improper and had slipped. In our regular reading of the psalms, we came to that portion of Psalm 18 that says, "my feet did not slip." David did not fall; in His sovereignty, God took him.

In answer to the prayer of a devastated father experiencing bone-crushing grief, the Lord led me to proceed with a talk I was preparing for a men's group at a rather liberal church. Although they excused me from my obligation, I felt called to speak. What I had to say that day came from a broken heart. A friend recorded my message and, without telling me, had it reproduced in a small pamphlet that has been printed in several languages well over a million times. Many have come to faith in Christ because of its message. This is only one of many things the Lord showed our family that came about through David's being taken from us at the vibrant age of twenty.

July 6

LOREN KRUSE, editor, *Successful Farming*, the nation's largest paid-circulation farm magazine, with 1.4 million readers; he joined its staff in 1976 after working as science editor at Oklahoma State University; also editor of *Corn Farmer* and *Soybean Grower* and author of two books on farming; president-elect of the Iowa 4-H Foundation; vice president for public relations, Fellowship of Christian Farmers International; he and his wife, Elizabeth, own and manage a crop, livestock, and Christmas tree farm in Grundy County, Iowa.

Forget the former things;
do not dwell on the past.
See, I am doing a new thing!
Now it springs up; do you not perceive it?
I am making a way in the desert
and streams in the wasteland. . . . (Isaiah 43:18–19, NIV)

These verses are a great encouragement to me as I deal with ever-increasing and often rapid change in my own life and business and in the lives of the farm families I serve. Change usually makes us apprehensive. But through God all things are possible. He even changed the way to eternal life for us—by giving us His Son, Jesus, so that we might be saved simply by believing in Him!

July 7

IVY KU, Harvard University student; 1994 graduate, Meadowcreek High School, Norcross, Georgia, with 4.0 average; six-time piano champion in statewide competitions; president, Atlanta Chinese Christian Youth, and editor, *Eye-Witness Newsletter* for Asian American youth in the southeastern United States, 1993–94; one of 150 Coca-Cola Scholars Foundation and 100 Tandy Technology 1994 scholarship recipients.

The fear of the LORD is the beginning of knowledge,
but fools despise wisdom and discipline.
(Proverbs 1:7, NIV)

Knowledge is a primary quest in every person's life. Why else do we go to school? Yet so many people search in the wrong places. Their heads are full of information, but they are unfulfilled. Ultimate knowledge and wisdom come not from books or research, but from believing in the One who is the Truth. This verse constantly reminds me to believe in the Truth of God and not the truth of people. Whatever I learn in this life will be nothing compared with the surpassing greatness of knowing Jesus as my Lord.

July 8

MARY BETH LAGERBORG, publishing coordinator, MOPS International, Inc. (Mothers of Preschoolers ministry); coauthor, with Mimi Wilson, family mealtime activity book, *Table Talk,* and cookbook, *Once-a-Month Cooking;* author of *Incessant Drumbeat* biography of New Guinea missionaries Larry and Shirley Rascher.

Where can I go from your spirit?
Or where can I flee from your presence?
If I ascend to heaven, you are there;
if I make my bed in Sheol, you are there.
If I take the wings of the morning
and settle at the farthest limits of the sea,
even there your hand shall lead me,
and your right hand shall hold me fast.
If I say, "Surely the darkness shall cover me,
and the light around me become night,"
even the darkness is not dark to you;
the night is as bright as the day,
for darkness is as light to you. (Psalm 139:7–12, NRSV)

In 1989 I flew to Irian Jaya on the island of New Guinea to research a biography I was writing on Larry and Shirley Rascher,
missionaries with the Evangelical Alliance Mission. I traveled
alone and would be met in Irian Jaya by the Raschers' son,
whom I had never met. I cried throughout the flight from Denver
to Los Angeles, frightened and thinking that I must be out of my
mind to be doing this. Yet I had never sensed more profoundly
the Lord's leading than in this project. On the fourteen-hour
flight from Los Angeles over the Pacific, I peered out the window into the seamless blackness of night. The little square
window perfectly framed the Big Dipper. It was to me a wink
from God. He would watch over me and was pouring out His
blessings upon me. I will always associate this beautiful portion
of Scripture with the Lord's tender care for me on that journey
to "the farthest limits of the sea." These verses also speak to me
of the Lord's care of the Rascher family through their trials and
triumphs in Irian Jaya.

July 9

TOM LANDRY, Pro Football Hall of Fame head coach,
Dallas Cowboys, twenty-nine seasons, tying NFL record for
coaching the same team for longest number of consecutive
years; led team to victories in Super Bowls VI and XII and to appearances in three other Super Bowls; posted twenty consecutive
winning seasons and eighteen playoff appearances; All-Pro in
New York Giants defensive secondary, 1954.

I can do all things through Him who strengthens me.
(Philippians 4:13, NASB)

The thing I discovered soon after I became a Christian—I was
thirty-five before I committed my life to Christ—is that you've
given yourself to Christ and yet you're not relying on Him 100
percent. You're relying on yourself to solve your problems. But I
didn't have the same feeling after I came across this verse.

I knew then that it was God who was directing my life; it was Christ in me.

July 10

BERNHARD LANGER, professional golfer; Masters champion, 1993, 1985; winner of more than thirty international tournaments; native of Anhausen, Germany; he and fellow Masters champion Larry Mize are international editors of the *Links Letter*, bimonthly Christian newsletter for pro and amateur golfers, based in Annandale, Virginia.

> *In reply Jesus declared, "I tell you the truth, no one can see the kingdom of God unless he is born again."*
> *(John 3:3, NIV)*

In 1985, my first year on the U.S. Tour, I won the U.S. Masters in Augusta, Georgia. I won seven tournaments on five continents and was ranked number one in the world. I had a beautiful young wife and had achieved everything I could ever have dreamed of. The problem was, something was missing. My priorities were golf, golf, golf, and more golf, then myself, and finally a little time with my wife. Every now and then, I prayed. I went to church. But if my golf game was not good, my whole life was miserable and I made everyone around me miserable.

The week after I won the 1985 Masters, my wife, Vikki, and I went to the Bible study on the tour. That evening was the first time in my life that I heard I needed to be "reborn." It didn't make any sense to me. So at the end of the study, I asked what it meant to be "reborn." PGA Tour chaplain Larry Moody opened the Bible and showed me John 3:3. He went on to explain that the only way to have eternal life is through Jesus Christ—that He died for our sins. And it is not through our deeds or good behavior that we receive eternal life, because we will always fall short of God's standard. After hearing this, it was natural for me to ask the Lord into my life and let the Holy Spirit reign within me. My wife felt the same, and she also accepted Christ as her Savior. Since then, I have seen tremendous changes in her life, my own life, our relationship as husband and wife, and the way we treat our friends and others in this world.

July 11

STEVE LARGENT, U.S. congressman, Oklahoma's First District, elected in November 1994, fifth former National Football League player to serve in Congress; member of the Pro Football Hall of Fame; in fourteen seasons as a Seattle Seahawks wide receiver, he set NFL records (since broken by others) for receptions, 819; yards, 13,089; touchdowns, 100; consecutive games with a reception, 177; and 1,000-yard seasons, 8; NFL Man of the Year, 1988, for on-field play and off-field humanitarian efforts; selected for Pro Bowl seven times.

> For the eyes of the LORD range throughout the earth to strengthen those whose hearts are fully committed to him. . . . (2 Chronicles 16:9, NIV)

I have adopted this Scripture as my life verse. The first line exemplifies God's tireless pursuit of a love relationship with us. The entire message of the good news of Jesus Christ is about God's effort to reach out to us. The second phrase states clearly why God pursues a relationship with us—to strengthen us. Strengthen us physically, spiritually, and emotionally. And finally, the last phrase lays out the prerequisite. We must be a people whose hearts are fully committed to Him. We cannot serve two masters. God asks us for nothing less than our whole-hearted and undivided devotion and commitment to Him. He deserves nothing less.

July 12

DAVID LARSON, M.D., president, National Institute for Healthcare Research, Rockville, Maryland; former senior researcher with the National Institute of Mental Health, Department of Health and Human Services, and National Institutes of Health; coauthor of the three-volume *The Faith Factor: An Annotated Bibliography of Clinical Research on Spiritual Subjects,* of *The Costly Consequences of Divorce: Assessing the Clinical, Economic, and Public Health Impact of Marital Disruption in the United States,* and of numerous articles on the impact of religious commitment on physical and mental health and on other facets of mental health research.

> *Wisdom begins with respect for the LORD.*
> *And understanding begins with knowing God,*
>   *the Holy One.*
> *If you live wisely, you will live a long time.*
> *Wisdom will add years to your life.*
> *(Proverbs 9:10–11, New Century Version)*

As a researcher, I was somewhat doubtful that religious commitment had clinical benefit. But research is showing that "Proverbs Works." Not only do the religiously committed have less stress, but they cope better with their stress. In addition, they have fewer drug and alcohol problems, less depression, and much lower rates of suicide. They enjoy their lives, their marriages, and even their sexuality more than do the less religious. And yes, study after published study is showing that the religiously committed live longer. Several millennia after Solomon claimed that a personal relationship with God extends your lifetime, we can now say it with data. That's right, Solomon, God is good—really good!

July 13

ROBERT R. LAVELLE, executive vice president, Dwelling House Savings and Loan Association, in the Hill district of Pittsburgh, Pennsylvania, and president, Lavelle Real Estate, Inc.; since 1957 when he became involved with Dwelling House, the

S & L has grown to nearly $18 million in assets and 5,000 savers from forty-six states and has made more than 1,000 mortgage loans in the Hill district's predominantly black neighborhoods, helping increase home ownership from 12 percent in 1960 to more than 40 percent in 1994; one of his sons, Robert M. Lavelle, is the S & L's president.

> *But seek ye first the kingdom of God, and his righteousness; and all these things shall be added unto you.*
> *(Matthew 6:33, KJV)*

I grew up hearing the Bible from an evangelist father. I saw the Word of God lived in the numerous moves we made (five) as my father "went wherever the Lord told him." He died in Pittsburgh in 1925. I was nine years old at the time, the sixth of eight children. Since we never had any money, I resolved to try to make some. I thought I could be good and still make money, so I set out to do so. The quest led to a night high-school diploma and two college degrees while I worked during the day. At age forty-seven, a "good citizen, civic servant, father of two sons, husband of one wife," and running two businesses, Lavelle Real Estate and Dwelling House Savings and Loan Association, I realized the truth of Jesus' statement in the sixth chapter of Matthew. Verse 24 was hard to understand—"Ye cannot serve God and mammon"—but verse 33 led me to Christ after a ten- to fifteen-year struggle. I finally realized that although I was a respected person in the church and community, and knew all about Christ, I didn't know Him personally as Savior and of the need to make Him Lord. I had been seeking the idol gods of this world. I accepted His offer of salvation and set on the path of seeking Him first, instead of worldly possessions. That journey continues in the marketplace today.

July 14

VICKI HARRELL LEAVELL, former model in New York City and discipleship leader with Impact, a ministry to people in the fashion and arts industries; Miss South Carolina 1984; singer, songwriter, speaker in churches and schools.

> *Delight yourself in the LORD*
> *and he will give you the desires of your heart.*
> *Commit your way to the LORD;*
> *trust in him and he will do this. . . . (Psalm 37:4–5, NIV)*

I believe a possible meaning of these verses is that, as I commit myself to the Lord and enjoy living for Him, He will place the desires He wants me to have in my heart. Then my life can begin to glorify Him. I won, for example, the Miss South Carolina pageant (my desire) in order to share Christ (God's desire). I modeled in New York City (my desire) in order to be a light in the darkness (God's desire). I recorded an album of songs I wrote (my desire) in order to reach young people and lead them to Jesus (God's desire). I married a preacher who loves Jesus (my desire) in order to continue our separate ministries together (God's desire). God's desires became my desires and the Lord worked them together for His purposes and glory.

July 15

DAVID LEESTMA, director, NASA Flight Crew Operations, Houston; NASA astronaut, flight engineer on space shuttle *Atlantis* in 1992 and *Columbia* in 1989 and mission specialist on *Challenger* in 1984; U.S. Navy captain who graduated first in class at U.S. Naval Academy, 1971.

> *Trust in the LORD with all thine heart; and lean not unto*
> *thine own understanding. In all thy ways acknowledge*
> *him, and he shall direct thy paths. (Proverbs 3:5–6, KJV)*

In my line of work, in engineering, flying airplanes, and flying in space, a lot of times you can start depending a lot on yourself. But if you continue depending on yourself, you're going to go astray. You forget that God's in control. These verses always bring me back to what's really important: everything works out a lot better when you trust in God, acknowledge that He's in charge, and follow His direction. It may not be easy. It may not be the way everybody else thinks you should go. But if you follow God's lead, it's going to work for the best.

July 16

MAX LENNON, president, Mars Hill (North Carolina) College; president and chief executive officer, Eastern Foods, Atlanta-based food manufacturer and distributor, 1994–96; president, Clemson University, 1986–94; previously, vice president for agricultural administration and executive dean for agriculture, home economics, and natural resources, Ohio State University, and dean of the college of agriculture and director of the agricultural experiment station, University of Missouri at Columbia.

> *"For I was hungry and you gave me something to eat, I was thirsty and you gave me something to drink, I was a stranger and you invited me in, I needed clothes and you clothed me, I was sick and you looked after me, I was in prison and you came to visit me." Then the righteous will answer him, "Lord, when did we see you hungry and feed you, or thirsty and give you something to drink? When did we see you a stranger and invite you in, or needing clothes and clothe you?" The King will reply, "I tell you the truth, whatever you did for one of the least of these brothers of mine, you did for me."*
> *(Matthew 25:35–40, NIV)*

The best advice on how to grow. Moment by moment, put God first and others above self.

July 17

TOM LESTER, actor who costarred in the films *Benji* and *Gordy* and played Eb on *Green Acres* and Pete Maravich in *The Pistol*.

> *Do not let this Book of the Law depart from your mouth; meditate on it day and night, so that you may be careful to do everything written in it. Then you will be prosperous and successful. (Joshua 1:8, NIV)*

Our hope of victory and wisdom necessary for success depends on our constant attention and adherence to the written law. We should not become judge and jury, however, by interpreting the law through rationalization, experience, or ethics or by validating whether something has biblical value from within ourselves. God validates His Word through the Holy Spirit.

July 18

RON LEWIS, U.S. congressman, Kentucky's Second District, elected in May 1994; he had been pastor of White Mills Baptist Church, Hardin County, since 1980; former owner of Alpha Christian Bookstore, Elizabethtown.

> *And we know that all things work together for good to them that love God, to them who are the called according to his purpose. (Romans 8:28, KJV)*

This verse is perhaps my favorite because it lets us know that ultimately we can rest easy, knowing that God is in control when things are bad. It has certainly comforted me many times. It also is a fine example of the importance and power of faith: the entire weight of the world does not rest on our shoulders.

July 19

BOB LILLY, member of the Pro Football Hall of Fame for his fourteen years as a Dallas Cowboys defensive tackle; he was the first player drafted by the new franchise in 1961; named to eleven Pro Bowls; member of the College Football Hall of Fame as an All-American at Texas Christian University; currently, a public speaker and landscape photographer of the Southwest.

For God so loved the world, that he gave his only begotten Son, that whosoever believeth in him should not perish, but have everlasting life. (John 3:16, KJV)

Speaking to a group of judges once, I told them that the Lord would save them even if they were on their deathbeds. I quoted John 3:16—a verse I first learned as a child—as a promise of this. Several years later, a woman called who was the wife of one of the men in the audience at that judges' meeting. Recounting how her husband had called upon the Lord to save him just before he died of cancer, she wanted to say thanks for that message being given so that her husband could hear it and use it when he most needed to.

July 20

ROBERT L. LINDSEY, Southern Baptist representative to Israel, 1944–87, including fifteen years as pastor of Narkis Street Baptist Church, Jerusalem; former lecturer at Hebrew University and Ben Gurion University; author of *Jesus, Rabbi and Lord* and *A Hebrew Translation of the Gospel of Mark.* (He died in May 1995.)

I will go before thee, and make the crooked places straight: I will break in pieces the gates of brass, and cut in sunder the bars of iron: And I will give thee the treasures of darkness, and hidden riches of secret places, that

thou mayest know that I, the LORD, *which call thee by*
thy name, am the God of Israel. (Isaiah 45:2–3, KJV)

I recall the first intimations I had that God might want me to live
and work as a pastor among the Jews. I put them aside. Again
that call came to me. Now I wanted a sign. Finally I found my
sign in Isaiah 45. I realize more every day how much these words
had to do with my life. What I had seen were indeed impossibilities—gates of brass. I have lived to see gate after gate broken before me. My first gate of brass was the difficulty of getting to
Palestine as a young student just out of college and without
funds. I did pray and I did believe that God would break that
gate. Before long, it was falling—money came from friends, I
worked overtime, and my parents aided me. I left for Palestine in
February 1939 and remained there a year and a half.

I had no more arrived in Palestine than another gate of brass
rose stolidly before me. I wanted to communicate with the
people of the land. The learning of Hebrew, not to mention
Arabic, stood in the way. After a few weeks of intensive study
and imitation, however, I found myself greeting friends, passing
pleasantries, and inquiring for directions. This gate of brass was
crumbling! But long before the second gate of brass was really
open, the third one appeared—the disadvantage of not being
able to understand the way these people thought, to perceive
what they wanted and what made them tick. Perhaps it was because my experience as a Baptist was so different from that of
being a Jew. For me, my religion had been a matter of choice,
even as a child. I had walked down an aisle to accept Jesus as
Lord and, in this way, became a Baptist as well. The Jews I met,
I discovered, were Jews mainly because they had come into the
world as children of Jewish parents. Their religion was completely a matter of circumstance. And many of them found the
faith of their fathers not to their liking.

Slowly I began to see that the creation of the state of Israel was to be the response of men born as Jews who sought to overcome their limitations of birth. A formal faith was less important than the freedom to live as a Jew in a country in which the majority were Jews. The Jews in Israel—the Israelis—have achieved this struggle for national freedom, and I have watched them through many fascinating years. I have also sat with them, shared with them, prayed with them, learned from them, and received a warmer friendship than I could return. Strangely enough, all this has strengthened my Baptist faith, for I have seen them looking for Christ, and finding Him, and they have made it possible for me to know Him better and witness for Him better.

July 21

ART LINKLETTER, radio and TV personality on NBC's long-running *People Are Funny* and CBS's *House Party;* featured performer in various other specials, TV dramas, and motion pictures; winner of two Emmy Awards; author of twenty-three books, including *Kids Say the Darndest Things,* 1957, one of the top-fifteen best-sellers in publishing history, *Drugs at My Doorstep,* 1973, after the death of his daughter from a drug overdose, and most recently, *Old Age Is Not for Sissies.*

> *The LORD is my shepherd; I shall not want. He maketh me to lie down in green pastures: he leadeth me beside the still waters. He restoreth my soul: he leadeth me in the paths of righteousness for his name's sake. Yea, though I walk through the valley of the shadow of death, I will fear no evil: for thou art with me; thy rod and thy staff they comfort me. Thou preparest a table before me in the presence of mine enemies: thou anointest my head with oil; my cup runneth over. Surely goodness and mercy shall follow me all the days of my life: and I will dwell in the house of the LORD for ever. (Psalm 23, KJV)*

I was adopted eighty-two years ago in Moosejaw, Saskatchewan, Canada, by a warm and wonderful man named John Fulton Linkletter (who was a Baptist evangelist) after being abandoned by my biological parents. My first memories go back to watching him speak on street corners with the traditional trio of musicians exhorting the crowd to give up sinful living and accept Jesus. I, at age five, played the triangle. In those early days my favorite Bible verse was "Jesus wept" because that was the only one I could remember. Today, after experiencing the joys and vicissitudes of a long and satisfying life, I fall back on the familiar and much-beloved Twenty-third Psalm, concerning the Lord being the shepherd of His people. Since I have "walked through the valley of the shadow of death" both personally, with an aneurysm, and as a parent, with the tragic loss of two of my five children, I have turned to this psalm for solace and comfort. I think it is one of the most significant passages in the Bible, and it was quoted to me following my daughter Diane's death by my friend Norman Vincent Peale, who called me from New York to solace me at that terrible moment. On the other side of the picture, my life has been happy and successful beyond my fondest dreams, so I can truly say "my cup runneth over," and I am sure that having a Baptist minister father up in heaven waiting for me—with his recommendation—I will eventually "dwell in the house of the Lord forever."

July 22

ROB LOOS, partner in Taweel-Loos & Company, film-TV production company in Studio City, California; producer, with partner George Taweel, of *McGee and Me!,* all-time top-selling Christian video series and finalist for two awards during the 1991 New York Film Festival; former director of development for *Star Search* and other shows produced by Bob Banner Associates; former head of creative affairs for Republic Pictures Studios.

Suppose you went to a friend's house at midnight, wanting to borrow three loaves of bread. You would shout up to him, "A friend of mine has just arrived for a visit and I've nothing to give him to eat." He would call down from his bedroom, "Please don't ask me to get up. The door is locked for the night and we are all in bed. I just can't help you this time." But I tell you this—though he won't do it as a friend, if you keep knocking long enough he will get up and give you anything you want—just because of your persistence. And so it is with prayer—keep on asking and you will keep on getting; keep on looking and you will keep on finding; knock and the door will be opened. Everyone who asks, receives; all who seek, find; and the door is opened to everyone who knocks.
(Luke 11:5–10, TLB)

I've found this illustration to be deeply important to those of us who are trying to impact the television and film world with new, moral, quality, family programming. We are carrying a message and a set of values not universally appreciated or understood. In our dogged determination to get great films to happen, we constantly run up against closed doors, yet we know if we keep pushing forward, continually lifting up our concerns in prayer, God will always give us an answer. *McGee and Me!* is an example of a project bathed in prayer from its inception. Consequently, through the Lord's work in our lives, it has been able to achieve the impossible: bring together top Hollywood professionals in the business; become the most popular kids' Christian video series yet; and be the first home video ever to air on network television, ABC. We keep on asking, praying, searching, and knocking for all sorts of new projects that can affect a generation of kids with quality values and moral imperatives, and we lean on verses like Luke 11:5–10 to help us make it through our journey.

July 23

ANNE GRAHAM LOTZ, president, AnGeL Ministries, communicating messages of biblical exposition; international speaker at seminaries, universities, conferences, and churches; second of Ruth and Billy Graham's five children; author of *The Vision of His Glory* on the Book of Revelation.

This book of the law shall not depart out of thy mouth; but thou shalt meditate therein day and night, that thou mayest observe to do according to all that is written therein: for then thou shalt make thy way prosperous, and then thou shalt have good success. (Joshua 1:8, KJV)

Success from God's point of view is not measured by the accumulation of wealth, a problem-free life, or good health. Rather, it is measured by the individual's observance of and obedience to the Word of God. I want to be successful in God's eyes.

July 24

SUSIE LUCHSINGER, country/gospel singer featured on ten albums, most recently *Come as You Are* and *Real Love*; Christian Country Music Association Female Vocalist of the Year, 1994, 1995; younger sister of country music star Reba McEntire.

Consider it all joy, my brethren, when you encounter various trials, knowing that the working of your faith produces patience. (paraphrase of James 1:2–3)

The word *working* reminds me of sourdough bread. It has potato flakes and sugar, and it "works" the starter to produce a nice, round, brown loaf of bread. So the trials and tribulations in our lives work our faith to produce patience.

July 25

SHANNON W. LUCID, NASA astronaut since 1979; the first woman to fly in space five times: as a mission specialist in 1996 aboard the space shuttle *Atlantis,* then working aboard the Russian space station *Mir,* setting women's and American space endurance records of 188 days; *Columbia* in 1993, which logged a shuttle record fourteen days in space; *Atlantis* in 1991 and in 1989, when the *Galileo* spacecraft was deployed to explore Jupiter; and *Discovery* in 1985; daughter of missionaries to China; six weeks after her birth in 1943, her family was placed in a prison camp by the Japanese.

> *If it be so, our God whom we serve is able to deliver us from the furnace of blazing fire; and He will deliver us out of your hand, O king. But even if He does not, let it be known to you, O king, that we are not going to serve your gods or worship the golden image that you have set up. (Daniel 3:17–18, NASB)*

Like so many others, I have always wanted to be doing the Lord's will. This passage—along with Micah 6:8: "He has told you, O man, what is good; / And what does the LORD require of you / But to do justice, to love kindness, / And walk humbly with your God?" (NASB)—always comes to mind when I am faced with an important decision.

July 26

BILL MACK, member of the Country Music Disc Jockey Hall of Fame and Texas Country Music Hall of Fame; heard on 50,000-watt WBAP, 820 AM, Fort Worth, Texas, as "The Midnight Cowboy," midnight to 5:00 A.M. Sunday through Thursday; twenty-year cohost of *Country Crossroads* with country comedian Jerry Clower, heard weekly on more than 1,000 radio stations and now in video syndication; his other credits include emceeing the *Buck Owens Show* and numerous other country music programs.

For God so loved the world, that he gave his only begotten Son, that whosoever believeth in him should not perish, but have everlasting life. (John 3:16, KJV)

Being an all-night disc jockey on a radio station heard throughout the United States, I have learned that "night people" are different. There is a tremendous amount of loneliness during those wee hours of the morning. I know, because on the telephone I talk with people from practically every avenue of life and am asked almost nightly: "What can I do to escape this loneliness?" I've had several people inform me that they were on the brink of suicide because of loneliness, illness, or heartache. I always advise them to seek counseling as soon as possible and, realizing the hour may prevent immediate help, I refer them to that old faithful biblical verse, John 3:16. I have found tremendous comfort personally through this great Scripture and have sought to share its value with others.

July 27

GAVIN MacLEOD, actor featured in two long-running TV series, as Captain Merrill Stubing on *The Love Boat* and Murray Slaughter on *The Mary Tyler Moore Show,* and in numerous other TV and film roles; host, with wife Patti, of *Back on Course* weekly half-hour Trinity Broadcasting Network program; other religious activities have included spokesman for The Bible League, a ministry dedicated to worldwide Scripture distribution.

For nothing is hidden, except to be revealed; nor has anything been secret, but that it should come to light. . . .
(Mark 4:22, NASB)

Before I was born again, I made many deals only to discover later that I had trusted the wrong people, and contracts I had agreed to were open to several interpretations, which, when all was said and done, left me with little alternative but to pay off the other parties. In most cases, to sue would have cost a lot of money. And who could know in advance which interpretation a judge or jury would decide on? Such errors cost me a fortune. Now, before I sign anything, I seek godly counsel and pray Mark 4:22 over any pending negotiations, and it has made a big difference in my life.

July 28

BARBARA MANDRELL, Grammy-winning country performer; two-time Country Music Association Entertainer of the Year; six-time People's Choice Awards' Favorite All-Around Female Entertainer; author of autobiography, *Get to the Heart: My Story,* on New York Times best-seller list six months; featured on some twenty-five albums.

> *And we know that all things work together for good to them that love God, to them who are the called according to his purpose. (Romans 8:28, KJV)*

If there's a decision to be made, I simply put it in God's hands and things just begin to fall into place.

July 29

ROBBIE MARONEY, Oklahoma City real estate agent whose husband, Mickey, was among the 168 people killed in the April 19, 1995, bombing of the Alfred P. Murrah Federal Building; Mickey had been a special agent with the U.S. Secret Service for twenty-four years; in addition to Robbie, Mickey Maroney is survived by three grown children, Alice, Darin, and Mickey.

For I know the thoughts and plans that I have for you,
says the Lord, thoughts and plans for welfare and peace,
and not for evil, to give you hope in your final outcome.
(Jeremiah 29:11, amplified)

My pastor, Mark Hartman, had come over to meet with me before Mickey's funeral service. He wanted to learn something
about Mickey by thumbing through his Bible. But I told him
Mickey did not mark in his Bible; it was just not something that
he did. But as Mark was going through the Bible, he found
where Mickey had typed out Jeremiah 29:11 on his computer,
and then cut it out and placed it right at Jeremiah 29, like a
bookmark. It was meaningful to him for some reason, and now
it means a lot to me. We do have the assurance that the Lord has
something really good for us as Christians. Our final outcome is
going to be great. Mickey knew the Lord and now is in heaven,
in a much better place. And I know God has something really
good in store for me. I just believe that. All things happen for a
reason; it's His plan. We can't really say why—sometimes we
want to—but we just have to remain faithful in whatever challenges come our way.

July 30

KELSEY MARSHALL, director, Office of Accessibility, John
F. Kennedy Center for the Performing Arts, Washington, overseeing architectural and program access for patrons and performers with disabilities (she herself has multiple sclerosis);
musician, painter, and screenwriter in her spare time; previous
positions include special adviser for disability issues, Office of
Intergovernmental Relations, U.S. Department of Housing and
Urban Development, and staff member for Senator Richard G.
Lugar of Indiana.

The word that came to Jeremiah from the LORD: *"Arise, and go down to the potter's house, and there I will let you hear my words." So I went down to the potter's house, and there he was working at his wheel. And the vessel he was making of clay was spoiled in the potter's hand, and he reworked it into another vessel, as it seemed good to the potter to do. Then the word of the* LORD *came to me: "O house of Israel, can I not do with you as this potter has done? says the* LORD. *Behold, like the clay in the potter's hand, so are you in my hand, O house of Israel. . . ."* (Jeremiah 18:1–6, RSV)

An active expertise. Always having an objective based on accomplishment. Still subject to unforeseen "changes" during the process. Skill in making the most of what one's got. Satisfaction and pride in the ability to fashion something to be one's own. Uniquely full of wonder.

The first six verses of chapter 18 of the Book of Jeremiah are treasures to me. As an artist, I immediately understand the potter's challenge, identifying with the elements involved in creating an art form and his determination to exercise his giftedness and do something "good." As a person with disabilities, I immediately recognize the vital relationship. Rather than my becoming DIS-abled, "spoiled clay" as it were, the Master Potter has reworked my life; He has taken what on a human level others may discount as weakness or inability and has fashioned it into another "vessel," a personality capable of being filled with His grace. Indeed, the Master Potter, well aware of what was happening when disability entered and seemingly altered my life, has instead made His creation differently able to reflect His glory. Such craftsmanship. As it has seemed good for Him to do. And I am the richer, the consequences professionally and personally immeasurable.

July 31

WILLIAM MARTIN, professor of sociology, Rice University, Houston; author of *A Prophet with Honor: The Billy Graham Story*, numerous other books, and articles on religion and culture in such magazines as *The Atlantic, Harper's,* and *Esquire*.

But let justice roll down like waters,
and righteousness like an everflowing stream.
(Amos 5:24, RSV)

In this verse, the prophet Amos proclaims the word of the Lord to a people who had come to believe that the form of religion was more important than its substance. To them, God says, "I take no delight in your solemn assemblies" (verse 21) but, instead, He desires actions and character that manifest a deeper commitment to Him and His will. From the tumultuous 1960s when I was coming to maturity until the present, this Scripture has reminded me that, though love has many dimensions, it should always embody—at the least—justice and a humble spirit of righteousness.

AUGUST

August 1

BILL McCARTNEY, founder of the Promise Keepers men's movement; head football coach, University of Colorado, 1982–94; 1990 national champions with an Orange Bowl victory over Notre Dame; named UPI Coach of the Year, 1989, 1990; editor of *What Makes a Man?* and author of autobiography, *From Ashes to Glory;* former defensive coordinator, University of Michigan.

> *. . . for where your treasure is, there your heart will be also. (Matthew 6:21, NIV)*

Many of us think that we follow our hearts. But Jesus clearly states that we follow our treasure (or focus). May our prayer be: Jesus, please be my treasure, my focus. Only then will our hearts wholeheartedly desire Christ.

August 2

MARILYN McCOO, former member, Fifth Dimension vocal group, which won six Grammys and was honored with a star on Hollywood's Walk of Fame; she also won a Grammy for rhythm-and-blues duo with husband Billy Davis, Jr., "You Don't Have to Be a Star (To Be in My Show)" and, more recently, was among the featured vocalists in the 1993 Grammy winner *Handel's Messiah: A Soulful Celebration;* cohost for the Children's Miracle Network Telethon and Lou Rawls's *Parade of Stars* telethon for the United Negro College Fund; host on former TV series *Solid Gold* who also has played guest roles on numerous shows.

> *Trust in the LORD with all thine heart; and lean not unto thine own understanding. In all thy ways acknowledge him, and he shall direct thy paths. (Proverbs 3:5–6, KJV)*

I quote these verses to myself very often and derive a lot of strength from them—especially in times of confusion or difficulty.

August 3

ROBIN Y. McDONALD, executive director, Capitol Hill Crisis Pregnancy Center, Washington, D.C.

> *I love the LORD, for he heard my voice;*
> *he heard my cry for mercy. . . .*
> *How can I repay the LORD*
> *for all his goodness to me?*
> *I will lift up the cup of salvation*
> *and call on the name of the LORD.*
> *I will fulfill my vows to the LORD*
> *in the presence of all his people.*
> *(Psalm 116:1, 12–14, NIV)*

I have often found this passage to be a blessed reminder that God's grace is the core of my commitment. When my work in pro-life ministry or my efforts at reconciliation within the church seem particularly daunting (or even when my efforts meet with some success), this Scripture calls me back to my true purpose. It is my faith in Christ and my vow to love and serve Him that motivate my actions, not the issues themselves. They are but expressions of my faith. I will ever strive to be a living sacrifice to God, for as the phrase from an old hymn admonishes: "Love so amazing, so divine, demands my soul, my life, my all."

August 4

SCOTT McGREGOR, Baltimore Orioles pitcher, 1976–86; had 1–1 record in two World Series, 1979, 1983; 1981 All-Star; currently pastor, Rock Church, Dover, Delaware.

> ... If anyone else thinks he has reasons to put confidence in the flesh, I have more: circumcised on the eighth day, of the people of Israel, of the tribe of Benjamin, a Hebrew of Hebrews; in regard to the law, a Pharisee; as for zeal, persecuting the church; as for legalistic righteousness, faultless. But whatever was to my profit I now consider loss for the sake of Christ. What is more, I consider everything a loss compared to the surpassing greatness of knowing Christ Jesus my Lord, for whose sake I have lost all things. I consider them rubbish, that I may gain Christ and be found in him, not having a righteousness of my own that comes from the law, but that which is through faith in Christ—the righteousness that comes from God and is by faith. (Philippians 3:4–9, NIV)

This Scripture was given to me at 2:00 A.M. the night before the final game of the 1983 World Series, which I was to pitch. I was tossing and turning all night until this point, and finally I prayed, "Lord, help me, please." The Lord led me to this Scripture and put it to me like this: If you want the glory like Paul could have had, since you are a pro athlete, in the World Series you must also live with this anxiety and fear. But if you let go and count it loss, you will be free of the outcome tomorrow.... The rest is history. I pitched a five-hit shutout and we were the world champs. Thank you, Jesus!

August 5

ERIC McGREW, twenty-five-year Delta Air Lines pilot who, by sharing his faith, thwarted a suicidal hijacker.

And he said unto me, "My grace is sufficient for you, for my power is made perfect in weakness." Most gladly therefore will I rather glory in my weaknesses, that the power of Christ may rest upon me. That is why, for Christ's sake, I delight in weaknesses, in insults, in hardships, in persecution, in difficulties. For when I am weak, then am I strong. (paraphrase of 2 Corinthians 12:9–10)

I had never been totally helpless before—until a hijacker appeared in the cockpit and pointed a gun at me on March 14, 1986. Somehow he had entered the aircraft after the passengers had exited and then had ushered the crew off. He told me to line up the DC–9 on the runway, take off, and then dive to a crash because he wanted to die. I started thinking about myself; I didn't want to die. Then the thought came, "You're pretty selfish, aren't you?" Yes, I admitted. "What about him? He's going to die, too. Is he going to heaven?" I didn't know. But I knew it's not fair if I knew how to get to heaven and he didn't, so I decided I wasn't going to take off until I told him how to get to heaven. I turned to him and said, "I just have one thing to tell you before we go, and then I'll be ready," then shared with him what Scripture says about what a person has to do to get to heaven. And when I was finished, God's power came through my weakness and the man decided not to go through with it. The older I get, the more I am coming to understand that God's power is perfected when we are weak, and that is totally contrary to the world's way of thinking. The world's way is to be strong, aggressive—intimidate 'em. But actually, if we retreat from ourselves and our aggressive personalities and let God take control, we can be super strong.

August 6

MICHAEL J. MCMANUS, "Ethics and Religion" syndicated columnist in ninety newspapers; author of *Marriage Savers,*

Insuring Marriage: 25 Proven Ways to Prevent Divorce, and *50 Practical Ways to Take Our Kids Back from the World;* organizer of "Community Marriage Policies" in fifty cities involving interdenominational clergy efforts to reduce divorce through expanded premarital counseling and the use of older, mentor couples; former *Time* magazine correspondent and newspaper reporter; Emmy winner, 1973, for televised town meeting series in metro New York.

> *Submit to one another out of reverence for Christ.*
> *(Ephesians 5:21, NIV)*

I think this is the key verse for how men and women should build a marriage. If men and women are willing to submit to one another out of reverence for Christ, that basically is the key to marital happiness. Ephesians 5:22, "Wives, submit to your husbands as to the Lord," is probably the most misinterpreted verse of the Bible in regard to husbands and wives. That's why 5:21 is so important. And a little farther down in the same chapter, the apostle Paul says husbands are to love their wives as Christ loved the church, being willing to die for her. Marital happiness for most people is the key to overall happiness. One can have a right relationship with God—or at least think he or she has a right relationship with God—and not have a right relationship with one's spouse. If the relationship with one's spouse is not healthy and vital, I think it blocks communication with the Lord. But if the Lord is a third partner of a marriage, it's going to work.

August 7

LARRY MELANCON, winningest apprentice jockey, 1972; finished fourth in 1976 Kentucky Derby, first in 1986 Bluegrass Stakes.

> *Casting all your care upon him; for he careth for you.*
> *(1 Peter 5:7, KJV)*

Sometimes when we're praying, we think we shouldn't bring this or that up to God because it's too little. But God wants to hear from us, regardless of whether it's a small problem or a big problem. He really cares for us whatever position we're in; He wants to meet our needs. Just be open to Him.

August 8

MIKE MERRIVAL, Native American bivocational minister among the 28,000 Lakota people on the 1-million-acre Pine Ridge Indian Reservation in South Dakota; former activist in the American Indian movement.

> By this we know love, because He laid down His life for us. And we also ought to lay down our lives for the brethren. But whoever has this world's goods, and sees his brother in need, and shuts up his heart from him, how does the love of God abide in him? My little children, let us not love in word or in tongue, but in deed and in truth. (1 John 3:16–18, NKJV)

Ministering here is very tough; the spiritual battle is so strong I call it the "trenches." Satan has a stronghold here on the reservation. A friend said to me, "I would never put my family in that situation." But if you don't teach your children how to get into the trenches when they're young, when they're older they might not be able to handle it. I praise the Lord that, so far, my three children—their ages are fifteen, thirteen, and twelve—are not involved in drugs and alcohol like I was when I was young. At the age of twelve, we were already drinking; at the age of thirteen, we were served at the bar. I praise the Lord that my children know Jesus Christ as their Lord and Savior and they love Him. They've been able to say no to alcohol and drugs and are being positive role models in this community.

The life I once lived here on the reservation—you could say I was probably one of the worst people here. I was into trouble, into alcohol and drugs. The change in my life started in 1973 during the radical American Indian movement days. I was involved with them; my cousin and I had a gun in our car, on the seat, and it accidentally went off and shot me through the stomach. As I lay on the ground dying, I just asked the Lord for forgiveness. I said, "Forgive me, Lord. I'm a sinner. Forgive me, Jesus." And I knew right there I was forgiven. And I just told the Lord at the time, "Lord, if You let me live, I'll do anything You want." From that point forward, the Lord started to change the events in my life. At the hospital, they said it was a miracle I had even lived. The surgeon said, "Son, there was nothing we could do for you. All we could do was patch a few things and close you up. It's only by the hand of God that you're living."

The next day, I would have been with the guys at the takeover at Wounded Knee and, two years later, the shoot-out that killed the two FBI men. I went to an Upward Bound summer college program, and it seemed the Lord just kept turning me this way and that way. I finally met a lady who was a Christian, married her, and in 1981 I accepted Christ as my Lord and Savior. I was involved in Indian religion before, like sun dance, medicine, and sweat lodges. When I share with people from my heart, they can't say, "You don't know anything about it," because I've been there. I tell them I've been to the sun dance, to the sweat lodge, and I never found a personal relationship with God until I accepted Jesus Christ.

August 9

NORMAN MILLER, chairman of the board, Interstate Battery System of America, Inc., marketers of the country's top-selling replacement battery; employee with Interstate thirty-plus years who started with his father's distributorship in Memphis, Tennessee; cofounder, Interstate Batteries Great American Race, world's richest vintage car race.

*And do not fear those who kill the body, but are unable to
kill the soul; but rather fear Him who is able to destroy
both soul and body in hell. . . . (Matthew 10:28, NASB)*

When I first became the CEO of Interstate back in 1974, I had
not firmed up in my mind how scripturally "obedient" I could
be in my decision making and daily behavior in running the
company. The acceptable consensus appeared to be that business required more of a "when in Rome, do as the Romans do"
mentality if you wanted to succeed, and I certainly had a fear of
what business failure might bring. While all these thoughts were
going 'round and 'round in my mind, God led me to this
Scripture in my Bible reading one day. Right then I decided I
was going to do my very best every day to live a faithful, Christ-
pleasing life—including in business—knowing that after I complete my time here on earth, I will stand before God Almighty
Himself to give an account of the life I have lived.

August 10

BRYANT MILLSAPS, executive director, Tennessee Higher
Education Commission, coordinating board for the Tennessee
Board of Regents and University of Tennessee System; Tennessee
secretary of state, 1990–93; former chief clerk, Tennessee House
of Representatives.

*When they saw the courage of Peter and John and realized
that they were unschooled, ordinary men, they were as-
tonished and they took note that these men had been with
Jesus. (Acts 4:13, NIV)*

This is the standard by which every Christian should seek to
live: when we walk away from any encounter, whether we are
relating to our families, our work associates, other members of
the body of Christ, our neighbors, or the person at the gas station or the grocery story, that they would look at us, reflect on

our countenance, language, attitude, and testimony, and say, "There goes someone who has clearly been with Jesus." When we make Jesus Lord of our lives, He, through the outpouring of the Holy Spirit through us, reaches out and touches the lives of those people with whom we come in contact daily.

August 11

MADELINE MANNING MIMS, four-time Olympian (1980, 1976, 1972, 1968); women's track captain of three U.S. teams; 1968 gold medalist in the 800 meters, setting new world record; 1972 silver medalist member of the 4 by 400 meter relay team; founder and president of Friends Fellowship, Tulsa, national ministry to incarcerated women; inspirational speaker, singer featured on six gospel albums.

> *Being confident of this very thing, that he which hath begun a good work in you, will perform it until the day of Jesus Christ.... (Philippians 1:6, KJV)*

My confidence, which brings great peace in my life, does not stem from my own abilities to accomplish my goals successfully, but in knowing that when I accepted Jesus as Lord and Savior of my life I accepted Father God's plan for my future. Now I am simply walking in steps that have been ordered for me as Jesus lives out the Father's will through me by His Spirit.

August 12

FRANZ MOHR, retired chief concert technician after forty years with Steinway & Sons; author, with Edith Schaeffer, *My Life with the Great Pianists;* during World War II, he became a Christian while reading Scripture after a bombing raid had destroyed his hometown in Germany.

> *For by grace you have been saved through faith; and that not of yourselves, it is the gift of God; not as a result of*

works, that no one should boast. For we are His work-
manship, created in Christ Jesus for good works, which
God prepared beforehand, that we should walk in them.
(Ephesians 2:8–10, NASB)

I have known the Lord for over forty years, and I must say it
gets better and better all the time. God has a plan for each of
our lives, and there is no greater joy for any Christian than to be
where God wants us to be. I remember when I first got saved
about forty years ago. I got so excited about Jesus that I didn't
want to do anything else but become a preacher and preach this
glorious gospel of our Lord Jesus Christ. But the doors were
closed for me to study theology in Germany at that time. Yet
God had other plans for my life. I became a piano tuner—and a
piano tuner to many artists. I traveled the world with my tuning
hammer and Bible, and I preached on the side all along.

As I reflect back on my life, it is absolutely marvelous to have
learned this one thing: God has a tremendous high calling for
each of us. And there is no happier life than this. But the important thing is that we let Him do His work of grace in us on a
day-by-day basis, that we make ourselves available to Him in
the morning. My prayer is always the same in the morning,
"Lord, here I am. I do not know what will happen on this day. I
make myself available to You. Let me be sensitive to the leading
of the Holy Spirit." And it is absolutely marvelous to see, then,
what God in His mercy and His love is doing as we are sensitive
to the Holy Spirit and His leading—the people He brings into
our lives to be a testimony to. Many times I reflect back in the
evening and say, "Lord, well, I blew it here and there, but I saw
Your hand upon it, and I thank You so very, very, very much for
what You have done on this day."

Our walk is a walk by faith. We never know what God will
do tomorrow or the day after tomorrow. But for this day, He
gives light for each step. But this is all on a foundation of prayer.

Prayer is the most important thing in my life, this communication between God and us through the Lord Jesus Christ.

August 13

ART MONK, Hall of Fame–bound wide receiver, holding NFL records for most career catches, 934, and most consecutive games with a catch, 180; after fourteen seasons with the Washington Redskins, including three Super Bowl championships, he signed with the New York Jets as a free agent in 1994 and the Philadelphia Eagles in 1995; sponsor of "I Have a Dream" program of support for Washington, D.C., youth to pursue a college education; among the founders of the Good Samaritan Foundation assisting Washington's needy.

> ... *Christ Jesus came into the world to save sinners—of whom I am the worst. But for that very reason I was shown mercy so that in me, the worst of sinners, Christ Jesus might display his unlimited patience as an example for those who would believe on him and receive eternal life.* (*1 Timothy 1:15–16, NIV*)

I did a lot of things as a young man that I look back on and really regret doing, to the point where, back then, I didn't feel worthy of being saved. I had been raised in the church. I was born into a very believing family, with my mother and father and sister all Christians. But I rebelled. I didn't think I needed Christ and didn't want anything to do with Him. I was just a young kid, was very successful in sports, and went from high school to college on a scholarship.

After doing well in college, I was drafted by the Redskins. But even with all the accomplishments, I began to feel a lot of emptiness and loneliness. I had everything I wanted yet still felt something was missing. I started going to some Bible studies in 1987 and, upon doing that, all the things I had been taught by my parents and by the church and things close friends had been trying to tell me—those things just came flooding back, and I realized the impact of what they had been trying to get across. I knew then that I needed Christ, that He was what I was looking for. And He's made all the difference.

Before we give our lives to Christ, I think everyone has the same feeling of not being worthy to be a part of the kingdom of God. We're all born sinners. These verses helped me understand that no matter how sinful I had been, or how bad I thought I was as a person, Christ truly died for everyone. In fact, while we were still sinners He died. It wasn't that we were good and holy people and He died for us. He died for us when we were at our worst. When I gave my life to Christ, obviously my life changed, and the emptiness and loneliness just kind of went away. And I began to realize, as Romans 8:1 says, that "there is now no condemnation for those who are in Christ Jesus." Even though there will be times when we fall short, when we sin and do things we aren't supposed to, as long as we repent and ask for forgiveness, we are indeed forgiven.

August 14

PAM MOORE, director of intercessory prayer, Dallas Baptist University; curator of the university's Corrie ten Boom Collection honoring the Dutchwoman who was imprisoned with other members of her family in a Nazi concentration camp for hiding Jews in their home during World War II. An assistant to ten Boom for seven years until ten Boom's death in 1983 at age ninety-one and a former Christian worker in Africa and Eastern Europe, Moore is the author of *The Five Silent Years of Corrie ten Boom, Safer Than a Known Way,* and, with husband Carey, *If Two Shall Agree.*

"... not as I will, but as you will." (Matthew 26:39, NIV)

One early spring evening when I was a young woman of twenty-one, I made a prayer in which I relinquished my own will to the will of God. It happened at a Christian conference center near my home in southern England and I made the prayer as honestly as I knew how. Through the words of a speaker to my church's youth group, I had come to understand something of the great price the Lord Jesus had paid for me by His death on the cross. My prayer that night echoed the words of the Lord Jesus to His Father just before His death, "Not my will but yours be done." I wept as I made the prayer, but not sentimentally. There was a price to be paid, and I knew it. I was a shy, often angry, rebellious young woman who realized this was a momentous night in her life. "Not my will but yours be done" meant that I gave up my right to my own way, and it included the previous fear that I might be called to mission work—which would mean leaving my protective family, probably undertaking dreaded public speaking, and possibly remaining single. But from the moment of my prayer to this time three decades later, I have seen God answer prayer. His will did indeed involve the things I had previously feared, but I have been given undreamed-of privileges—in mission service in East Africa, in the Netherlands as a co-worker of Brother Andrew, as assistant to Corrie ten Boom for seven years at the end of her life, and as director of intercessory prayer at Dallas Baptist University. The prayer of total surrender to the will of God is the key to answered prayer for every Christian. There is nothing He cannot do through a man or woman who is willing to say, "Not as I will, but as you will."

August 15

VALERY MOORHEAD, wife of U.S. Congressman Carlos Moorhead of California; one of the founders of Project Nehemiah, a ministry operating an orphanage in the Andes mountains of Peru, for children whose parents were killed by the Shining Path guerrilla movement, and ten Sunday feeding centers in Lima; artist who does oil paintings with a group of congressional wives who put on a yearly show of their work, with benefits in previous years for Project Nehemiah and for construction of a Smithsonian Native American museum in Washington, D.C.

> *. . . God . . . is the blessed controller of all things. . . .*
> *(1 Timothy 6:15, Phillips)*

Most of our life goes along like normal people's lives—a series of ups and downs but, mostly, many good and wonderful things. But in the summer of '94, my husband and I got hit with so many things. Two of our very good friends died. Our daughter-in-law had a miscarriage. A home we moved to in Glendale had major problems that were not disclosed, so there were big expenses trying to settle all of that. And I was saying, "Lord, what's going on here?" I was relating these dilemmas to Maxine Dean, a strong Christian woman who has been my husband's administrative assistant the whole twenty-plus years he's been in office. "Val, I've got a great verse for you," she said. And I just nearly broke down on the phone and cried because it was so perfect. I had been trying to get all my ducks in a row, trying to get these problems solved myself, totally going ahead of the Lord, and the verse just brought me up short. I thought, I'm going to put this on my refrigerator, right up there in plain sight for me to use while working in the kitchen, opening the refrigerator, and so forth, as these problems come up. (It helped me not to double-dip into the refrigerator as well!) This verse has been a wonderful thing to have, to think about, to ponder. He is in control of *all* things, and what a joy to rest in that fact.

August 16

ANNIE M. MORGAN, mother who, with her husband, Walter, raised twelve sons and six daughters on a forty-acre farm near Marianna, Florida; the Morgans, who were married in 1945, now have forty-seven grandchildren.

The LORD is my shepherd; I shall not want. He maketh me to lie down in green pastures: he leadeth me beside the still waters. He restoreth my soul: he leadeth me in the paths of righteousness for his name's sake. Yea, though I walk through the valley of the shadow of death, I will fear no evil: for thou art with me; thy rod and thy staff they comfort me. Thou preparest a table before me in the presence of mine enemies: thou anointest my head with oil; my cup runneth over. Surely goodness and mercy shall follow me all the days of my life: and I will dwell in the house of the LORD for ever. (Psalm 23, KJV)

The Twenty-third Psalm helped me put the Word of God into reality in my life. We raised eighteen beautiful children by faith in God. This psalm helped me in my Christian growth. Times of crisis and decisions in life were made easier as a result of these verses. Recently I slipped and fell on my back. I suffered contusions. This Scripture was a mainstay in my recovery. I knew I couldn't heal and worry at the same time. The Lord is my shepherd, and I love all the words of God.

August 17

ELISA MORGAN, president, MOPS International, Inc. (Mothers of Preschoolers), since 1989, Denver-based ministry founded in 1973 to address needs of mothers with children from infancy to kindergarten; mother of an elementary school–age daughter and son; host of syndicated weekday radio program *Mom Sense;* author of five books, including *Prayers from a Mother's Heart* and *Mom to Mom;* former dean of women, Colorado Christian University, Denver.

He tends his flock like a shepherd:
He gathers the lambs in his arms
and carries them close to his heart;
he gently leads those that have young. (Isaiah 40:11, NIV)

This verse is part of a chapter focusing on God calling His people out of captivity in Babylon and home to Himself. God uses the analogy of shepherd and sheep to express His tender concern for His people. Close to His heart, they can draw on the guidance and compassion He daily supplies. When it's ten at night, you've been up since five, and you have three more loads of wash and a set of bottles to prepare, you need to be carried. When you're racing from baseball practice to committee meetings to dental appointments, you need guidance. When you climb the stairs during what you thought was nap time to discover that your eighteen-month-old has baptized his crib with his messy diaper, you need to be cradled. Close to His heart. That's where He says He'll put us, we who have young. I don't know about you, but I can't think of a better place to be.

August 18

PATRICK MORLEY, Orlando business and real estate executive who launched Patrick Morley Ministries in 1992 focusing on spiritual awakening and reconciliation in America; author of several books, including *The Man in the Mirror,* named best Christian-living book of 1990 by the Evangelical Christian Publishers Association, and most recently, *The Seven Seasons of a Man's Life* and *Two Part Harmony;* teacher of a weekly businessmen's Bible study.

> . . . *God was reconciling the world to himself in Christ, not counting men's sins against them. And he has committed to us the message of reconciliation. We are therefore Christ's ambassadors, as though God were making his appeal through us. . . . (2 Corinthians 5:19–20, NIV)*

I love Jesus with all my heart. So I'm always surprised to meet someone who doesn't love Him, too. Why wouldn't someone love Jesus? The way I figure, the only reason anyone of right mind would not love Jesus is that he or she does not yet realize who Jesus is. Fortunately, we have the high privilege of inviting our friends to join the family, the eternal kingdom of Christ. It's found at the foot of the cross. But there are obstacles. The nature of life is tragic. Each day our ministries will take us to places of loneliness, despair, death, fear, brokenness, exhaustion, emptiness, evil, pain, and persecutions. The world is full of death and decay. The nature of the kingdom, however, is "righteousness, peace, and joy in the Holy Spirit" (Romans 14:17). Though we are associated with tragedy much of the time, our lives are not tragic. Rather, we are agents of the kingdom—Christ's ambassadors. A physician's office is a place of sickness. But how would you feel if you went to see the doctor and the staff was mopey and depressed? You would run! The problem, of course, is that we are all subject to the daily aches and pains of living in a world held hostage by sin. Yet if we appear without hope, there can be no hope. What message do you send? Is it the message of reconciliation? Above all else, our lives should pulsate with the love of Christ—the Great Physician—"as though God were making his appeal through us." We belong to Jesus. He has a purpose for our lives. We are ambassadors of the kingdom, not pallbearers of the kingdom.

August 19

HENRY M. MORRIS, president emeritus, Institute for Creation Research, El Cajon, California, which he founded in 1970; editor of the *Defender's Study Bible: Defending the Faith from a Literal Creationist Viewpoint* and author of nearly fifty books; cofounder, Christian Heritage College, El Cajon, in 1970, serving initially as vice president for academic affairs, then president, 1978–80; former professor of hydraulic engineering and Department of Civil Engineering chairman, Virginia Polytechnic Institute, and professor and head of the Department of Civil Engineering, University of Southwestern Louisiana.

Knowing this first, that there shall come in the last days
scoffers, walking after their own lusts, And saying, Where
is the promise of his coming? for since the fathers fell
asleep, all things continue as they were from the beginning
of the creation. For this they willingly are ignorant of, that
by the word of God the heavens were of old, and the
earth standing out of the water and in the water: Whereby
the world that then was, being overflowed with water, per-
ished. . . . (2 Peter 3:3–6, KJV)

This has been a key passage in connection with our ministry of promoting true scientific biblical creationism wherever we can, and has been accompanied by much evidence of God's guidance and blessing. This prophecy is being remarkably fulfilled today, with the philosophy of "evolutionary naturalism" ("all processes of nature today are operating just as they have since the beginning of the universe, without divine initiation or intervention") dominating all science and education in Christendom and thus negating faith in God's promise of future consummation. The prophecy also reveals, however, that the answer to such willful ignorance on the part of modern intellectuals is to recognize and apply the overwhelming evidence—both biblical and scientific—for primeval special creation of all things, together with the later worldwide Noahic hydraulic cataclysm.

August 20

DONALD W. MUNRO, executive director, American Scientific Affiliation, 2,000-member organization dedicated to fidelity to Scripture and integrity in the practice of science; head of Houghton (New York) College's department of zoology/biology, 1969–94.

For by him all things were created: things in heaven and
on earth, visible and invisible, whether thrones or powers

or rulers or authorities; all things were created by him and
for him. He is before all things, and in him all things hold
together. (Colossians 1:16–17, NIV)

Although there are many verses in the Bible I hold dear, these verses have sustained me as a professional biologist struggling to understand how God created the universe. These words from God bring me back to the source. The "him" in these verses is the Lord Jesus Christ who created everything for His glory, and He continues to hold it together. If He ever lets it go, it appears that the whole creation would fly apart, but I trust Him to maintain His work. The more I study biology and understand the intricacies of the cell and cellular interactions in organisms, the more amazed I become at His awesome creative powers. Yet there are so many more things to research and try to comprehend. Hallelujah, what a Savior! I am so glad that He is my redeemer.

August 21

CHRISTI MYERS, reporter, 13 Eyewitness News, KTRK-TV, Houston; former syndicated medical reporter, News and Information Weekly Service; honored by the Jewish Federation of Greater Houston in 1989 for a series of reports helping to secure freedom for a Soviet Jewish family.

> *Dear brothers, is your life full of difficulties and temptations? Then be happy, for when the way is rough, your patience has a chance to grow. So let it grow, and don't try to squirm out of your problems. For when your patience is finally in full bloom, then you will be ready for anything, strong in character, full and complete. If you want to know what God wants you to do, ask him, and he will gladly tell you, for he is always ready to give a bountiful supply of wisdom to all who ask him; he will not resent it.*

But when you ask him, be sure that you really expect him
to tell you, for a doubtful mind will be as unsettled as a
wave of the sea that is driven and tossed by the wind; and
every decision you then make will be uncertain, as you
turn first this way, and then that. If you don't ask with
faith, don't expect the Lord to give you any solid answer.
(James 1:2–8, TLB)

During difficult times in my life, these verses seemed to place the
problems in perspective. While I really wanted to "squirm out
of my problems," instead I should have been expecting tough
times—even looking forward to them! I wanted God to give me
a quick solution. But He doesn't because the Bible says testing is
necessary. And it's certainly not over yet, either! To get through
the testing, He offers us an out—verses 5–8. All we have to do is
ask for wisdom—wisdom to understand the difficulties and wisdom to guide us through them. But what do we do? I tend to
pray for His wisdom and then use my own. I live in a world of
deadlines, and it never works when I try to put God on my
timetable instead of changing my deadlines to meet His. To remind myself of that, I read verse 8 with verses 2–4. When we
have difficulties, we must not only go to God and ask for wisdom, but ask "with faith." Sometimes that is harder for me to
do than to deal with the original difficulties. But at least we have
a blueprint, a "user's guide" to deal with life's downs. As for
me, I'm glad James placed these sections of Scripture next to
each other.

August 22

STEVE NAGEL, NASA astronaut since 1979; colonel, USAF;
commander of space shuttle flights of *Columbia* in 1993 and
Atlantis in 1991; pilot of *Challenger*'s 1985 flight and crew
member aboard *Discovery* earlier in 1985.

When I consider your heavens,
the work of your fingers,
the moon and the stars,
which you have set in place,
what is man that you are mindful of him,
the son of man that you care for him?
You made him a little lower than the heavenly beings
and crowned him with glory and honor.
(Psalm 8:3–5, NIV)

About ten minutes after liftoff, *Columbia*'s engines had shut down right on time and we were coasting toward the apogee (highest point) of the insertion orbit where we would perform a small burn to establish the final circular orbit. I picked up the checklist and said, "Let's see, where are we?" My pilot, Tom Henricks, always quick and witty, said, "Space!" And indeed we were. That first look out the windows on any shuttle mission is an unforgettable moment—the beauty of the Earth is over-whelming, and the sensation of speed is dramatic at this initial low altitude. At that point, the commander usually has to re-mind the crew that they need to get back to work or else experi-ence a premature, unplanned entry into the atmosphere in about thirty minutes!

My most memorable moments from all these missions have been the views of Earth from orbit. Night or day is equally im-pressive. Most of the time we are too busy to reflect on what we are seeing, but on every mission I have found at least one or two opportunities to look out the windows for extended periods, as much as an entire orbit (about ninety minutes). The richness of the colors of deserts, jungles, and mountains contrasted against the jet-black sky is hard to describe, and even the best pho-tographs do not reveal the beauty that is actually present. It is at these times that verses like Psalm 8:3–5 come to mind and I give thanks to God for the beauty of His creation, the great privilege that is mine to be there, and for another safe excursion into space.

August 23

REBEKAH NAYLOR, missionary physician at the Baptist Hospital, Bangalore, India, since 1973.

Trust in the Lord with all thine heart; and lean not unto thine own understanding. In all thy ways acknowledge him, and he shall direct thy paths. (Proverbs 3:5–6, KJV)

Life is filled with decisions, small and large, but there need not be confusion at any point. I do not need to understand but I must trust, submit, and acknowledge the Lord and then know that He will direct. This promise of direction has been fulfilled in my life over and over again.

August 24

HATTIE NEWELL, nurse, San Bernardino, California, and founder of E.F.I. (Exhortation, Faith, Intercession), a ministry underscoring the importance of knowing the Bible; former member of Jim Jones's People's Temple who served as a bodyguard to his wife, Marceline.

I can do all things through Him who strengthens me. (Philippians 4:13, NASB)

On November 18, 1978, my whole world was shattered. Twelve members of my family, including my mother, two sisters, and three brothers, along with 900 followers of the Reverend Jim Jones, committed suicide or were murdered in the remote jungle of Jonestown, Guyana. When I saw the lists of those who had died on the evening news special report, and saw my family's names listed among the dead, all I could do was cry. Because of the loyalty I still felt for Jim Jones, I could not bring myself to hate him at that moment for what he had done to my family. But in February 1979, when I finally left San Francisco behind me, I was filled with anger and bitterness for the man and cause I had loved and supported for six years. I was struggling to find answers to why this had happened to me and my family. My life was going downhill fast. I felt so far away from God I thought there was no way He would help me or could help me. Jim Jones had been my source for answers for six years. Now he was gone. Who would be my source for help now?

In 1982 God sent Debbie Seitz (Dodd), a Christian lady, into my life and she invited me to go to Immanuel Baptist Church with her. After attending for a few weeks, I heard pastor Rob Zinn speak the words in a sermon that would change my life forever: "Would you love God and serve Him even if you never get answers to your questions?" I knew God was speaking directly to me. I said, "Yes, Lord, I will love You and serve You, even if I never get answers." Because Jesus Christ is now in my heart, I can deal with the pain and heartache of my past and also deal with the trials and storms in my future, because He gives me the strength to make it through.

In 1993 I faced my biggest test. On the fifteen-year anniversary of Jonestown, the pain hit me like a Mack truck. I cried as never before. The pain would not go away. I thought of friends who had committed suicide, but I knew that was not the answer. I asked the Lord, "When will the pain go away?" I remembered Pastor Rob saying that sometimes we shed tears to water someone else's garden. I said, "Lord, someone's garden is flooding right now." I felt God saying, "You are going through this right now so that others will not have to suffer the same pain." God sustained me through that time of crisis. He was my strength and my shield. I can truly say that I can do all things through Him who gives me strength.

August 25

FERN NICHOLS, president, Moms in Touch International, Poway, California, which she founded in 1984, now with groups of mothers in fifty states meeting one hour each week to pray for their children and schools and with contacts in forty-five countries; author of *Moms in Touch International,* a book with guidelines for starting and developing MIT prayer groups.

> *. . . Pour out your heart like water before the face of the Lord; lift up your hands toward Him for the life of your young children. . . . (Lamentations 2:19, amplified)*

The theme verse for Moms in Touch International is Lamentations 2:19. I have truly experienced this verse over and over again as I have prayed for my four children. There have been times of extreme anguish in my soul as I have come before the Lord pleading, asking, and crying out for mercy, praying that God would protect them from the world, the flesh, and the devil.

Yes, my heart has poured out like a waterfall, many times through tears, before the face of the Lord as I have actually lifted my hands, fully surrendering my child to God. As I surrender my child, it's as though I physically lift him to the Lord and place him in His hands. I have found that my children are too heavy to carry. Can you imagine physically having to carry your child all day long? Yet that's what I do emotionally and mentally when I worry, fret, and am anxious about them. God never intended for us to carry them. We are reminded in 1 Peter 5:7 of "casting all your anxiety upon Him, because He cares for you" (NASB). Worrying and fretting are mentally, emotionally, and physically exhausting. I am so thankful that as I pour my heart out to God, He helps me to understand that I am doing my part, for truly the very best thing I can do for my children is to pray for them. God then tenderly reminds me that as I give my children to Him, He will do His part, for only He can change a heart.

At the same time, pouring out my heart with other moms in a Moms in Touch group has been the support thread that has kept me hanging on, especially during troublesome times or crises. In times when my children were not walking with the Lord, the supportive prayers of the other moms would give me the strength, inspiration, and hope to persevere. When the group would pour their hearts out like water for the very "life" of my child, I not only felt humbled but also very special that they would take the time to love my child through intercessory prayers. There truly is healing in sharing one another's burdens in prayer. I knew that when I left the MIT hour of prayer, I could be certain that everything shared and prayed would be held in strictest confidence and that my prayer concern would be taken only to their prayer closets.

I'm so very grateful that I can pray without embarrassment with other moms who carry the same heavy burdens for their children. I have seen over and over again the answer to the promise from Jesus in Matthew 18:19–20, ". . . if two of you agree on earth about anything that they may ask, it shall be done for them by My Father who is in heaven. For where two or three have gathered in My name, there I am in their midst" (NASB).

August 26

DON NICKLES, U.S. senator, Oklahoma; youngest Republican ever elected to the Senate, at age thirty-one in 1980; chairman, Senate Republican Policy Committee; Oklahoma state senator, 1978–80; former vice president and general manager, Nickles Machine Corp., Ponca City, Oklahoma.

A new commandment I give unto you, That ye love one another; as I have loved you, that ye also love one an-

other. By this shall all men know that ye are my disciples, if ye have love one to another. (John 13:34–35, KJV)

This command to love others as Christ has loved us, if followed, would change the world for the better.

August 27

PEGGY NOONAN, speechwriter for Presidents Reagan and Bush, 1984–89; author of *What I Saw at the Revolution*, about her White House days, and *Life, Liberty, and the Pursuit of Happiness.*

> *This is the day which the Lord hath made; we will rejoice and be glad in it. (Psalm 118:24, KJV)*

I often think of these words on a beautiful morning. They remind me to be grateful. They remind me that there is an unseen order and coherence in the world and that the order and coherence were created and are governed by God, who knows every hair on my head and who made this butterfly.

August 28

KATHLEEN NORRIS, author of *Dakota: A Spiritual Geography*, chronicling her spiritual pilgrimage in returning to the Great Plains in the early 1970s from New York City, and *The Cloister Walk*, concerning monasticism and celibacy; poet whose works include *Falling Off*, *The Middle of the World*, and *Little Girls in Church*; 1993 Guggenheim grant recipient.

> *O God, make haste to my rescue,*
> *Lord, come to my aid! (Psalm 69:2, Grail trans.)*

I recently spent several months with a monastic community and learned that for more than 1,500 years Benedictine men and women have spoken these words to open their afternoon and evening prayers. I now find the verse coming into my mind and heart at all hours of the day and night, and I welcome it as a simple prayer and as reassurance of God's presence in all circumstances.

August 29

WILL NORTON, JR., dean, College of Journalism and Mass Communications, University of Nebraska, Lincoln, since 1990; formerly professor of journalism, University of Mississippi, where he joined the faculty in 1974, department chairman, 1977–90; former copy editor at the *Chicago Tribune*.

> *Therefore, my beloved brethren, be steadfast, immovable, always abounding in the work of the Lord, knowing that in the Lord your labor is not in vain.*
> *(1 Corinthians 15:58, RSV)*

After an exhilarating declaration of the resurrection, the apostle Paul tells us that the power that raised Jesus is available to us through Him. In other words, he tells us the relevance of the resurrection for our lives. My roommate in college gave me this verse at the end of my freshman year. When I have been discouraged and aware of my sin and weaknesses and failures, this verse has encouraged me. It reminds me that the Lord has the power to work—even through me.

August 30

DEBORAH NORVILLE, anchor, TV's *Inside Edition*; coanchor, *CBS News*'s "America Tonight," 1994; correspondent, *CBS News*'s "Street Stories," 1992–94; 1989 Emmy winner for coverage of the democratic revolt in Romania. Her media work has included ABC Radio's weeknight call-in *Deborah Norville Show*; cohost and, earlier, news anchor of NBC's *Today* show and anchor of *NBC News at Sunrise*.

I can do all things through Him who strengthens me.
(Philippians 4:13, NASB)

When sometimes it looks like the mountain is too high or there's too much garbage coming my way, this has always been a verse that comes to mind.

August 31

SAM NUNN, U.S. senator from Georgia, 1972–96; former chairman, Senate Armed Services Committee and the Senate's Permanent Subcommittee on Investigations; cochair, Strengthening of America Commission, a bipartisan group of business, political, education, and labor leaders addressing such issues as a balanced federal budget, the income tax system, and health care reform.

> *For I was an hungred, and ye gave me meat: I was thirsty, and ye gave me drink: I was a stranger, and ye took me in: Naked, and ye clothed me: I was sick, and ye visited me: I was in prison, and ye came unto me. Then shall the righteous answer him, saying, Lord, when saw we thee an hungred, and fed thee? or thirsty, and gave thee drink? When saw we thee a stranger, and took thee in? or naked, and clothed thee? Or when saw we thee sick, or in prison, and came unto thee? And the King shall answer and say unto them, Verily I say unto you, Inasmuch as ye have done it unto one of the least of these my brethren, ye have done it unto me. (Matthew 25:35–40, KJV)*

There are many portions of the Bible that have guided and sustained me through many different and difficult times in my life. I try to use the lessons taught in the Old and New Testaments in my professional and personal life. I believe that, as a country and a society, we must begin to stress a return to the basic values of tolerance and charity for one another, such as the actions reflected in one of my favorite passages, Matthew 25:35–40. These values are basic tenets not only of Christianity, but also of many of the world's other religions.

SEPTEMBER

September 1
KIM ODEN, captain, U.S. bronze medalist volleyball team, 1992 Olympics; two-time Broderick Award winner as the top collegiate volleyball women's player while at Stanford University.

Yes, the Lord hears the good man when he calls to him for help, and saves him out of all his troubles. The Lord is close to those whose hearts are breaking; he rescues those who are humbly sorry for their sins. The good man does not escape all troubles—he has them too. But the Lord helps him in each and every one. (Psalm 34:17–19, TLB)

This psalm is a blueprint of what God wants from me, and it states God's promises to hear and respond to my prayers. It puts to rest the myth that the Christian life is lived on a bed of roses. But it explains that when life does get a bit rough, the Almighty God is with me and will help me. That is an incredible comfort to my mind and soul—to know that whether the situation is good or bad, my God is there.

September 2
ROSEMARIE OEHLER, artist whose exhibit of more than one hundred oil paintings covering the overthrow of communism in Eastern Europe and the former Soviet Union, Russian refugees in Europe, and contemporary Russian life, has toured the United States and several European countries; founder and president, Arts for Relief and Missions, Inc., Warrenville,

Illinois, a ministry linking the arts to missions and ministry endeavors, such as a 1993–94 project with World Vision to provide more than $1.2 million worth of vegetable seeds and children's vitamins to an agriculturally depressed area southwest of Moscow.

> *. . . God, who gives life to the dead and calls into being that which does not exist. (Romans 4:17, NASB)*

Working to see the arts reclaimed in this century for the glory and honor of God has often been a labor in isolation. This verse has been central to my work and ministry, stirring me to abandon myself fully and absolutely to His sovereignty when I need the miraculous to occur in order to continue that which I've been called to do. So often He has given life to my dead hopes and called into being, by the breath of His mouth, things of which I could only dream, because they were not yet in existence. Through much prayer, and through the power of His might in response to prayer, He created that which could not be—because He is the God who will always be the great I Am.

September 3

JOHN OFFERDAHL, five-time Pro Bowl linebacker in eight seasons with the Miami Dolphins; board member, Einstein Bros. Bagels, with 300 outlets across the country; NFL "Extra Effort" recipient for food distribution after Hurricane Andrew struck south Florida in September 1992; winner of several 1986 rookie-of-the-year honors; 1985 Mid-America Conference Defensive Player of the Year at Western Michigan University.

> *Therefore, since we are surrounded by such a great cloud of witnesses, let us throw off everything that hinders and the sin that so easily entangles, and let us run with perseverance the race marked out for us. Let us fix our eyes on Jesus, the author and perfecter of our faith, who for the*

joy set before him endured the cross, scorning its shame,
and sat down at the right hand of the throne of God.
Consider him who endured such opposition from sinful
men, so that you will not grow weary and lose heart.
(Hebrews 12:1–3, NIV)

As I have been challenged in football and will continually be challenged in my Christian life, and as a husband and father, I find that these verses supply the "brass tacks" for happiness and eternal reward. In these verses, I see a need for (1) *accountability* to God and to the "great cloud of witnesses" who have gone before us; (2) *perseverance* to endure through hardship; (3) *direction* to run the race already "marked out for us" by God; (4) *focus*—keeping our eyes fixed on Jesus; (5) *confidence* that allows us to "scorn the shame" of those who doubt Jesus' work on the cross; and (6) *hope,* rooted in God's encouragement, to not grow weary or lose heart!

September 4

LLOYD JOHN OGILVIE, U.S. Senate chaplain since February 1995; pastor of First Presbyterian Church, Hollywood, California, 1972–95; author of forty-five books and general editor of the thirty-two-volume *Communicator's Commentary;* formerly featured on *Let God Love You* national weekly telecast and daily radio broadcast.

> *Thus says the LORD:*
> *"Let not the wise man glory in his wisdom,*
> *Let not the mighty man glory in his might,*
> *Nor let the rich man glory in his riches;*
> *But let him who glories glory in this,*
> *That he understands and knows Me,*
> *That I am the LORD,*
> *exercising lovingkindness, judgment,*

and righteousness in the earth.
For in these I delight," says the LORD.
(Jeremiah 9:23–24, NKJV)

This is one of two favorite passages that have sustained me through the ups and downs of living the Christian life. The other, from the New Testament, comes out of my favorite epistle of Paul, the one he wrote to Timothy from prison at the end of his life, when he reminded Timothy not to be timid, not to be taken into cowardice: "Therefore I remind you to stir up the gift of God which is in you through the laying on of my hands. For God has not given us a spirit of fear, but of power and of love and of a sound mind" (2 Timothy 1:6–7, NKJV). Very often, in times of need, immense challenge, or opportunities, I repeat these verses. They reorient my focus, keep my priorities clear, and have opened me to receive supernatural power. I ask myself, Do I glory in the Lord above anything else, anyone else, any position? When my answer is yes, then I'm open to receive the genuine power of the Spirit of God through the anointing of Jesus Christ. And then I know that God has not given me a spirit of fear; He has given me a spirit of power, of love, and of a healed, sound mind to think His thoughts and live out His will.

September 5

TOM OSBORNE, head football coach, winner of back-to-back national championships at the University of Nebraska (1995, 1994) and twelve Big Eight titles; winningest active coach in NCAA Division I-A with at least ten years on the sideline, .819 percentage; each team in his twenty-three years as Nebraska head coach has won at least nine games, and he is the first coach in Division I-A history to reach 200 wins at one school; among civic activities, he and his wife, Nancy, founded the Husker Teammates program matching Nebraska football players with local junior high students in a big-brother relationship; author of *More Than Winning.*

Whoever finds his life will lose it, and whoever loses his life for my sake will find it. (Matthew 10:39, NIV)

What this verse has meant to me is that we often try to save our lives in many ways, primarily through the acquisition of position, power, wealth, and prestige—all of which, although inherently innocent in their nature, can really get in our way if they become of high priority in our lives. On the other hand, Jesus was saying that if any man would lose his life for His sake he will begin to find it. When we put Christ and His values and His kingdom first in our lives, then our lives begin to take on a perspective and a focus they would otherwise lack.

September 6

PAUL OVERSTREET, country music songwriter and performer; named BMI country Songwriter of the Year five consecutive years, 1987–91; 1991 Grammy winner for "Love Can Build a Bridge" performed by the Judds and 1987 winner for "Forever and Ever, Amen" performed by Randy Travis; winner of Country Music Association Song of the Year, 1988 for "Forever and Ever, Amen" and 1987 for "On the Other Hand" performed by Travis; also featured on seven solo albums.

Then he said to his disciples, "The harvest is plentiful but the workers are few." (Matthew 9:37, NIV)

That's what our life is all about—to work for the Lord.

September 7

JACK PADDON, actuarial vice president, New York Life Insurance Company; chairman of the Society of Actuaries' Individual Mortality Committee, former chairman of the society's

Education/Examination Committee; actuarial adviser, Evangelical Free Church of America's and Interserve's pension plans.

> *Therefore, my dear brothers, stand firm. Let nothing move you. Always give yourselves fully to the work of the Lord, because you know that your labor in the Lord is not in vain. (1 Corinthians 15:58, NIV)*

This verse concludes one of the most significant chapters of Scripture. First Corinthians, verse 15 is a profound apologetic for the truth of Christ's resurrection, His second coming, and His victory over death and the grave. Humanly speaking, as Solomon said in Ecclesiastes, "Everything is meaningless!" But when what we do seems meaningless and in vain humanly speaking, we are assured that death has no power over us and we will be forever transformed at Christ's coming. Because this is so, we can affirm with gratitude that our faith, as well as our work for God, whether sacred or secular, will always be meaningful and productive in His sight.

September 8

RAYMA C. PAGE, public education consultant and speaker; president, National School Boards Association, 1982–83; member of NSBA's board of directors, 1972–84; president, Florida School Boards Association, 1974–75; Lee County (Florida) School Board member, 1968–86; member of numerous other education-related boards, commissions, and advisory councils.

> *We can make our plans, but the final outcome is in God's hands. We can always "prove" that we are right, but is the Lord convinced? Commit your work to the Lord, then it will succeed. The Lord has made everything for his own purposes—even the wicked, for punishment. Pride disgusts the Lord. Take my word for it—proud men shall be*

punished. Iniquity is atoned for by mercy and truth; evil is avoided by reverence for God. When a man is trying to please God, God makes even his worst enemies to be at peace with him. A little, gained honestly, is better than great wealth gotten by dishonest means. We should make plans—counting on the Lord to direct us.
(Proverbs 16:1–9, TLB)

I have read Proverbs 16 over and over and carried its essence with me for support. It comforts me as well as uplifts me, often when I least expect it; there's always something new in it for me. Proverbs 16:1–9 talks to people who are in positions of leadership or responsibility. The rest of the chapter fits in, too, but the first nine verses really cut through everything and leave no doubt about what God expects.

I became involved in the political arena through education. I did not run for public office because I was a Christian; I ran because I believed I had something to offer the governance of public education in Lee County, Florida. But a love for the Lord and an understanding of His guidance went with me. I was elected to the local school board (the first woman in those womanless days) and moved on to be president of the state and national school board associations, with lots of other experiences spread over twenty-five years. At the outset, I was not prepared for the new experiences in the political world and knew I would need lots of guidance from God's Word.

Being a politician and being a Christian are very much alike. You are in the limelight all the time, answering to your constituency or answering to the Lord. A politician can never go back to being just the man or woman on the street after serving in public office, and a person who has lived a true Christian life will never be looked upon the same again by his or her peers. We are always watched.

September 9

CHRISTOPHER PARKENING, classical guitarist who has performed with the New York Philharmonic, the National Symphony, and the Chicago, Cleveland, Philadelphia, San Francisco, Los Angeles, and numerous other orchestras, at the White House, and on numerous TV programs; student of the late Andrés Segovia; featured on more than a dozen albums.

> *And he said unto me, My grace is sufficient for thee: for my strength is made perfect in weakness. Most gladly therefore will I gather glory in my infirmities, that the power of Christ may rest upon me. Therefore I take pleasure in infirmities, in reproaches, in necessities, in persecutions, in distresses for Christ's sake: for when I am weak, then am I strong. (2 Corinthians 12:9–10, KJV)*

While folding up a hideaway bed during the summer of 1992, I caught my ring finger between the metal bars that close like scissors. The result was a swollen and lacerated finger—and a lot of pain! Worse than the pain was the fact that in just six days I was scheduled to play the guitar in concert in front of 10,000 people at the Hollywood Bowl. Some of my family members prayed with me, and I had complete peace that if the Lord wanted me to play, His grace would be sufficient. I did play the concert—in some pain and with a finger that was still swollen—but the Lord was gracious. What should have been one of my worst concerts was actually one of my best. This was an unusual situation, but praying before a concert is the usual practice for me. I depend on the Lord's grace and I strive to bring glory to His name through my music.

September 10

ROSA PARKS, seamstress and NAACP member whose refusal to surrender her seat to a white man on a segregated bus sparked the 1955 bus boycott in Montgomery, Alabama, which gave national prominence to Martin Luther King, Jr.; author of five books, including *Rosa Parks: My Story* and *Quiet Strength*, with Gregory J. Reed.

> *The LORD is my shepherd; I shall not want. He maketh me to lie down in green pastures: he leadeth me beside the still waters. He restoreth my soul: he leadeth me in the paths of righteousness for his name's sake. Yea, though I walk through the valley of the shadow of death, I will fear no evil: for thou art with me; thy rod and thy staff they comfort me. Thou preparest a table before me in the presence of mine enemies: thou anointest my head with oil; my cup runneth over. Surely goodness and mercy shall follow me all the days of my life: and I will dwell in the house of the LORD for ever. (Psalm 23, KJV)*

During my school days, the Twenty-third Psalm was a part of our devotions, when we had devotions in school. And at church it was one of the favorite psalms that we enjoyed reading and thinking about. During the time of our boycott, we did much praying and we had mass meetings at the various churches, where people would come in and testify and relate their experiences. It was very helpful that we had the churches and could gather strength from one another and encourage each other to continue the struggle throughout that long year of boycotting the buses. I look back on those days and remember the Spirit within us and our faith and hope that things would be better, and I still have that same faith. When we face any obstacle, any discouragement, that faith is a strong attribute to have.

September 11

NINA PARUSHEV, Ph.D. exercise physiologist in Bulgaria who, with husband Parush, specialized in biomechatronics, a technical medicine used in Olympic training and in rehabilitation to increase the body's capacity for physical activity; a former third-generation Communist; she and her husband embraced Christianity in a Bulgarian Baptist church in 1990.

> *Rejoice, young man, while you are young, and let your heart cheer you in the days of your youth. Follow the inclination of your heart and the desire of your eyes, but know that for all these things God will bring you into judgment. . . . [The] dust returns to the earth as it was, and the breath returns to God who gave it.*
> *(Ecclesiastes 11:9, 12:7, NRSV)*

The power of this passage had a tremendous impact on my thinking and style of life. Raised in a Communist country, I had never heard the name of Jesus, and it was easy for me reading through the Book of Ecclesiastes to agree with the author's statement that "all is vanity." In my early thirties, I had reached many goals and found no satisfaction. I saw myself as "nothing new under the sun." Work, ambitions—nothing seemed to be worthy, everything a disappointment. But this wonderful poetry opened my eyes to see the beauty of the eternal and to realize that only God's presence in my life is able to make things worthy. My system of evaluating the world around me was changed. I was saved!

September 12

PARUSH PARUSHEV, Bulgarian scientist with a Ph.D. in applied mathematics who, with wife Nina, specialized in biomechatronics, a technical medicine used in Olympic training and in rehabilitation to increase the body's capacity for physical activity; a former Communist party member whose grandfather was among the founders of communism in Bulgaria; he and his wife embraced Christianity in a Bulgarian Baptist church in 1990.

> *. . . for whoever is not against you is for you.*
> *(Luke 9:50, NRSV)*

In communism, I was taught all my life in an opposite way, that whoever is not with us is against us. Thus, we had enemies everywhere. This verse helped me to look on the teaching of our Lord as a peace-bringing message—in diverse communities, from ancient times till today. Christianity is not an exclusive, elitist phenomenon only for chosen people, but an open-minded faith, recognizing human values even in the imperfection of all people. There is no better instruction from our Lord to build bridges with people of various persuasions for the future both of humanity (in a universal sense) and of the world (in an ecological, stewardship sense). And for us in the Eastern European countries, this verse provides the best foundation for starting a process of healing and restoration after so many years of ideological exclusiveness and forced brainwashing regarding "the one and only truth of Marxism-Leninism."

September 13

CURTIS PECK, news editor/sports, *St. Louis Post-Dispatch*, since 1987; executive editor, *The Edmond (Oklahoma) Evening Sun*, 1985–87; previous newspaper slots were in Mexico, Missouri; Danville, Illinois; Cocoa, Florida; and Memphis, Tennessee.

Though he slay me, yet will I trust in him. . . .
(Job 13:15, KJV)

This has been a most meaningful verse in my growth as a Christian. I am awed by such a declaration of faith from a man who has been ravaged by Satan in every possible way—losing family, fortune, and health. Yet Job refuses to be dislodged from what he knows is absolute truth: God is in control. His tenacious faith has inspired me to make this verse my prayer continuously, that no matter what God chooses to send my way, "yet will I trust in him" who is the rock of my salvation.

September 14

JOHN M. PERKINS, founder and publisher, *Urban Family* magazine; cofounder and chairman, Christian Community Development Association, encompassing 300 organizations engaged in inner-city initiatives; founder and president, Harambee Christian Family Center, Pasadena, California, operating an elementary school and other youth ministries; founder and president emeritus, Voice of Calvary Ministries, based initially in Mendenhall, Mississippi, now in Jackson, launching a number of medical clinics, literacy and youth programs, cooperative stores, and other community development efforts in the state; author or coauthor of nine books, beginning with his *Let Justice Roll Down* 1976 autobiography and including *He's My Brother,* with former Ku Klux Klansman Thomas A. Tarrants III.

> *I am crucified with Christ: nevertheless I live; yet not I, but Christ liveth in me: and the life which I now live in the flesh, I live by the faith of the Son of God, who loved me, and gave himself for me. (Galatians 2:20, KJV)*

Like most people, I had traditionally thought there was a God in heaven and He was going to reward people who did good and send them to heaven and punish others. But I had never thought of a God who really loved me, because I grew up without a mother and father. I grew up without the certainty of love, and without that certainty, I think I was a person who was really seeking love. But I never felt worthy of love, because I never had that unmerited love that a mother and a father give. So when I heard that God loved me, that became an important part of my life—that I am loved by a holy God. I had come to the place where I understood God is Creator and all-powerful, so to be loved by this God was really significant. I think that's what really brought me to faith.

I have come to believe that is the most central message of the whole gospel: God is expressing His love toward us in sending Jesus to die for us. And it's become also a means of understanding sacrifice, that the life I'm now living—it's Christ's life living itself out through me, and that's a sacrificial life. I need to offer something to that. Not to get to heaven. But in gratitude for what He's done for me.

September 15

KAREN PHILLIPS, executive director, Abyssinian Development Corp., thirty-employee Harlem-based nonprofit organization initiated by Abyssinian Baptist Church in 1987, since fostering various business development and social service projects and creating 500 low-, moderate-, and middle-income housing units.

> *Yea, though I walk through the valley of the shadow of death, I will fear no evil; for thou art with me. . . .*
> *(Psalm 23:4, KJV)*

When I had nightmares as a child, this was a passage I was taught to help me survive my fears. Now, in managing a nonprofit organization that has created $50 million in investments to the distressed community of Harlem, I repeat this verse to help me through everything from community meetings and bumpy airplane flights to negotiations of difficult real estate deals and risky business ventures.

September 16

STU PHILLIPS, Montreal native who became a member of the Grand Ole Opry in 1967; featured on twelve albums; ordained as an Episcopal priest in 1980; rector of Saint James the Less Episcopal Church, Madison, Tennessee.

> *. . . Lord, I believe; help thou mine unbelief.*
> *(Mark 9:24, KJV)*

I recall a time in the early seventies when I was invited to do some singing with a tour group in the Holy Land. One morning we ascended Mount Arabela, a scene where, according to some scholars, Jesus retreated to pray and at other times addressed a "multitude." The summit of this mountain hovered as a cliff one mile straight up from the little town of Megiddo. The summit itself consisted of a rock formation shaped very much like a throne, which jutted out precariously over the cliff looking down on Megiddo. In front of the "throne," the terrain was a grassy field with a gentle slope resembling a natural amphitheater. Having been a professional entertainer all my life, I wondered, rather skeptically, how Jesus was able to be heard by a vast multitude without a pretty decent public address system. I thought I'd test the Lord on this one and asked one of the people traveling with us, Harry Yates, husband of Joanne Cash and brother-in-law of Johnny Cash, if he would walk out on the grassy field some 300 yards while I sat on the "throne." When he reached his spot, I said in a normal speaking voice, "Harry, can you hear me?" whereupon Harry responded with my precise words, "Harry, can you hear me?" I felt goose bumps all over and sat there contemplating God's Word for a long time, repeating the words of the man who appeared before the Lord after a miracle of God: "I believe Lord. Help thou my unbelief."

September 17

JANE O. PIEROTTI, motivational speaker and communications consultant; president, Counterpoint, Inc., Memphis, Tennessee, which she founded in 1986; member, transition team for Memphis mayor W. W. Herenton; first female vice president of Holiday Inns, initially of marketing for the hotel services division, then hotel group human resources, and later, public relations and communications; previously, in twelve years with IBM, she was the corporation's first female sales representative, first female marketing manager, then branch manager (Madison, Wisconsin), and later, national marketing manager for the Memory Typewriter.

But seek ye first the kingdom of God, and his righteous-ness; and all these things shall be added unto you.
(Matthew 6:33, KJV)

Until six years ago, I was an atheist. Thanks to the grace of God and the power of His Word, my life has been transformed. I have now made the Word of God the final authority in my life. When I do what Matthew 6:33 instructs, everything else works. As I learned the teachings about tithing and God's biblical eco-nomics, the connection became clear between sowing and reap-ing bountifully.

Two years ago, God began to deal with me about tithing my time to Him. At first I gulped. Most of our lives are like a re-make of *Beat the Clock.* Mine, in fact, was like the plate-spin-ning performance at the circus—trying to keep balance among family, career, travel, commitment to God, church, community work, and friends. My time on the road added even more com-plexity. When the Lord began to deal with me about tithing my time, my first thought was: Net or gross? "Awake" hours or the full twenty-four hours a day? I decided to do it right. Let's see ... twenty-four hours a day ... that's 2.4 times seven days a week. That's 16.8 hours a week. It seemed impossible.

But I've learned that with God's Word, if I quit trying to rea-son it out and go with what the Word says, He always "perfects that which concerns me." After adding up the time I had already committed to the Lord (church on Sunday morning and evening and Wednesday night, intercessory prayer group on Tuesday night), I committed to getting up an hour earlier every morning to spend time in prayer and fellowship with Him. I drew a line in the dirt and said, "Okay, Lord, you get the first fruit of my time."

As I began to tithe my time to the Lord, everything in my life began to work out. Business came in easier. People began doing favors for me. I had time enough to complete work, spend time with family, and give something back to the community. As I continue to put God first in not only my finances, but my time, He keeps my course steady and creates peace with my schedule. I've learned you can't outgive God. I've also learned to sow seeds toward needs. If I need money, I have to sow money into His kingdom. If I need love, I have to sow love into someone else's life. If I need time, I must sow time. God is the God of multiplication and return. This has been the greatest time-management lesson of my life.

September 18

T. C. PINCKNEY, retired U.S. Air Force brigadier general; his assignments included director, Far East Region, Office of the Secretary of Defense; special assistant to USAF Chief of Staff; commander, Sixty-seventh Tactical Reconnaissance Wing, Bergstrom Air Force Base; White House National Security Council staff member; F–4 pilot in Vietnam; political science instructor, Air Force Academy.

The heavens declare the glory of God; and the firmament sheweth his handiwork. (Psalm 19:1, KJV)

This verse is especially meaningful to me for two reasons. First, my experiences as an Air Force fighter pilot impressed me almost daily with the overwhelming power and beauty that God displays in His cloud-columned halls and, simultaneously, with my own puny and fragile nature. Second, my favorite recreation is backpacking long distances (I have walked the Appalachian Trail from Georgia to Maine and the Pacific Crest Trail from the Mexican border to Canada). To stand atop a mountain with the world laid out at your feet, to thrill to one breathtaking view of God's handiwork after another, to be dependent for drink upon the cold, clear flow from quiet springs or rushing brooks, to wake warm in your sleeping bag on a frigid night under un-countable stars stretched across His firmament inescapably marks the very real presence of the Father and the truth and beauty of this verse.

September 19

JOANNA B. PINNEO, photographer, *St. Petersburg Times* in Florida; *National Geographic* contributor for "Who Are the Palestinians?" June 1992, "Europe Faces an Immigrant Tide," May 1993, "Sonoran Desert: Anything but Empty," September 1994, "Europe's First Family: The Basques," November 1995; first-place winner, magazine feature series, Palestinians, *Washington Photojournalism Review*, 1993; former staff photographer, *U.S. News and World Report*, and special assignment photographer, Southern Baptist Foreign Mission Board, who has worked in more than fifty countries.

> *But seek first his kingdom and his righteousness, and all these things will be given to you as well.*
> *(Matthew 6:33, NIV)*

When I feel off track personally I often turn to Matthew 6:33. I remember one time a few years ago when I was feeling confused about directions. One whole week, so many things I opened, read, or heard seemed to turn up this verse. It was so astounding when I opened the Bible there, it was the theme of the Christians in Photojournalism newsletter that arrived that week, someone at work mentioned it, and someone quite separate mentioned it. Finally, I was digging through some boxes I hadn't gone through in a while looking for something, and written in bold letters in a pile of papers was Matthew 6:33. I sort of fell/sat on the floor and said aloud in a prayer, "All right, all right, I get the message!" So when things are particularly unclear, this verse really helps straighten things up.

September 20

WESLEY G. PIPPERT, director, University of Missouri School of Journalism's Washington Program and former UPI correspondent in Washington, D.C., and the Middle East.

Mercy and truth will meet,
Justice and peace will kiss each other.
(Psalm 85:10, trans. from Hebrew)

As a Christian, I find truth in Jesus, and this discovery leads me to be kind and merciful, to be just in all that I do, and to be peaceable. As a journalist, I see my primary task as the pursuit and publication of truth, and this verse tells me that in my professional pursuit of truth I will seek out the dimensions of mercy, justice, and peace in whatever assignment I have or story I cover.

September 21

ALVIN PLANTINGA, professor of philosophy and director of the Center for Philosophy of Religion, University of Notre Dame, since 1982; professor of philosophy, Calvin College, Grand Rapids, Michigan, 1964–82; former associate professor at Wayne State University, Detroit, and instructor at Yale University; president, Society of Christian Philosophers, 1983–86; author of twelve books.

I know, O LORD, that your laws are righteous,
and in faithfulness you have afflicted me.
May your unfailing love be my comfort,
according to your promise to your servant.
(Psalm 119:75–76, NIV)

Bad things often happen to God's people; perhaps your friend is dying of cancer, or you yourself or your children or parents are suffering, or you are distressed by the terrifying suffering our world contains. These things can cause us to take the wrong attitude toward God, to take toward Him an attitude of suspicion, or distrust, or resentment, or anger. The psalmist, however, strikes it right: he doesn't know why God afflicts him, but he rests in his knowledge that God is faithful and just in permitting him to suffer, and he asks God for the comfort He has promised. Of course it isn't always easy to attain this attitude, but perhaps one thing that helps is the reflection that God Himself was willing to suffer to make it possible for us to live triumphantly.

September 22

WILBUR PLAUGHER, cofounder, Fellowship of Christian Cowboys; rodeo clown for some forty-five years, former rodeo competitor who won more than a dozen all-around cowboy titles, ProRodeo Hall of Fame member; actor in several films and TV series, including *Daniel Boone* and *Run, Appaloosa, Run.*

For God so loved the world, that he gave his only begotten Son, that whosoever believeth in him should not perish, but have everlasting life. (John 3:16, KJV)

When I'm asked to sign my autograph, I include John 3:16 on every occasion. It's the way God provided through His Son, Jesus, for us to be with Him forever. It's the only reason for me to live—to share with others the way, the truth, and the life.

September 23

GARY PLAYER, one of only four golfers to win the four major championships: Masters, 1978, 1974, 1961; U.S. Open, 1965; British Open, 1974, 1968, 1959; PGA Championship, 1972, 1962; only player ever to win British Open in three different decades; winner of PGA Seniors Championship, 1990, 1988, 1986.

The LORD is my shepherd; I shall not want. He maketh me to lie down in green pastures: he leadeth me beside the still waters. He restoreth my soul: he leadeth me in the paths of righteousness for his name's sake. Yea, though I walk through the valley of the shadow of death, I will fear no evil: for thou art with me; thy rod and thy staff they comfort me. Thou preparest a table before me in the presence of mine enemies: thou anointest my head with oil; my cup runneth over. Surely goodness and mercy shall follow me all the days of my life: and I will dwell in the house of the LORD for ever. (Psalm 23, KJV)

It's very easy to have faith when you're successful. The most important thing is to have faith in adversity. Before the Masters tournament in 1961, I spent a day with Billy Graham at his home in the Carolinas. He said to me that every time something happened in the tournament that wasn't very good, what you've got to do is be grateful for the difficulties and say thank you to the Lord. In the tournament, many occasions arose when I was having difficulty and I said thank you. In the last round, I was leading Arnold Palmer by four shots. I had a seven at number 13 and a six at number 15 and still went on to win the tournament by one shot. The entire Twenty-third Psalm, if you pray hard and pay attention to it, can help you so much in life. It teaches you patience. There's courage in it. There's great peace in it.

September 24

LARRY W. POLAND, founder, chairman, and chief executive officer, Mastermedia International outreach to film and television leaders in Hollywood and New York; former president, Miami Christian College, and founder of the first Christian radio station in the city; former director, Agape Movement, international volunteer service organization of Campus Crusade for Christ; author of five books and commentator on *The Mediator* daily radio broadcast.

Dear friends, if our hearts do not condemn us, we have
confidence before God and receive from him anything we
ask, because we obey his commands and do what pleases
him. (1 John 3:21–22, NIV)

The terror that unbelievers feel in approaching God and the impotence of Christians who should have supernatural power to deal with life are both tied to the same problem, an unclean conscience. In working with Hollywood leadership, I have discovered that those who live in sin want nothing to do with God, to say nothing of having "confidence" in His presence. Even believers who are not practicing holiness have no boldness in God's presence and are timid and powerless in their prayers. The state of total cleansing—and the clear conscience that results—coupled with willful obedience to God's commands takes the worry out of being close and assures the spiritual power to conquer.

September 25

MARGARET FISHBACK POWERS, poet whose 1964 poem "Footprints" has been reprinted more than a million times; author of *Footprints: The True Story Behind the Poem That Inspired Millions;* Christian worker in Mexico as codirector of Little Peoples Ministry.

> . . . *I will never leave thee, nor forsake thee.*
> *(Hebrews 13:5, KJV)*

This was my special verse after being struck by lightning as a youth. And it was my special verse before I was engaged—the "Footprints" beach scene along Echo Lake, Ontario.

September 26

GHILLEAN T. PRANCE, director, Royal Botanic Gardens outside London, England; formerly a staff member at the New

York Botanical Garden for twenty-five years, rising from research assistant to senior vice president for science, and director of graduate studies at the Instituto Nacional de Pesquisas de Amazonia in Brazil, where he established various study programs involving conservation of the Amazon rain forest; author of nine books and editor of eight others.

> *The earth is the* LORD's, *and all it contains,*
> *The world, and those who dwell in it. (Psalm 24:1, NASB)*

This verse reminds me that the nature that I study is the creation of God and not something that has happened by chance. This verse calls us as Christians to a closer stewardship of creation. However, the verse does not end there; it reminds us of God's care, not only for His world or cosmos, but also for the people who dwell in it. This loving care was later expressed in the way in which He sent His only Son because He so loved the world.

September 27

ROSE PRICE, Fort Lauderdale, Florida, Holocaust survivor of five years at Dachau and other Nazi concentration camps; native of Skarzysko Kamienna, Poland, and granddaughter of a rabbi shoemaker; her father was killed by anti-Semitic thugs when she was ten years old; for a time, she and her thirteen-year-old sister worked in a Nazi munitions factory to avoid imprisonment, with her job being to crawl inside airplane motors and tighten bolts and screws; her mother died at Treblinka death camp.

> *Therefore, if anyone is in Christ, he is a new creation;*
> *the old has gone, the new has come! All this is from God,*
> *who reconciled us to himself through Christ and gave*
> *us the ministry of reconciliation; that God was reconciling*
> *the world to himself in Christ, not counting men's sins*

against them. And he has committed to us the message of reconciliation. We are therefore Christ's ambassadors, as though God were making his appeal through us. We implore you on Christ's behalf: Be reconciled to God. God made him who had no sin to be sin for us, so that we might become the righteousness of God.
(2 Corinthians 5:17–21, NIV)

A pastor said the Lord gave him this Scripture for me while he was praying for the ministry I was scheduled to have in his church. I later read it and asked the Lord, "Is it mine?" And He said, "Why don't you read it again slowly?" And I read it word for word. And yes, it was mine, because the ministry God has given me is reconciliation and forgiveness.

In 1981, I was to speak on reconciliation at a "Berlin for Jesus" rally of Christians in Germany. I didn't want to go back; it took me six months of wrestling with the Lord to accept the invitation. I had become a believer in Jesus in 1971. My oldest daughter came home and brought Jesus into the house. I shook her and said, "Do you have any idea what I went through because of this Jesus? Haven't you ever wondered why you don't have any cousins, aunts, uncles, or grandparents?" Two days later, I threw her out. But then my husband became a believer and my youngest daughter became a believer. It was very, very hard for me. I had had twenty-seven operations. They were illnesses, and all the illnesses stemmed from unforgiveness. You see, all the atrocities, all the sufferings of the Jews in Europe were done in the name of Christ. In the camps, the Nazis would tell us we were there because we killed Christ. When I was a little girl, I was hit over the head with a cross by a priest. My crime was that I walked on the sidewalk where the church was. The only thing of Christ I knew was hate. But my daughter would say, "It wasn't the Jesus of the Bible; it was the church that did those awful things." And after a year, I said, "Yes, Lord." Still, I suffered from unforgiveness.

As the time came for me to speak in Berlin, I began to panic; all the old painful memories came rushing back to haunt me, along with all the hatred and anger. "Why did I ever come back here?" I asked myself. "I am betraying my parents and everyone who was killed by Nazi hands. Their blood was spilled by these people!" But as I spoke, I gave forgiveness. The miracle is that it was the Lord. It wasn't me. I will not take any credit at all for it. It is to His credit completely.

September 28

ANNE PURCELL, coauthor with husband Ben of *Love and Duty*, a book about his five years as a prisoner of war in Vietnam and her efforts in the POW/MIA movement for his release.

> *Consider it pure joy, my brothers, whenever you face trials of many kinds, because you know that the testing of your faith develops perseverance. Perseverance must finish its work so that you may be mature and complete, not lacking anything. If any of you lacks wisdom, he should ask God, who gives generously to all without finding fault, and it will be given to him. (James 1:2–5, NIV)*

I did not know if I was a wife or a widow. I was in limbo. A very uncertain future lay ahead of us with my husband being MIA (missing in action) in Vietnam. I was a Christian, and it was wonderful to read that what I must face was going to be helpful to me if I would see it through with God's help. There were many decisions to make. The most important one at the beginning was, "Where do we live?" I began to ask God that question and He told me very clearly, "Go to Columbus, Georgia, and wait." In the months and years that followed there were many other questions, and I tried always to ask God for wisdom in making those decisions that affected not only my life but the lives of five wonderful children.

September 29

BEN PURCELL, Georgia state representative; coauthor with wife Anne of *Love and Duty;* one of the highest-ranking officers taken prisoner during the Vietnam War; retired U.S. Army colonel.

> *Even though I walk*
> *through the valley of the shadow of death,*
> *I will fear no evil,*
> *for you are with me;*
> *your rod and your staff,*
> *they comfort me.*
> *You prepare a table before me*
> *in the presence of my enemies. (Psalm 23:4–5, NIV)*

In mid-August of 1968 I was in solitary confinement as a prisoner of war in a camp southwest of Hanoi. I was being interrogated by a rather antagonistic individual who demanded that I condemn myself as a criminal of war and my country as an aggressor in South Vietnam. When I refused to do either, the interrogator became very irate and threatened me with a trial that could result in a sentence of life in prison or even death. He further stated, however, that if I would only "refirm my thinking" (i.e., deny myself and disallow my love and loyalty for my country), conditions would become better for me and I would be placed in a cell with another American and be permitted to return to my family when the war ended. Otherwise, the trial would take place soon. "Now, go back to your cell to consider your crimes and be prepared to return this afternoon to refirm your thinking!"

Anxious for my personal welfare, yet determined not to turn my back on America, I spent that noon hour in prayer, asking God for courage to face whatever was in store for me. After two hours of agony I heard the guard coming to unlock the cell so I could return to the interrogation room. As he inserted the key in the lock, the words of the Twenty-third Psalm came to mind and I felt a peace in my heart greater than any other I had ever known. I was no longer anxious for my welfare because I knew beyond any question who held the keys to my prison cell, and it wasn't that Vietnamese interrogator, but God Himself.

September 30

DAN QUAYLE, U.S. vice president, 1989–93; chairman, Hudson Institute's Competitiveness Center for helping America meet the challenge of global competitiveness; author, *Standing Firm,* autobiographical account of his vice presidency, and *The American Family: Discovering the Values That Make Us Strong,* with Diane Medved; U.S. senator from Indiana, 1981–89; U.S. congressman, 1977–81.

I will say of the LORD, He is my refuge and my fortress: my God; in him will I trust. (Psalm 91:2, KJV)

As a Christian, I have made prayer a constant in my life; not a day goes by when I don't conduct some kind of conversation—no matter how quiet and casual—with God. I believe in daily prayer, because faith has to be more than a crutch and more than an emergency matter.

OCTOBER

October 1

AL QUIE, governor of Minnesota, 1979–83; Minnesota congressman, 1958–78; chairman of the 1996 Greater Twin Cities Billy Graham Crusade.

James and John, the sons of Zebedee, came forward to him and said to him, "Teacher, we want you to do for us whatever we ask of you." And he said to them, "What is it you want me to do for you?" And they said to him, "Grant us to sit, one at your right hand and one at your left, in your glory." But Jesus said to them, "You do not know what you are asking. Are you able to drink the cup that I drink, or be baptized with the baptism that I am baptized with?" They replied, "We are able." Then Jesus said to them, "The cup that I drink you will drink; and with the baptism with which I am baptized, you will be baptized; but to sit at my right hand or at my left is not mine to grant, but it is for those for whom it has been prepared." When the ten heard this, they began to be angry with James and John. So Jesus called them and said to them, "You know that among the Gentiles those whom they recognize as their rulers lord it over them, and their great ones are tyrants over them. But it is not so among you; but whoever wishes to become great among you must be your servant, and whoever wishes to be first among you must be slave of all. For the Son of Man came not to be served but to serve, and to give his life a ransom for many." (Mark 10:35–45, NRSV)

When I got into government and was in Congress, as I was doing my devotions, I was searching the Scriptures for what one ought to do, and I came across these verses where Jesus teaches about serving others. Jesus is really telling us how to be leaders—servant leaders: if you want to be great, then be the slave of all. That's about 180 degrees away from the way human beings think to get power and authority. But it is the way Jesus asked us to do it.

October 2

DOYLE RAHJES, president, Kansas Farm Bureau, 1983–94; farmer whose son, Ken, and nephew, Robert, operate the family farm in Phillips County, producing wheat and milo and raising cattle.

> *But seek first his kingdom and his righteousness, and all these things will be given to you as well.*
> *(Matthew 6:33, NIV)*

My parents taught me as a child and as an adolescent to respond to temptation by asking myself the question, "Would this be something Jesus would do or is this a place that Jesus would go?" This proved to be a measure of accountability that always held the standard high. I am forever grateful for that standard. Bible standards for measurement and accountability are most important in my personal life. Matthew 6:33 has provided me with the basic standard for making decisions. When we seek God's will first, it is a natural phenomenon that a Spirit-led life will be abundantly filled. I testify to that abundant life. My life has been spent, up to now, in the agricultural industry, farming, ranching, and representing agriculture through a farm organization. Weather, markets, and other uncontrollable factors create an unfriendly environment for farmers and ranchers that can be frustrating if not cruel. My personal challenges have been changed to

blessings—sometimes by doors opening; at other times, closing—
when I have met them in the light of Matthew 6:33.

October 3

BARBARA REYNOLDS, *USA Today* Opinion Page columnist; she joined the newspaper's staff in 1983 as an editorial
board member and Inquiry Page editor; cofounder, former international editor, *Dollars and Sense* magazine for black professionals; author, *And Still We Rise,* featuring interviews of fifty
black role models, and *Jesse Jackson: America's David,* 1985,
updated from the initial 1975 release as *The Man, the Movement, and the Myth;* former media work includes *Ebony* assistant editor and *Chicago Tribune* urban affairs reporter, then
Washington correspondent; 1987 recipient, Southern Christian
Leadership Conference's Dr. Martin Luther King, Jr., Drum
Major for Justice Award.

> *If a man therefore purge himself from these, he shall be a*
> *vessel unto honour, sanctified, and meet for the master's*
> *use, and prepared unto every good work. Flee also youth-*
> *ful lusts: but follow righteousness, faith, charity, peace,*
> *with them that call on the Lord out of a pure heart.*
> *(2 Timothy 2:21–22, KJV)*

The Lord began calling me through that Scripture maybe fifteen
years ago. And we've been working on it all these years, to my
ordination as a minister at Greater Mount Calvary Holy Church
in Washington, D.C., in May 1995. It really has taken that long
to purge me, to make me a sanctified vessel that can be used.
The Lord can't really use you for His good works if you are full
of anger, bigotry, spite, venom. You have to empty those out so
more of the Holy Spirit can come in you. My flesh, my weaknesses have to get out so more of Him can come in. You cannot
have two competing forces in the same vessel at the same time.

The Lord's calling was a long process. It was not one thing. Years ago, I was awakened one night and told to go tell the news that "Babylon is falling." Through the years, I was born again. The Lord encouraged me to go to divinity school and get a degree from the Howard School of Divinity here in Washington. I was just brought along—dragged along at first, then wooed, and then encouraged. Now I feel I'm at the *kairos* moment. I cannot go back and I can't stay still. I've got to go forward.

October 4

NAOMI RHODE, president, National Speakers Association, 1993–94; professional speaker based in Phoenix; former dental hygienist and president of the Arizona State Dental Hygienists Association; author of two books, *The Gift of Family: A Legacy of Love* and *More Beautiful than Diamonds: The Gift of Friendship.*

> *Let the words of my mouth and the meditation of my*
> *heart*
> *Be acceptable in Thy sight,*
> *O* LORD, *my rock and my redeemer. (Psalm 19:14, NASB)*

Having been a Christian since I was six and raised in a pastor's family, I had a wonderful start in my faith and it has grown deeper and deeper and is extremely meaningful to me. I truly feel called to be "light and salt" in the secular world, and on secular platforms primarily, although I also do some speaking in the Christian marketplace. For my life as a professional speaker, this is one of the most significant verses in Scripture. I use it as a prayer before every single speech and have done so for more than twenty years.

October 5

BOBBY RICHARDSON, New York Yankees second baseman, 1955–66; Most Valuable Player, 1960 World Series; runner-up to Mickey Mantle as American League MVP, 1962; World Series record holder with thirty consecutive games and most hits and runs batted in in a Series; seven-time All-Star.

Delight yourselves in the Lord, yes, find your joy in him at all times. Have a reputation for gentleness, and never forget the nearness of your Lord. Don't worry over anything whatever; tell God every detail of your needs in earnest and thankful prayer, and the peace of God, which transcends human understanding, will keep constant guard over your hearts and minds as they rest in Christ Jesus. (Philippians 4:4–7, Phillips)

Dick Houser (Kansas City Royals manager) had been diagnosed as having a tumor and doctors had given him maybe six months to live. I was sitting in my office and the phone rang. It was Dick and he said, "Can you encourage me from the Scriptures?" I shared with him Philippians 4. He said, "Okay, that's all I needed." In the next few months, he was a radiant Christian, sharing Christ at every opportunity.

October 6

ROBERT RIETH, executive director, Media Fellowship International, an evangelical ministry to the entertainment and media community, with chapters in Los Angeles, New York, and more than thirty other cities; former Lutheran seminary professor and, earlier, pastor for nearly twenty years; he led pregame services for professional basketball and baseball teams in Seattle, 1977–86.

And thou shalt love the Lord thy God with all thy heart, and with all thy soul, and with all thy mind, and with all thy strength. This is the first commandment. And the second is like, namely this, Thou shalt love thy neighbour as thyself. There is none other commandment greater than these. (Mark 12:30–31, KJV)

My desire is to make loving God my first priority, not just with my heart, but with my mind, soul, and strength. When we love someone deeply, everything we do is done with our loved one in mind. If my first love is God, I can begin my day secure in the fact that He is my comfort and my encouragement. My attention can then be turned to the second commandment—loving my neighbors. They shouldn't have to earn my love any more than I have to earn God's love. Love for others means that I care for them unconditionally. My actions toward them are to be charitable, honorable, and of the highest integrity. I can't truly love in my own strength, but love comes from God.

October 7

H. W. "SALTY" ROBERTS, horsemen's parking lot attendant, Gulfstream Park in Florida, since 1953; founder of Race Track Chaplaincy in 1971, now with full-time chaplains at some sixty racetracks in North America.

But he answered and said, It is written, Man shall not live by bread alone, but by every word that proceedeth out of the mouth of God. (Matthew 4:4, KJV)

I was in a crisis situation back in 1966, contemplating suicide because I had been everywhere, seen everything, and done everything, and I was a walking dead man. I was asking, How do you live?—not make a living—but, How does a man live to get peace, joy, happiness, and fulfillment out of life? I had failed to learn how to do that and I was tired of living yet scared of dying. So I cried out to God in my crisis and said, "God, how do I live?" And He drove me right to the Word ... the Bible. I looked over at my dresser, put down the shotgun I had and the bottle of whiskey, got to my feet, and dug out a pocket-sized booklet of Bible verses. The first page of the booklet said man does not live by bread alone but by every word that proceeds out of the mouth of God. That was like a light going on in Salty Roberts. I got ahold of that, and from that moment on, God gave me Jesus to guide and direct and give me the hope that tomorrow would be better than those times I had in the past.

October 8

DALE EVANS ROGERS, star of numerous films and *The Roy Rogers Show* on NBC from 1951 to 1957; featured in the Roy Rogers–Dale Evans Museum, Victorville, California; author of several inspirational books, including *Angel Unaware* and *Happy Trails* with husband Roy Rogers and, most recently, *Say Yes to Tomorrow* with Floyd W. Thatcher.

> *And we know that all things work together for good to them that love God, to them who are the called according to his purpose. (Romans 8:28, KJV)*

This Bible verse has sustained me through many tests, trials, and deep valleys since I was called by the Spirit of the living Christ to give my life to Him in 1948. I was called to serve Him and His purpose for my life. He has never disappointed me in working out my salvation. My trail has been hard at times but always blessed afterward.

October 9

FRED ROGERS, creator of *Mister Rogers' Neighborhood* in 1968, longest-running program on PBS, viewed in some 8 million households and child-care settings; winner of three Emmy and two Peabody awards for children's programming; ordained as a Presbyterian minister, 1962; author of twelve children's books and of *Mister Rogers Talks with Parents, You Are*

Special, and *Dear Mister Rogers;* as a young college graduate in 1951, he was hired for the floor crew of such NBC-TV shows as *The Lucky Strike Hit Parade* and *The Kate Smith Hour* and then in 1953 became producer of *The Children's Corner,* a live one-hour program on WQED, Pittsburgh.

> *For God's foolishness is wiser than human wisdom, and God's weakness is stronger than human strength.*
> *(1 Corinthians 1:25, Anchor Bible)*

There isn't a more surprising place for God to appear than in a manger or on a cross. Throughout His life, Jesus demonstrated the vulnerability and the power of showing and sharing God's love. Whenever I write a script or a song or walk into the studio for a taping, I pray, "Let some word that is heard be Thine." That's really all that matters. Through television we have a wonderful opportunity to show and tell our children that they really matter, even when they're very little. It's not just the adult symbols of our world that have value, but how children interpret and respond to those symbols. We have a unique chance to communicate the fact that childhood—open, honest, vulnerable childhood—lies at the very basis of who people are and what they become.

October 10

ROY ROGERS, star of numerous western films and *The Roy Rogers Show* on NBC from 1951 to 1957; featured in the Roy Rogers–Dale Evans Museum, Victorville, California; subject of *Roy Rogers: King of the Cowboys* by Georgia Morris and Mark Pollard; author with wife Dale Evans of *Happy Trails.*

> *For God so loved the world, that he gave his only begotten Son, that whosoever believeth in him should not perish, but have everlasting life. (John 3:16, KJV)*

This is my favorite verse because it is the great promise of God to anyone who will believe and trust Jesus Christ. This verse changed my life in 1948, and the Lord has been the strength of my life ever since.

October 11

LULU ROMAN, comedienne, singer on *Hee Haw* during its twenty-five-year syndicated run on TV; member of the Grand Ole Opry; featured on thirteen albums; winner of Gospel Music Association 1985 Dove Award for best album by a secular artist for *You Were Loving Me.*

> *Behold, I am the* LORD, *the God of all flesh: is there any thing too hard for me? (Jeremiah 32:27, KJV)*

Years ago when I first got saved this verse was special because of God just bringing me through the hard times, the drug abuse, and almost losing my life at my own hands. Through the years it has grown to be even more precious, helping me through times when, even though I had a relationship with Jesus, I still held a lot of anger against God as my Father. I was born in a home for unwed mothers and dumped in an orphan's home when I was barely two and felt God had allowed that to happen. In these recent years, I have come to realize how much God is my Father, how much He loves me, how much He covers and protects me, and how His mercy is new every day in my life.

October 12

PAUL R. ROOT, education department chairman, Ouachita Baptist University, Arkadelphia, Arkansas; former high-school history teacher in Hot Springs, Arkansas, named by Bill Clinton, then Democratic presidential candidate, as one of his best teachers; Clinton's gubernatorial staff liaison to religious groups, 1983–87.

Let not your heart be troubled: ye believe in God, believe
also in me. (John 14:1, KJV)

This verse, coupled with John 3:16, gives me assurance that I
have life eternal with Jesus. And it gives me historical perspective as I assist students in preparing for a life of service in God's
work—that we work according to His plan, not in reaction to
current events.

October 13

HUGH ROSS, president, director of research, Reasons to
Believe ministry committed to harmonizing the words of the
Bible and the facts of nature, and minister of apologetics, Sierra
Madre (California) Congregational Church; former research fel-
low in radio astronomy, California Institute of Technology;
author of several books, including *The Fingerprint of God*,
Genesis One: A Scientific Perspective, *The Creator and the*
Cosmos, and *Creation and Time*.

I know your deeds. See, I have placed before you an open
door that no one can shut. I know that you have little
strength, yet you have kept my word and have not denied
my name. (Revelation 3:8, NIV)

The open door God has placed before us is the door of scientific
discovery. The more scientists discover about the universe, including life, the more sharply the evidence focuses on the God of
the Bible as the one who planned it, shaped it, and still holds it
together, just as the Bible says. Since the Bible speaks truthfully
about these matters, we can also trust its message about the purpose of all things—that people everywhere would embrace their
salvation in Jesus Christ and thus form an eternal, personal relationship with Him. Some people are upset by what the facts say
and refuse to accept them. But nothing and no one can change

the facts. As a ministry, we have "little strength" in terms of our human financial resources. But by God's grace we can and will proclaim the facts, keep His Word, and never deny His name.

October 14

RICHARD ROSS, youth ministry consultant, Baptist Sunday School Board, Nashville, since 1984; one of the coordinators of the board's "True Love Waits" national campaign for sexual abstinence among teens until marriage; minister of youth at Tulip Grove Baptist Church, Nashville, since 1984 and at Royal Haven Baptist Church, Dallas, the previous twelve years.

I have no greater joy than to hear that my children are walking in the truth. (3 John 4, NIV)

Certainly this verse is important to me as I observe my only son, Clayton. Even at age five, he brings me joy as he chooses actions that honor God. This verse also sums up my relationship with teenagers, which now stretches over twenty-five years. The entire quarter-century has been rich, but 1994 was the most joyful of all. Several hundred thousand Christian teenagers have joined the True Love Waits movement as a way to publicly affirm a private decision to be sexually pure. Their exuberance and boldness at rallies and demonstrations and in media appearances have filled my heart with joy. And the story isn't over yet. Every spiritual awakening has begun among the young and has been preceded by a renewed emphasis on moral purity and repentance. Deep in my heart, I believe God is calling out a great host of Christian young people, cleaning them up morally, and strengthening them to be strong and bold—so that He can place them at the forefront of a sweeping revival. What a joy for youth leaders to see our spiritual children not only walking in truth, but leading the parade!

October 15

KYLE ROTE, JR., chief executive officer, Athletic Resource Management, Inc., Memphis-based sports agency representing about forty pro athletes; only American-born player to win a major professional soccer league scoring championship and author of *Complete Book of Soccer* and *Beyond the Goal;* three-time champion of the *Superstars* TV competition, 1977, 1976, 1974; periodic sports commentator on CBS and PBS, host of ESPN's *Just for Kicks,* former USA Cable *Game of the Week* announcer for eight years, and actor in five films.

> This is what the LORD says:
> "Let not the wise man boast of his wisdom
> or the strong man boast of his strength
> or the rich man boast of his riches,
> but let him who boasts boast about this:
> that he understands and knows me,
> that I am the LORD, who exercises kindness,
> justice and righteousness on earth,
> for in these I delight," declares the LORD.
> (Jeremiah 9:23–24, NIV)

Our core identity should never come from what we've done or not done, what we've accomplished or what we've failed at. An athlete may brag about his or her athleticism, a businessman about his banking account, a beauty queen about her physical attractiveness. We may brag about our social standing or popularity among a group of people. But our primary identity in life comes from nothing that we can do, nor from the symbols of our culture, whether they be cars, money, status, or power. The mandate of God, speaking to us through the prophet, is that our primary identity is to come from what Jesus Christ did on the cross and who we are as children of God.

Who I am is Kyle Rote, Jr., a child of God by faith in Jesus who happened to have played professional soccer, who happened to have won the *Superstars* three times, who happens to be a father and a husband. Those other roles can be very important—and notably the last two, father and husband—but even they don't take the place of my identity as one of His own through Christ.

So when we ask what it is that makes us important, if the answer is anything but the blood of Jesus Christ, then we're off on a tangent that ultimately can deceive us. Jesus is not to be just a part of our lives, He's not to be prominent in our lives—He's to be preeminent, above all things, above who I am as an athlete, above who I am as a businessman, above who I am even as a father and as a husband. He's whom I need to rejoice in first and foremost.

October 16

SAM RUTIGLIANO, head coach, Cleveland Browns, 1978–84; two-time UPI Coach of the Year, AFC; author of autobiography *Pressure;* currently head football coach, Liberty University, Lynchburg, Virginia.

Faith is the assurance of things hoped for, the certainty of things you cannot see. (paraphrase of Hebrews 11:1)

On August 16, 1962, my daughter Nancy was killed in an auto accident. There was no way I was capable of handling that crisis, let alone wanting to go on with my life. Through that tragedy my wife and I came to know the Lord. God impacted my life and it has never been the same since. It also has given me an "attitude of gratitude" in reaching out to help others.

October 17

JAMES P. RYAN, founder, The Ryland Group, Inc., one of the top three builders in the United States, constructing 10,000 houses a year in twenty-eight cities; he left the business in 1982 to devote himself full-time to the Ryan Family Foundation, which has funded more than 500 nonprofit programs, including work among Palestinians overseas, and provided management training to 300 nonprofit organizations since its founding in 1977.

> *Thou wilt keep him in perfect peace, whose mind is stayed on thee: because he trusteth in thee. (Isaiah 26:3, KJV)*

There's a plaque on my desk that says this given to me by a high-school friend, Ted Fletcher, founder of Pioneers missionary agency. I think he saw that part of who I am is a person who tries to get a lot done and doesn't like to "talk" being a Christian but to "be" and "do" it. Sometimes people like me run the risk of forgetting that God loves the people we're trying to help more than I do. And if I catch myself getting overly concerned about a project not doing well or moving slowly, I have to remember that I'm not God. God is. The plaque helps remind me that peace comes when I know He's in heaven and He's still in charge.

October 18

JIM RYUN, U. S. congressman, Kansas's Second District, elected in November 1996 election; silver medalist, 1,500 meters, 1968 Olympics in Mexico City; U.S. Olympic team member, 1972, 1968, 1964; former two-time world record holder in the mile; his 3:55.3 mile in 1965 still stands as a high-school world record; *Sports Illustrated* Sportsman of the Year, 1966; author of two books on Christian themes and an autobiography, *In Quest of Gold: The Jim Ryun Story.*

> *Jesus answered and said to him, "Most assuredly, I say to you, unless one is born again, he cannot see the kingdom of God." Nicodemus said to Him, "How can a man be born when he is old? Can he enter a second time into his*

mother's womb and be born?" Jesus answered, "Most assuredly, I say to you, unless one is born of water and the Spirit, he cannot enter the kingdom of God. That which is born of the flesh is flesh, and that which is born of the Spirit is spirit. Do not marvel that I said to you, 'You must be born again.' The wind blows where it wishes, and you hear the sound of it, but cannot tell where it comes from and where it goes. So is everyone who is born of the Spirit." (John 3:3–8, NKJV)

Whenever I autograph anything, I always put this Bible reference with it. I want people to know this life-changing truth. No matter how successful or how famous an individual is, his worth is not in his own works but in the work our Lord Jesus did on the cross for every person who accepts His wonderful gift of salvation. Our "ticket" to heaven is Jesus, and our peace on this earth and the value of our lives are proportional to the extent to which we obey and live by the Father's commands. On the day of judgment, the only thing that will matter is if I have intimately loved and served Jesus as my Lord and Savior. And the only way I can begin to understand the ways and teachings of Christ is to become His disciple by becoming "born again" in the Spirit.

October 19

RACHEL SAINT, missionary in Ecuador; sister of Nate Saint, one of five missionaries killed in 1956 in making initial contact with the Auca tribe of Ecuador; she later took up work among the Aucas. (She died on November 11, 1994, two months after dictating these words to her pastor, James Smith, in Quito, Ecuador.)

". . . Those who have never been told of Him shall see and those who have never heard shall understand."
(Romans 15:21, Berkeley)

When I told the Lord I wanted to serve Him as a foreign missionary, I asked that He would guide me along the line by Scripture. I didn't trust my own leading. I asked the Lord to guide me through His Scriptures. The verse that has meant the most to me, Romans 15:21, is one the Lord gave me before I ever went to study linguistics to become a Bible translator. From this verse I knew the Lord wanted me to go to a completely unreached ethnic group. It was very clear to me that I should go to people who had never heard the truth of God's Word. Now almost fifty years later, I can say that the Lord led me very definitely. When I visited my brother, Nate, in Ecuador, he told me he didn't fly over the Aucas; he flew around them. After asking questions, I knew it was the Auca Indians (as they were then known) of Ecuador to whom the Lord wanted me to go.

Five years of praying later, I arrived in that tribe with my language assistant, Dayuma, who took me back to her hitherto unreached people. Before that, her people had killed five American missionaries, including my own brother. But after she came to know the Lord, she wanted to go back to her people and did so at the risk of her life. After a week or so, I went with her. Both of our lives were threatened from time to time. What I can say now is that many of the Waodani Indians (formerly known as Aucas) have come to know and believe in the Lord and follow Him. God has been more than faithful to His part of the call. It has been my joy to watch the Lord reach the hearts of those who knew nothing before I came, except about demons, witch doctors, and sorcerers. What a joy to let these people know that God has a Son whose name is Jesus, who gave His life for them—for they knew nothing, absolutely nothing, about a God of love and forgiveness and nothing at all about His Son. I praise the Lord for the many who now understand and I pray for those who yet do not understand and do not see what God has planned for the Waodani-Aucas.

October 20

CHERYL PREWITT SALEM, Miss America 1980; featured on five gospel albums; author, with Kathryn Slattery, of *A Bright Shining Place*; mother of two sons.

He that dwelleth in the secret place of the most High shall abide under the shadow of the Almighty. I will say of the LORD, He is my refuge and my fortress: my God; in him will I trust. Surely he shall deliver thee from the snare of the fowler, and from the noisome pestilence. He shall cover thee with his feathers, and under his wings shalt thou trust: his truth shall be thy shield and buckler. Thou shalt not be afraid for the terror by night; nor for the arrow that flieth by day; Nor for the pestilence that walketh in darkness; nor for the destruction that wasteth at noonday. A thousand shall fall at thy side, and ten thousand at thy right hand; but it shall not come nigh thee. Only with thine eyes shalt thou behold and see the reward of the wicked. Because thou hast made the LORD, which is my refuge, even the most High, thy habitation; There shall no evil befall thee, neither shall any plague come nigh thy dwelling. For he shall give his angels charge over thee, to keep thee in all thy ways. They shall bear thee up in their hands, lest thou dash thy foot against a stone. Thou shalt tread upon the lion and adder: the young lion and the dragon shalt thou trample under feet. Because he hath set his love upon me, therefore will I deliver him: I will set him on high, because he hath known my name. He shall call upon me, and I will answer him: I will be with him in trouble; I will deliver him, and honour him. With long life will I satisfy him, and shew him my salvation. (Psalm 91, KJV)

Psalm 91, the entire chapter, has helped me know that no matter what I am going through in life there is one special secret hiding place I can run to where the enemy, Satan, cannot find me. It has been especially helpful knowing I can "dwell" there and not just "visit." As I grow older and my children are growing, I find it beneficial to pray all of Psalm 91 in the first person and over my loved ones by name. For example: "I dwell in the secret place of the most High and I abide in the shadow of the Almighty." This not only is a reminder to myself that God is always with me, protecting me, and sending angels to guard over me at all times, but it's also nice to be able to pray it out loud and remind the devil that he can't do one thing to interfere with my Father God and me. Isn't that great? Just relax, you have the best accommodations to be had, a deluxe suite with Father God, and Satan can't seem to find the address!

October 21

DAVID SATCHER, M.D., Ph.D., director, U.S. Public Health Service's Centers for Disease Control and Prevention, and administrator, Agency for Toxic Substances and Disease Registry; president, Meharry Medical College, Nashville, 1982–93; former positions include chairman and professor in Morehouse School of Medicine's department of community and family medicine, Atlanta; faculty member at King-Drew Medical Center, Los Angeles, and director of its Sickle Cell Research Center; and UCLA School of Medicine faculty member.

> *And we know that in all things God works for the good of those who love him, who have been called according to his purpose. (Romans 8:28, NIV)*

When I look back over my life, there have been a lot of ups and downs, if you will, but I think what's so encouraging is when you put it all together it seems there is a pattern of hope, that things do move in a very positive direction. It helps you not to get too low when things go bad or too high when things go well, when you're always seeking to put things in the context of God's will.

October 22

ARTHUR L. SCHAWLOW, winner of the 1981 Nobel Prize in physics; professor of physics, emeritus, Stanford University, member of the faculty since 1961, department chairman, 1966–70; best known for his work on lasers, he was president of the American Physical Society, 1981, president of the Optical Society, 1975, and California Scientist of the Year, 1973; physicist with Bell Telephone Laboratories, 1951–61.

The heavens declare the glory of God; and the firmament sheweth his handywork. (Psalm 19:1, KJV)

Joseph Haydn set this thought magnificently to music in his oratorio *The Creation* as "The heavens are telling the glory of God." From a religious point of view, scientific research is a worshipful activity, for it enables us to reveal more of the wonders of God's creation. While a scientist is actively participating in research, he or she must concentrate on the problem at hand, rather than thinking all the time of why it is being done. But when discoveries emerge, large or small, we see a little more of the beauty and harmony of the universe.

October 23

BRET SCHUNDLER, mayor, Jersey City, New Jersey, since 1992; former positions include financial analyst at the economic forecasting firm of C. J. Lawrence; account executive at Salomon Brothers; field director in Iowa, Georgia, and New Jersey for the 1984 Gary Hart presidential campaign; and executive assistant to U.S. Congressman Roy Dyson of Maryland.

Dear friends, let us love one another, for love comes from God. Everyone who loves has been born of God and knows God. Whoever does not love does not know God, because God is love. (1 John 4:7–8, NIV)

Even though the infinity of God is much greater than any limited image, definition, or understanding we can keep in our minds, we all need a way to think of God. As children, we tend to think of God as an old man with a white beard who lives among the clouds. That image seldom works for us once we grow into adulthood. First John 4:7–8 provides me with an understanding of God that works for me as an adult. It gives me not only a way to think about God, but even more important, a way to become joined with Him!

October 24

ROGER SCHWEICKERT, vice president of corporate affairs, Charlotte Hornets of the National Basketball Association; former FBI special agent for twenty-two years.

> *Nay, in all these things we are more than conquerors, through him that loved us. For I am persuaded that neither death, nor life, nor angels, nor principalities, nor powers, nor things present, nor things to come, Nor height, nor depth, nor any other creature, shall be able to separate us from the love of God, which is in Christ Jesus our Lord. (Romans 8:37–39, KJV)*

My father died when I was nine years old, and this created a real financial struggle for my mother, who was left with the responsibility of caring for my older brother and sister and me. There was no insurance or benefits to help, but I had the great fortune of having a godly, hardworking mother, and her faith was infectious. During one particularly tough time, I was struck with concern for the future and perhaps sensed some urgency in my mother's efforts to make ends meet. I tearfully expressed these concerns to her. Sternly but lovingly, she took me aside and with great assurance said, "Son, if a man fears God, he won't fear anything else. If he doesn't fear God, he will fear everything else. This is a God-fearing family, and His love will see us through. Now let's finish our chores." Shortly afterward, our minister spoke about God's love that makes us more than conquerors through Him (Romans 8:37–39). I realized that was the heart of my mother's message to me. These words have been a source of strength since that day, and they have seen me through some difficult times as a child, during my military days, and in my career at the FBI.

October 25

VONDA KAY VAN DYKE SCOATES, Miss America 1965, only winner in pageant history also voted Miss Congeniality; public speaker, author of five books, featured on four albums.

> *And we know that all things work together for good to them that love God, to them who are the called according to his purpose. (Romans 8:28, KJV)*

Things don't always work out the way we plan—like being first runner-up for Miss Phoenix two years in a row! This verse assures me that while I cannot always have my own way, and things don't always work out the way I want them to, I don't have to worry because if God guides my life things will work out for His good.

October 26

RUTH SCOTT, resource management specialist, Olympic National Park, Washington State; her responsibilities include wilderness monitoring, planning, and restoration at 922,654-acre Olympic, 95 percent of which is designated wilderness; former National Parks Service staffer at Everglades, Great Basin, Bryce Canyon, and Denali National Parks, Klondike

Gold Rush National Historic Park, and Oregon Caves National Monument.

> *The creation waits in eager expectation for the sons of God to be revealed. For the creation was subjected to frustration, not by its own choice, but by the will of the one who subjected it, in hope that the creation itself will be liberated from its bondage to decay and brought into the glorious freedom of the children of God. We know that the whole creation has been groaning as in the pains of childbirth right up to the present time.*
> *(Romans 8:19–22, NIV)*

I have had the privilege of being called to be a steward of God's creation, to directly care for and protect remnants of the original "good" creation found in wilderness. This verse holds great significance for me as I look at a world where our human greed and exploitation have resulted in abuse of so much of God's created works. It echoes the agony I have come to feel for humankind and the rest of creation as I watch ecological functions and humankind's condition deteriorate. These verses reveal to me how creation is as deeply immersed in the consequences of our sin as we are. Though I feel tremendous pain and frustration expressed here, it also speaks to me of tremendous hope. God promises to renew creation along with His children, through Christ. The inevitable conclusion to the path of destruction we have chosen for ourselves and creation is not devastation, but redemption and joy when Christ reigns as king over a new creation!

October 27

WILLARD SCOTT, NBC *Today* show personality since 1980; weatherman at WRC-TV, Washington, D.C., 1968–80, whose broadcast career began as a page at WRC and weekend disc jockey at a local radio station in 1950; author of four books; honors include 1985 humanitarian in residence, National Society of Fund Raisers, and *Washingtonian* magazine's Washingtonian of the Year, 1979.

> *Blessed are the peacemakers: for they shall be called the children of God. (Matthew 5:9, KJV)*

It's a universal sentiment. It's one of the absolute truths. There's no controversy involved in it. There's nobody in the world who could deny that that is a truth.

October 28

GEORGE SENTER, former Southern Baptist missionary in Africa whose wife, Libby, and nine-year-old daughter, Rachel, were murdered in the Liberian town of Yekepa in November 1986; now remarried, he is pastor of Deep Creek Baptist Church, Wadesboro, North Carolina.

> *Trust in the LORD with all your heart*
> *and lean not on your own understanding;*
> *in all your ways acknowledge him,*
> *and he will make your paths straight.*
> *(Proverbs 3:5–6, NIV)*

I have used Proverbs 3:5–6 many times in attempts to minister to people going through various kinds of crises. Our minds are limited and we can't see all that is going on, especially when something bad happens to us. But we can trust an all-knowing God to handle the situation and even bring good out of what to us is a bad situation. These verses became very personal to me following the murders of my wife and daughter in 1986. What happened seemed so wasteful of human resources. Libby was the kind of person this world needs more of; Rachel was talented and smart and had so much potential. Why did the lives of these two useful people have to be cut short? It was beyond my understanding, but God knew what was going on. It didn't really matter whether I could understand what was going on. My responsibility was to trust God with the situation and leave it up to Him to accomplish His purposes through what had happened. This made it easier to accept what happened, and make the adjustments, and seek to continue to give myself in the Lord's service. I thank God that He can be trusted to handle this and many other situations that I don't understand.

October 29

SAMUEL SHAHID, executive director, Good News for the Crescent World, Fort Worth, Texas; teacher at the Arab Baptist Theological Seminary, Beirut, Lebanon, 1970–75; author of eighteen books in Arabic about Christianity and Islam.

> *Yea, though I walk through the valley of the shadow of death, I will fear no evil: for thou art with me; thy rod and thy staff they comfort me. (Psalm 23:4, KJV)*

While my family and I were in Lebanon and Chicago and now in Fort Worth, we have gone through several crises: war in Lebanon, tragedy in Chicago (our daughter's life hung in the balance for twenty-three days after she was hit by a car), and financial crisis in Fort Worth. But every time, the Lord made it clear that He stood beside me and lifted me up in spite of all the difficulties. When you feel you are not alone and somebody who is so powerful, sympathetic, and loving walks beside you and guides you in the valleys of this life, you realize that your burden is not as heavy as it seems. What is more frightening than the valley of the shadow of death? Yet even there God is walking with you.

October 30

RICKY VAN SHELTON, country music star featured on nine albums (five reaching platinum, 1 million in sales) and twelve No. 1 singles on *Billboard*'s country chart; winner of County Music Association's Horizon Award, 1988, and Male Vocalist of the Year, 1989; author of three children's books, *Tales from a Duck Named Quacker, Quacker Meets Mrs. Moo,* and *Quacker Meets Canadian Goose.*

> *Verily, I say unto you, Whatsoever ye shall bind on earth, shall be bound in heaven; and whatsoever ye shall loose on earth, shall be loosed in heaven. Again I say unto you, That if two of you shall agree on earth as touching any thing that they shall ask, it shall be done for them of my Father which is in heaven. (Matthew 18:18–19, KJV)*

A lot of demons have attacked me in various ways in different parts of my life, and I've just stood on the Word of God and commanded them to leave in the name of Jesus. And they go— they have to go; they have no choice.

October 31

HERBIE SHREVE, president, Christian Motorcyclists Association, Hatfield, Arkansas, with more than 40,000 members and 325 chapters in the United States, Canada, Latin America, and other countries and ten full-time evangelists; his father, Herb, and he founded the association in 1975.

> *He said: "Son of man, I am sending you to the Israelites, to a rebellious nation that has rebelled against me; they and their fathers have been in revolt against me to this very day. The people to whom I am sending you are obstinate and stubborn. Say to them, 'This is what the Sovereign LORD says.' And whether they listen or fail to*

listen—for they are a rebellious house—they will know
that a prophet has been among them. And you, son of
man, do not be afraid of them or their words. Do not be
afraid, though briers and thorns are all around you and
you live among scorpions. Do not be afraid of what they
say or terrified by them, though they are a rebellious
house. . . ." (Ezekiel 2:3–6, NIV)

Bikers are known as rebellious, rowdy, rough, and rejected.
When it seems I am only a small light in vast darkness, this passage reminds me that whether they listen or not, they will know
a man of God has been in their midst.

NOVEMBER

November 1

ARTHUR SIMON, director of the Washington office of Christian Children's Fund, nonsectarian humanitarian organization founded in 1938, now providing help to 2.5 million needy children in forty countries; president emeritus, Bread for the World, Christian citizens' movement he founded in 1974, lobbying in Washington for U.S. policies to address causes of hunger and poverty in the United States and overseas; author of four books and one with his brother, U.S. Senator Paul Simon, *The Politics of World Hunger;* former pastor of an inner-city church in New York City.

> *For by grace you have been saved through faith; and this is not your own doing, it is the gift of God—not because of works, lest any man should boast. For we are his workmanship, created in Christ Jesus for good works, which God prepared beforehand, that we should walk in them. (Ephesians 2:8–10, RSV)*

I like this statement of the apostle Paul because it tells us not only *how* we are saved, but *why* we are saved. We have frequently been content to know how we are saved. But that is only half of the good news. God did not rescue us in Jesus Christ to let us wander aimlessly through life. God gave us a purpose, and that purpose is the doing of good for others: works of justice, mercy, peace, and the care of the earth. We are not saved *by* our good deeds, because His Good Deed on the cross accomplished that, thank God. But we are saved *for* good deeds. That, too, is part of God's great plan for us.

November 2

MIKE SINGLETARY, Hall of Fame–bound Chicago Bears linebacker, 1981–92; contributed two fumble recoveries and thirteen tackles to Bears' Super Bowl XX championship capping the 1985 season; NFL Defensive Player of the Year, 1985, 1988; NFL Man of the Year, 1990, for on-field play and off-field humanitarian efforts; selected to Pro Bowl ten times; author, with Jerry Jenkins, of *Singletary on Singletary;* two-time Southwestern Conference Player of the Year at Baylor University.

> *Blessed is the man who perseveres under trial, because when he has stood the test, he will receive the crown of life that God has promised to those who love him.*
> *(James 1:12, NIV)*

The Bears had just won the Super Bowl. I had been named defensive player of the year. I was making good money. Kim and I were in our first year of marriage. And we were in the process of building my mom a house. All the things I had prayed for had happened. I should have been on top of the world. But I was at the very bottom. I was probably the most frustrated I had ever been as a person and couldn't figure it out.

One day I walked outside and said, "Lord, something's wrong here. I don't understand what's going on. I don't understand why You don't use me more. I don't understand with all of the things going on in my life why I'm so frustrated." And I felt like the Lord said, "Son, there are two things you need to do if you really want to get to know Me and if you want Me to use you more." So I said, "Okay, what's that?"

The first was to forgive my father. I'm the last of ten children, and I had hated my dad for leaving us and how we had to grow up. It was a very difficult thing to do, but I went back and forgave my dad. To this day, I love my dad and we're very close. The second thing the Lord said was—I don't say this is for everybody, but this is what the Holy Spirit said to me—to go back and confess to my wife my unfaithfulness during the times we were dating and when we were engaged and what I almost did during our first year of marriage. That was *extremely* difficult to do. I remember finding James 1:12 and looking at the trials I was going through at the time and realizing if I could just persevere there would be a crown at the end. That was a very difficult time; it took about a year and a half for my wife to be healed from the deep hurt and to trust me again. But once we came through that, there was peace and a clear conscience. The walk of faith transformed my heart and changed my life, and I definitely received a crown.

November 3

BOB SINGLETON, who, with Larry Haron in Singleton Productions, Inc., produces and directs the music for the PBS children's show *Barney and Friends* and has produced music and sound tracks for programs on NBC, PBS, and the Disney Channel and for such clients as American and Southwest airlines and the U.S. Air Force.

> *Now to Him who is able to keep you from stumbling, and to make you stand in the presence of His glory blameless with great joy. . . . (Jude 24, NASB)*

I have a picture in my mind from this verse of God the Father holding my hand and steadying me just as I have held my three daughters' hands while they were learning to walk and run. When my girls would trip, or stretch their legs beyond their own limits, I would catch them before they fell. In the same way, I'm reminded that God has chosen to hold me and never let me fall away from Him. He is always there, with a loving grasp that never tires. I'm also encouraged by this verse to risk. I can take risks for good, because I know that God will not let me stumble. Nothing I can do will separate me from standing in His presence with great joy. How liberating! I am free to be all that God wants me to be, because no matter how I blow it along the way, God my Father is there, keeping me from falling away from His care. I am free to stretch beyond what I see as my own limits and run with assurance toward the goals God sets for me.

November 4

STEVE SLOAN, director of athletics, University of Central Florida at Orlando; former athletic director at the University of Alabama and head football coach at Vanderbilt University, Texas Tech, Duke, and the University of Mississippi; All-American quarterback who led the University of Alabama to a national title in 1965; author of two books, *A Whole New Ball Game* and *Calling Life's Signals.*

> *Don't be selfish; don't live to make a good impression on others. Be humble, thinking of others as better than yourself. (Philippians 2:3, TLB)*

The deepest Christians I've met through the years all seem to possess the trait of genuine humility. It seems to me humility is part of the cement that makes the faith viable. True humility allows Christians to rise above themselves.

November 5

LINDA SMITH, congresswoman, Third District, Washington, elected in 1994, first person in the state's history to qualify for the primary-election ballot as a write-in candidate; member of the Washington senate, 1987–94, and Washington house of representatives, 1983–87.

> *... Clothe yourselves with humility toward one another, because, "God opposes the proud but gives grace to the*

*humble." Humble yourselves, therefore, under God's
mighty hand, that he may lift you up in due time. Cast
all your anxiety on him because he cares for you. Be self-
controlled and alert. Your enemy the devil prowls around
like a roaring lion looking for someone to devour. Resist
him, standing firm in the faith, because you know that
your brothers throughout the world are undergoing the
same kind of sufferings. (1 Peter 5:5–9, NIV)*

Soon after I was elected to Congress, an uneasiness was keeping
me awake that was, and still is, hard to define. I know I was
struggling with having the spotlight on me and what that
means. It's becoming clear to me that the spotlight often blinds
individuals to the needs of others around them. My husband,
Vern, read this passage to me one night and I found it comforting. It reminded me to be obedient to doing what is right. The
Scripture made it clear that God expects me to humble myself
and raise others up. And in His time, He will raise me up for His
glory. That makes my day-to-day challenges a much lighter load
as I trust in God and His timing and grace.

November 6

PHILIP SMITH, principal trumpet, New York Philharmonic;
fourth-generation Salvation Army member who directs and
plays in various brass ensembles; Juilliard School of Music graduate.

*Each one should use whatever gift he has received to serve
others, faithfully administering God's grace in its various
forms. If anyone speaks, he should do it as one speaking
the very words of God. If anyone serves, he should do it
with the strength God provides, so that in all things God
may be praised through Jesus Christ. To him be the glory
and the power for ever and ever. Amen.
(1 Peter 4:10–11, NIV)*

In what I do, I try to use my gifts to serve, specifically the gift of trumpet playing. Anytime I can, I try to give a witness, whether spoken or simply through a hymn as a selection. If I'm introducing a hymn, I try to note the relevance of the piece and what my faith is, the fact that I believe in the power of the Lord Jesus Christ and what this specific song means to me. I find that it (1) encourages me to be more bold in my faith and (2) is helpful to Christians, encouraging them to be bold. In presenting Jesus Christ, I want people to understand who He is specifically to me, that He is my Savior, He is someone who helps me, guides me, strengthens me—that you, like me, may have need for a Savior, that there may be things in your life you need to give over to Christ. I had a guest appearance at Carnegie Hall with a British brass band, the Black Dyke Mills Band, for example, and I used a new Salvation Army hymn, "Share My Yoke," on the program. It gave me the chance, on the apron of Carnegie Hall, to actually refer to "my yoke is easy and my burden is light," to quote Scripture and say to people: this is special to me, because there are times when I, and perhaps you, feel overburdened, overworked, and overdone and not able to cope and yet, with faith in Jesus Christ, with the power He has, we can give this over to Christ and allow Christ to help us.

November 7

SANDY SMITH, Sunday features and social issues writer, *The Tennessean*, Nashville, since 1988.

> "... I know the plans I have for you," declares the LORD, "plans to prosper you and not to harm you, plans to give you hope and a future. Then you will call upon me and come and pray to me, and I will listen to you. You will seek me and find me when you seek me with all your heart...." (Jeremiah 29:11–13, NIV)

This passage, more than any other in the Bible, is the one on which I stand. Daily. Being in the mainstream media is surely one of the most oppressive environments for a Christian. It doesn't help that my newspaper is one of the most liberal in the country. There are many days when I don't know why I do this for a living. But that's okay. God knows. Not only does He know why, but He's given me a plethora of promises: prosperity, safety, hope, and a future. All I have to do is call on Him—fairly easily. And He will listen to me. We hear all the time how powerful the media is—and it is—but the media's power can't compare to what we have when we call upon the Lord. There's nothing quite as secure as knowing that God, creator of the universe, has a plan for your life—even when you may not know what that plan is. But one look at the promises that follow assures me that whatever it is, it's outstanding.

November 8

SHEPHERD SMITH, president, Americans for a Sound AIDS/HIV Policy (ASAP), Washington, D.C., nonprofit organization he founded in 1987 dedicated to early HIV diagnosis, traditional public health interventions to halt the spread of HIV, compassionate care for all infected and affected by HIV, development of a vaccine as well as effective treatments and a health care system capable of treating all who become infected; member of the U.S. Centers for Disease Control's Ad Hoc Panel on STD/HIV and other AIDS-related panels.

Jesus then said to the Jews who had believed in him,
"If you continue in my word, you are truly my disciples,
and you will know the truth, and the truth will make you
free." (John 8:31–32, RSV)

For many people who have not grown up in this culture as Christians, committing their lives to Christ is kind of a traumatic experience. You think you're giving up a lot, rather than understanding that you're gaining a lot. Sometime after I had committed my life to Christ in 1979, one of the verses that helped me realize what I was gaining was John 8:32—knowing the truth and being set free. But I really didn't focus on John 8:31—following Christ's commands and truly being His disciples in order to know the truth and be set free.

In this culture, in this world, following His commands is not easy. There are so many diversions in America today it's hard even for discerning Christians to reject things that are not fundamentally good for us. A friend of mine who is a missionary overseas comes back every three or four years and is amazed each time by just turning on a TV at how much we have slipped toward degradation, in terms of language and story lines and nudity. Yet we don't understand that that's happening to us. As in C. S. Lewis's *Screwtape Letters,* if the devil set out to design a program to corrupt, he's done it here. It's not with bad things, but with good things. We have too much of everything, in my opinion, and that can be very corrupting.

Particularly with the AIDS issue and getting just a small amount of support from church people and churches, this is true. It's easy to turn your back on things that aren't very appealing, to walk by the person who's suffering, to not be the Samaritan. That's very easy as an American Christian. People say God's love and Christ's love are unconditional, and that's very, very true. But I think God asks us to do a lot to retain a relationship with Him. So sticking to John 8:31 has been the challenge in continuing my commitment to Christ. If you keep your eye on the truth, the truth does, in fact, set you free from the bondage of this society, of this world, and makes it possible to follow His commands.

November 9

STAN SMITH, member of the International Tennis Hall of Fame, Newport, Rhode Island; 1972 Wimbledon, 1971 U.S. Open singles champion; doubles champion, U.S. Open, 1980, 1978, 1974, 1968, with Bob Lutz; eleven-year Davis Cup competitor with a 15–5 record in singles and 20–3 in doubles; U.S. Intercollegiate singles champion, 1968, doubles champion 1967–68 with Bob Lutz; currently, associate director of player development, United States Tennis Association.

> *Trust in the LORD with all your heart*
> *and lean not on your own understanding;*
> *in all your ways acknowledge him,*
> *and he will make your paths straight.*
> *(Proverbs 3:5–6, NIV)*

These two verses capsulize for me what my faith should be about. If we trust Him with all our hearts, then we won't worry about anything else. He *will* direct us in every way if we have placed this trust in Him. When I'm struggling with situations in my life, I repeat this to myself over and over.

November 10

MIKE SPENCER, law enforcement officer, Fremont County, Colorado; president, Fellowship of Christian Cowboys, Colorado Springs, Colorado, 1989–94; former rodeo clown and barrel man.

> *But seek first his kingdom and his righteousness, and all*
> *these things will be given to you as well.*
> *(Matthew 6:33, NIV)*

I believe for success in whatever you do, you must be focused, have a good foundation, and set some goals. This verse gives you all three. You set your sights on Christ and His righteousness. In doing this, you build your foundation on His principles. When you pursue His righteousness, the needs of life will be taken care of and you will end up with a balanced life. This is not a way to justify doing nothing, however, because Christ doesn't allow for slothfulness.

November 11

RICK STANLEY, evangelist based in Fayetteville, Georgia; stepbrother of the late Elvis Presley whose book, *Caught in a Trap,* recounts childhood and, later, touring crew experiences with the singer; he credits his wife, Robyn, a high-school friend who kept in touch over the years, as a key influence in his conversion and overcoming drug abuse several weeks after Presley's death in 1977; guest speaker in several Billy Graham crusades and interviewed on such shows as *20/20* and *Larry King Live* and in *People* and other periodicals.

> *Let nothing be done through selfish ambition or conceit, but in lowliness of mind let each esteem others better than himself. (Philippians 2:3, NKJV)*

A picture of Mother Teresa in *Life* magazine has been locked in my mind for several years. There were two pictures in that issue that were powerful. The guy standing in front of the tank in Tiananmen square—that picture spoke to me about the willingness to stand alone. But that picture of Mother Teresa standing among starving kids in Calcutta and feeding them—we as Christians must develop an other-consciousness in order to reach the world. That lady is other-conscious. She lets others know that she cares. She's willing to lead with her life.

In this Scripture, the point that really gets to me is: nothing out of selfish ambition, but in lowliness of mind, consider others. When we get to the point as Christians that we're able to

look at those with AIDS and those who are on drugs and consider others better than we are, then they'll see Christ in us. In
evangelism, pastors want people down the aisle, and I'm for
that. But unfortunately everything but Jesus has become the
issue. Now it's: Are you a Republican or a Democrat? Do you
like Clinton? Are you pro-life? Are you pro-choice? Do you like
Rush Limbaugh? Do you think Jerry Falwell's doing the right
thing? And on and on. We're not other-conscious. When we
turn in on ourselves, we become *self*-conscious, and pettiness
and politics break out. But when we stay other-conscious, we'll
look out and see a hurting humanity and understand its great
need for Christ and meet that need.

November 12

WAYNE STAYSKAL, *Tampa Tribune* editorial cartoonist
since 1984, syndicated to newspapers across the country; previously editorial cartoonist for the *Chicago Tribune* and *Chicago
American;* his cartoons also have been published as several collections, most recently *Till Euthanasia Do You Part?*

> *Humble yourselves therefore under the mighty hand of
> God, that he may exalt you in due time. (1 Peter 5:6, KJV)*

Since reading this verse twenty years ago, I've carried an ever-
present mental image of God's strong hand that, under His
terms, provides every kind of protection and comfort.

November 13

DON STEPHENS, president and chief executive officer,
Mercy Ships, since 1978, and international director of relief and
development services, Youth With A Mission, since 1985;
Mercy Ships operates four relief ships, which have docked in
more than sixty ports worldwide in areas of natural disaster or
chronic need; the 522-foot, nine-story M/V *Anastasis* is the

world's largest nongovernmental hospital ship; the fleet's volunteer crew encompasses deck officers, doctors, nurses, engineers, and other professionals from more than thirty-five nations.

> *Arise, shine; for your light has come,*
> *And the glory of the* LORD *has risen upon you.*
> *For behold, darkness will cover the earth,*
> *And deep darkness the peoples;*
> *But the* LORD *will rise upon you,*
> *And His glory will appear upon you.*
> *(Isaiah 60:1–2, NASB)*

When my future seemed darkest, Jesus was my light. When all the media focus was on pain, death, and hopelessness, and depression attempted to bring the darkest of clouds, God's Word was my lamp to light my way. And when the Light of the World shone through His people, bondages were broken, the homeless were sheltered, the lost were found, the blind brought to first sight.

November 14

NOEL PAUL STOOKEY, member of Peter, Paul, and Mary some thirty years and performer with Bodyworks folk/eclectic Christian ensemble since 1979.

> *But you are God's "chosen generation," his "royal priest-hood," his "holy nation," his "peculiar people"—all the old titles of God's people now belong to you. It is for you now to demonstrate the goodness of him who has called you out of darkness into his amazing light. In the past you were not "a people" at all: now you are the people of God.... (1 Peter 2:9–10, Phillips)*

Years ago, while working on an album project, *State of the Heart,* I was touched by the calling of 1 Peter 2:9–10. As perhaps you're aware by virtue of my political activity with Peter and Mary, the thread of peacemaker has been woven throughout my life. And as I read that Christians are a "holy nation" who once "were not 'a people' . . . (but) now you are the people of God," I was struck once again that we are called by our faith to transcend national borders.

This was several years before the end of the Cold War; Russia was still considered a military threat. Much of the violence and repression in the Central American countries was being financed by our government, so that the "spread of communism" might be halted. That this policy should be supported by believers was puzzling to me, particularly in light of the Scriptures. How could we presume to think that believers in these other countries were any less "of one Spirit"? Were we so naive as to think that the genocide of war differentiated between "heathen" and "Christian"? And even if such a differentiation were possible, where is it written in the New Testament that *we* are empowered to judge the wicked?

The resultant song was called "The Come Away Suite," the most powerful performance of which occurred at a West Point chapel–sponsored concert on the U.S. Military Academy campus.

November 15

LEE STROBEL, teaching pastor and communications director, Willow Creek Community Church, the nation's second-largest congregation, in South Barrington, Illinois; former newspaper journalist for fourteen years, including seven at the *Chicago Tribune* as legal affairs editor; author of *What Jesus Would Say, Inside the Mind of Unchurched Harry and Mary,* and *Reckless Homicide.*

> Yet to all who received him, to those who believed in his name, he gave the right to become children of God. . . .
> (John 1:12, NIV)

Intrigued by my wife's conversion to Christianity, I came to church as an atheist on January 20, 1980, and first heard the gospel explained in a way I could understand it. I decided to spend the next portion of my life using my journalistic and legal training to investigate systematically whether there was any credibility to Christianity. That's what I did for a year and nine months, at which time I concluded that the evidence of history points compellingly toward Jesus Christ being who He claimed to be.

But I was stuck—what do I do next? That's when I read John 1:12, which spells out with nearly mathematical precision what it means to be adopted into God's family. In fact, the key verbs of that verse form an equation: *believe* + *receive* = *become*. I believed that Jesus Christ was the unique Son of God, that He died on the cross for my sins and was resurrected from the dead, and that He was offering eternal life as a free gift that cannot be earned. So I took the step of receiving that gift by repenting of my sin and embracing Christ as my forgiver and leader. And that's when I became one of His children, adopted forever into His family.

This was the last verse of the Bible that I read before becoming a Christian, so it holds special significance for me. And through the years since, I've used it time after time to help spiritual seekers cross the line of faith and put their trust in Christ. I thank God for such a succinct and simple summary of what it means to enter into His family.

November 16

SUZANNE STRUDWICK, professional golfer; native of Cheshire, England, who played on the WPG European Tour 1983–93, winning the 1989 French Open and 1991 AGF Paris Open; joining the LPGA Tour in 1992, she was named 1993 Rookie of the Year.

> O LORD, *thou hast searched me, and known me. Thou knowest my downsitting and mine uprising, thou under-*

*standest my thought afar off. Thou compassest my path
and my lying down, and art acquainted with all my ways.
For there is not a word in my tongue, but, lo, O LORD,
thou knowest it altogether. Thou hast beset me behind
and before, and laid thine hand upon me. Such knowledge
is too wonderful for me; it is high, I cannot attain unto it.
Whither shall I go from thy spirit? or whither shall I flee
from thy presence? If I ascend up into heaven, thou art
there: if I make my bed in hell, behold, thou art there. If I
take the wings of the morning, and dwell in the uttermost
parts of the sea; Even there shall thy hand lead me, and
thy right hand shall hold me. If I say, Surely the darkness
shall cover me; even the night shall be light about me. Yea,
the darkness hideth not from thee; but the night shineth
as the day: the darkness and the light are both alike to
thee. For thou hast possessed my reins: thou hast covered
me in my mother's womb. I will praise thee; for I am fearfully and wonderfully made: marvellous are thy works;
and that my soul knoweth right well. . . . Search me, O
God, and know my heart: try me, and know my thoughts:
And see if there be any wicked way in me, and lead me in
the way everlasting. (Psalm 139:1–14, 23–24, KJV)*

After my initial new birth in Christ at the age of eighteen in
1983, I put all my energies into the believer who originally
shared Christ with me, and not in Christ. My foundations were
on sand and not on the Rock. When I was tempted to stray back
into a life of disobedience to Christ, I did so. It wasn't until
1992–93 when I was joining the LPGA tour that I realized why I
was meant to be here. God has taken me on a journey of discovery and adventure, of seeing the world, myself, and finally Him.

I made the decision to play on the LPGA tour to start fresh
with my life and my faith. I had to do that away from the temp-
tations of home. I gained my LPGA card in October 1992 and

played well in 1993 and was named Rookie of the Year. I really felt God was with me all the way. I didn't have a sponsor, but I had a peace about the finances. Every time I ran low on funds, I'd have a good week! I really wanted to make a statement in my faith and my golf. I talked to my friends about the changes in my life and told them that Jesus was the reason. I wanted to support the Christian fellowship on the tour and get to know some new friends. That has been such a blessing. God knows me, He knows what I need, what I can take, how to stretch me to the limit and then a little more! I have come to know Psalm 139 as the way God has shown me that He knows me.

Right now, God is showing me that the limits we put on others and ourselves are wrong. God sets the limits but will always change them to what we can take. When we are low, He shows us we can rise above and move on, even if we think we cannot. When we are on a high, He shows us we can ride even higher than we ever imagined if we trust in Him and are open to receive Him always.

November 17

JIM SUNDBERG, catcher with the Texas Rangers and, earlier, Kansas City Royals and Chicago Cubs, ranking fourth in major league history in number of games caught, 1,927, and third in fielding percentage in 1,000-plus games (tied with Elston Howard and Bill Freehand), .993; member of the Royals' 1985 World Series champions; three-time All-Star, winner of six consecutive Gold Gloves for fielding; the Rangers' annual player honor for exemplary service on and off the field is named for him, the Jim Sundberg Community Achievement Award.

> Behold, thou desirest truth in the inward parts: and in the hidden part thou shalt make me to know wisdom.
> (Psalm 51:6, KJV)

David was known as a man after God's own heart because he shot straight with God and poured his heart out to Him. David knew he could trust God no matter what, and he found great security in that. It is a lesson to me, underscored by David's words in Psalm 51:6, that God desires truth in our inmost parts. We as Christians need to be more honest with God, ourselves, and others about our emotions.

November 18

ALLAN A. SWENSON, author of more than thirty gardening books, most recently, *Plants of the Bible and How to Grow Them*, and eight children's books; syndicated gardening columnist more than twenty-five years, writing for *Grit* and, formerly, United Media; featured on the Christian Broadcasting Network's *700 Club* gardening segments, "Let's Grow Together."

> *Judge me, O LORD; for I have walked in mine integrity: I have trusted also in the LORD; therefore I shall not slide. Examine me, O LORD, and prove me; try my reins and my heart. For thy lovingkindness is before mine eyes: and I have walked in thy truth. I have not sat with vain persons, neither will I go in with dissemblers. I have hated the congregation of evil doers; and will not sit with the wicked. I will wash mine hands in innocency: so will I compass thine altar, O LORD: That I may publish with the voice of thanksgiving, and tell of all thy wondrous works. LORD, I have loved the habitation of thy house, and the place where thine honour dwelleth. Gather not my soul with sinners, nor my life with bloody men: In whose hands is mischief, and their right hand is full of bribes. But as for me, I will walk in mine integrity: redeem me, and be merciful unto me. My foot standeth in an even place: in the congregations will I bless the LORD.*
> *(Psalm 26, KJV)*

In my small way, I have focused my life and writing on a special theme: "Let's Grow Together." I believe that by working together Christians of all denominations must and can make that critical difference in getting America back on the right track—of honesty, integrity, faith, and Christian values. There is a goodness and kindness in many people all across America. Unfortunately, too many good people remain quiet nonactivists in the face of continuing, daily assaults to all our senses by the violence, immorality, and rude and crude focus of so many newspaper articles and TV programs. It is time for that "silent majority" to speak up more forcefully.

November 19

JONI EARECKSON TADA, founder and president, JAF Ministries, dedicated to accelerating Christian ministry in the disability community; her autobiography, *Joni,* was made into a movie in which she re-created her life after a diving accident in 1967 that left her a quadriplegic; author of eighteen other books, including several for children; her *Joni and Friends* weekday radio program is aired on more than 800 stations, offering information and encouragement to those with disabilities and fostering disability awareness; presidential appointee to the National Council on Disability, during which time the Americans with Disabilities Act became law; painter and recording artist; first woman honored as Layperson of the Year by the National Association of Evangelicals.

> *For no matter how many promises God has made, they are "Yes" in Christ. And so through him the "Amen" is spoken by us to the glory of God.*
> *(2 Corinthians 1:20, NIV)*

Just think, every promise God has ever made finds its fulfillment in Jesus. God doesn't just give us grace, He gives us Jesus, the Lord of grace. If it's peace, it's only found in Jesus, the Prince of

Peace. Even life itself is found in the Resurrection and the Life. Christianity isn't all that complicated . . . it's Jesus.

November 20

ADON TAFT, religion editor during thirty-seven of his forty-four years with *The Miami Herald;* now a columnist on issues related to aging.

> *But God commendeth his love toward us, in that, while we were yet sinners, Christ died for us. (Romans 5:8, KJV)*

I identify myself in that verse as a sinner. Yet God loves me. He loved me long before I was aware of His love. He loves me in spite of my failure to live up to His standard. His love makes me want to live more for Him, to love Him more, and, consequently, to live more of a loving life toward my neighbor, whoever he is, wherever she is.

November 21

THOMAS A. TARRANTS III, co-pastor, Christ Our Shepherd Church, Washington, D.C.; before his conversion to Christianity in 1970, he was involved with the Ku Klux Klan in Mississippi and spent eight years in prison for terrorist activity; author of *The Conversion of a Klansman* and coauthor with John Perkins of *He's My Brother: Former Racial Foes Offer Strategy for Reconciliation.*

> *But because of his great love for us, God, who is rich in mercy, made us alive with Christ even when we were dead in transgressions—it is by grace you have been saved. . . . For we are God's workmanship, created in Christ Jesus to do good works, which God prepared in advance for us to do. . . . For he himself is our peace, who has made the two one and has destroyed the barrier, the dividing wall of hostility. . . . (Ephesians 2:4–5, 10, 14, NIV)*

Ephesians 2 is one of my favorite chapters in the Bible. The first half of the chapter speaks clearly and powerfully of how God in His rich mercy "made us alive with Christ" even when we were dead in sin. And it speaks about how this grace, which we receive only through faith in Christ, moves us to do good works already envisioned in God's plan for our lives. But it doesn't stop there. The second half of the chapter goes on to describe how our reconciliation with God leads us to reconciliation with others, that Jesus "destroyed the barrier, the dividing wall of hostility," which in those days separated Jew and Gentile—and in our own day separates black and white. This world continues to look for the visible manifestation of this reconciling, unifying power of the gospel that demonstrates the messiahship of Jesus our Lord.

November 22

GRANT TEAFF, executive director, American Football Coaches Association; head coach, Baylor University, 1972–92; six-time Southwest Conference Coach of the Year and 1974 Division 1-A Kodak Coach of the Year.

> *I beseech you therefore, brethren, by the mercies of God, that you present your bodies a living sacrifice, holy, acceptable to God, which is your reasonable service. And do not be conformed to this world, but be transformed by the renewing of your mind, that you may prove what is that good and acceptable and perfect will of God.*
> *(Romans 12:1–2, NKJV)*

These words from the apostle Paul convey so much practical information and knowledge. Paul convinced me, through his words, that God has a plan, a purpose, and a will for my life. This passage points out the importance of our mind and how, when that mind is changed, our whole nature can be transformed. God loved us enough to allow His Son, Jesus Christ, to die for us. If we believe that, it seems totally impossible that God would let us live without a plan, a purpose, and a will for our lives. Thanks to Paul, this became clear to me.

November 23

JOHN W. TEETS, chairman and chief executive officer, Viad Corp, Phoenix, Arizona, created as a spin-off of Dial Corp's services businesses in August 1996; as Dial's chairman and CEO, he presided over the restructuring of the former Greyhound Corp. conglomerate, encompassing such enterprises as bus lines and meatpacking, into a company focused on consumer products and services; he joined the company in 1963; named chief executive officer of the year by *Leaders* magazine, 1986, and top business speaker of the year by *Forbes* magazine, 1990.

> *For my thoughts are not your thoughts, neither are your ways my ways, saith the* LORD. *For as the heavens are higher than the earth, so are my ways higher than your ways, and my thoughts than your thoughts.*
> *(Isaiah 55:8–9, KJV)*

This passage is one of my favorites because it puts into perspective God's omnipotence. It unequivocally states that only God knows the whys and wherefores of His actions and the reasons behind His methods. His mysteries are His to know, and only He has the key to the Grand Plan. It is up to all of us, in our own way, to accept God's ways on faith. These verses seriously debunk the pontificating statements of secular prophets and preachers who tell us that only they know what God is thinking and the reasons behind His actions. It is clear that God's thoughts are God's thoughts and God's ways are God's ways—and His ways only!

November 24

JERRY THACKER, Fleetwood, Pennsylvania, businessman; author, *When AIDS Comes Home,* written under the alias Wayne Marshall, about his family's crisis with HIV.

> *Yet I am always with you;*
> *you hold me by my right hand.*
> *You guide me with your counsel,*
> *and afterward you will take me into glory.*
> *Whom have I in heaven but you?*
> *And being with you, I desire nothing on earth.*
> *My flesh and my heart may fail,*
> *but God is the strength of my heart*
> *and my portion forever. (Psalm 73:23–26, NIV)*

As a result of a blood transfusion given to my wife after the cesarean-section birth of our daughter in 1984, my wife and I, and our youngest child, are all having to deal with HIV, the virus that causes AIDS. It is a great comfort to know that by God's grace we are members of that "forever generation" that will be with God for all eternity. He will guide us each step of the way while we are on this earth, and when we die, He will take us home to live with Him in a beautiful place called heaven.

November 25

SUE THACKER, Fleetwood, Pennsylvania, wife and mother infected by HIV in the 1984 birth of her third child, Sarah, through a cesarean-section operation that required a transfusion; her husband, Jerry, and Sarah also became HIV-positive as a result of the tainted blood; "my husband and I started sharing our story in November 1993 to help people show the compassion of Christ to people who have AIDS."

> *But thanks be to God, which giveth us the victory*
> *through our Lord Jesus Christ. (1 Corinthians 15:57, KJV)*

I am HIV-positive and when I get discouraged I think of the victory we have in Christ—victory over sin, victory over circumstances, victory over death! Victory in the end when Christ returns to be recognized as King of Kings and Lord of Lords. This is the tremendous God that we serve!

November 26

KATHY THIBODEAUX, founder and director, Ballet Magnificat, national touring Christian ballet troupe based in Jackson, Mississippi; silver medalist, 1982 International Ballet Competition; wife of Keith Thibodeaux.

> *I am the* LORD, *the God of all mankind. Is anything too hard for me?. . . (Jeremiah 32:27, NIV)*

The Lord gave me this Scripture during the beginning stages of Ballet Magnificat. I guess He knew that many times I would have to be reminded of this truth. There were times when we didn't know how we were going to make it, when circumstances seemed too hard to handle. Then He would remind me of His Word—that He is God and nothing is too hard for Him to handle and take care of.

November 27

KEITH THIBODEAUX, executive director, Ballet Magnificat; featured as Little Ricky, TV son of Lucille Ball and Desi Arnaz on *I Love Lucy,* and author of *Life After Lucy,* with Audrey T. Hingley; husband of Kathy Thibodeaux; former drummer for David and the Giants, rock band that disbanded in 1974, reuniting five years later as a Christian band.

> *He is like a tree planted by streams of water,*
> *which yields its fruit in season*
> *and whose leaf does not wither.*
> *Whatever he does prospers. (Psalm 1:3, NIV)*

This Scripture has always given me a lot of inspiration and hope. I've liked that picture of a tree; I can see it in my mind. It's planted by this stream of beautiful, cool water. Its leaves don't wither; they are always green. It lives because of the water it's planted by. And the water, of course, is the Holy Spirit. When we are living in the Spirit, when we are planted in God, no matter what kind of hardships or trials come, we can be like this tree.

November 28

ANDRE THORNTON, Cleveland Indians first baseman, 1976–87, top right-handed home run hitter in Indians' history, two-time All-Star; president, Thornton Marketing and Consulting, Inc., and former president, Christian Family Outreach, both in Cleveland; cochairman, 1994 Northeastern Ohio Billy Graham Crusade; author of *Triumph Born of Tragedy*, with Al Janssen, about life after an auto accident that claimed his wife and young daughter.

> *Looking unto Jesus the author and finisher of our faith, who, for the joy that was set before him, endured the cross, despising the shame, and is set down at the right hand of the throne of God. (Hebrews 12:2, KJV)*

This verse has been pivotal in my life because it has always reminded me of the price Christ paid on the cross for me, yet He counted it as a joy.

November 29

DEBBYE TURNER, Miss America 1990, who earned a doctor of veterinary medicine degree from the University of Missouri at Columbia in 1991.

> *For whom He foreknew, He also predestined to be conformed to the image of His Son, that he might be the first-born among many brethren. Moreover whom He*

predestined, these He also called; whom He called, these
He also justified; and whom He justified, these He also
glorified. (Romans 8:29–30, NKJV)

This Scripture confirms to all of God's children that He has a specific plan and blueprint for our lives from the time of our conception—which means that our only responsibility is to seek and know the face of the Father. Then He takes the lead in molding, developing, and glorifying our lives.

November 30

ROBERT VERNON, retired Los Angeles assistant police chief whose office directed the city's 8,000-plus patrol officers; member of the L.A. Police Department thirty-eight years; author of two books, *L.A. Justice* and *L.A. Cop: Peacemaker in Blue.*

Trust in the LORD with all your heart,
And do not lean on your own understanding.
In all your ways acknowledge Him,
and He will make your paths straight.
(Proverbs 3:5–6, NASB)

When I was in high school, a missionary at our church spoke on these verses as kind of a formula for finding God's will for your life. That got my attention: three conditions to which, if we fulfill them as God gives us strength, He attaches a promise, an absolute commitment.

The first condition is "Trust in the Lord with all your heart." In understanding that, I had to come to realize the difference between simple belief and trust. Belief can be an intellectual exercise, "Yes, I believe that." Trust makes something very personal. I've experienced many things to help me understand that over the years. I was allowed once to fly with a Navy pilot and land on an aircraft carrier and, after spending the night there, catapult off the aircraft carrier with him the next day. I'd always wanted to do that; it had been kind of a secret dream. Yet when the time came to get in the jet to be catapulted off, I had some real reservations. I believed it could be done; I had watched fifty or more jets launched while I was there. Of course, I did it; it was the only way back. But I really appreciated the difference between belief and trust. This Scripture says we have to trust in the Lord with all our heart. We have to personally get involved with Him and not just believe in Him. The way I applied that in my life is I made a commitment to Him and asked Him to be my Savior and Lord. And it became very personal; I was involved.

The second condition is "Do not lean on your own understanding." Of course, the question is, If you don't lean on your own understanding, if you don't try to figure things out in life yourself, whose understanding do you accept? The obvious answer is He's saying, "Lean on me." Where do we find God's understanding? In the Bible primarily. And so, the second condition is, Once you've established a personal relationship with the Lord, with His enlightenment and help you search the Scriptures to dig out the principles to apply to your life. And as He gives you the strength, you live by them. Much—in fact most—of His will is revealed in the Bible. Although there may not be a lot of specifics of, Should I work for this company? Should I marry this particular woman? there are principles that will give you answers to a lot of specifics or rule out a lot of specifics.

Then the third step is "In all your ways acknowledge Him." Acknowledging is the opposite of ignoring. I think it means, as the early church fathers used to say, to "practice the presence." In other words, God is with me, God is watching me, God knows what I'm doing right now. And I find if I can keep that mentality in my life, if I'm conscious of God's presence, it affects my behavior. Acknowledging God means to bring Him in on the decisions. In prayer, communicate with Him. Specifically ask Him for direction.

And the promise, the commitment, then, is "He will make your paths straight." It's a Hebrew way of saying your path will be right in front of you. You won't need a map to find it, you won't get lost, you won't need a note from heaven. It'll be so obvious what God wants you to do that you won't be able to miss it.

DECEMBER

December 1

PAM VETETO, Batesville, Arkansas, minister's wife and mother of four children who, after the death of eight-year-old daughter Shauna from a brain aneurysm in 1985, has been a foster mother to more than one hundred children; at age seven, Shauna had told her parents she wanted to be a missionary.

For I know the plans I have for you, says the LORD. They are plans for good and not for evil, to give you a future and a hope. (Jeremiah 29:11, TLB)

God has not allowed tragic events to occur in my life to chastise me, test me, or prove Himself to me. He has allowed these events to guide me in what is His divine and wonderful will for my life. I do not always have to understand God's will, but I must accept His will in order to achieve His ultimate purpose in my life.

Shauna had made a profession of faith in Christ at age six and, at age seven, told my husband, Danny, and me she thought God was calling her to be a missionary. As a proud mother, I was so excited. A year later, when Shauna began experiencing severe headaches, we took her to a neurologist and prayed that God would help our little girl get better. To our horror, a CAT scan showed a mass at the base of Shauna's brain. Surgery to remove the aneurysm was scheduled. Our world was crashing in around us. We could not understand why God was allowing this to happen. Grasping for answers and seeking to find God's purpose, I thought maybe God would use this terrible ordeal to give

Shauna a great testimony when she became older. We had faith each day that the physicians would tell us they did not know how, but somehow Shauna had been cured. This, however, never happened. As the mother of an eight-year-old, I had been able to kiss away her hurts, drive away her monsters, and dry her tears. Now I was completely helpless to come to her aid. All I could do was sit beside her bed and watch my child grow weaker and weaker. I begged God to let my little girl live. However, this was not God's will. She died and, although I knew Shauna was now in the presence of the glorious God she loved so much, I felt alone, cheated, and completely deserted.

I prayed constantly for comfort and peace, for relief from the pain, but I could not get any relief from God. I told God if I could just feel Him, if I thought He was even listening, if I thought He even cared, maybe I could get through this nightmare. It seemed as if God was silent, as if He had completely turned His back on me. I kept going to church but found it difficult to sit in a pew without my daughter beside me. One day, I told God I was giving up. He knew how much I loved my daughter, He knew I could not make it without her, and He had taken her anyway. So He should understand that I was giving up. I would not ask anything of Him anymore and I expected Him not to ask anything of me.

But in this hour of deepest despair, I started feeling God's Spirit for the first time since Shauna's death. I really knew He loved me and would not leave me alone. He still had plans for my life. After some time, I told God I wanted to live abundantly again, but I had a huge void in my life and I asked Him to please help me fill that void. God answered that request with one of the most joyful and fulfilling experiences I could ever imagine: He led us into the foster care ministry.

More than a hundred needy children have stayed in our home, and we have adopted three of these. With all these children has come the opportunity to share God's love and concern.

It is very exciting watching each child grow in body and spirit. We have had the opportunity to see several of them come to a saving knowledge of Christ while in our care. I still believe in a God of miracles. He has worked a miracle in me. Each time children leave my home, they take a little part of me with them, but they also leave a part of themselves with me. God has taken a huge void and filled it with so many smiles, kisses, and I-love-yous, sometimes I think the void is about full and even over-flowing.

December 2

GEORGI VINS, former executive secretary, Council of Evangelical Baptist Churches in the former Soviet Union; one of five prisoners exchanged by the Soviet Union in 1979 for two spies held by the United States; president, Russian Gospel Ministries International, Elkhart, Indiana.

> *". . . For I know the plans I have for you," declares the*
> LORD, *"plans to prosper you and not to harm you, plans*
> *to give you hope and a future. . . ." (Jeremiah 29:11, NIV)*

This verse, written by God in my heart, strengthened my faith in the years of persecution, especially during my eight years' imprisonment in Siberian prisons and camps for my testimony of Christ. Atheism takes away spiritual values from men and women: God, the Bible, faith, morals, a future, hope. In exchange, atheism cannot give anything except hatred, cruelty, immorality, and emptiness. For seventy years, state atheism sought to destroy Christian values and Christians themselves in my homeland. But God had His eternal plans for Russia, and He is powerfully carrying out His purpose today. In Russia there is great religious freedom. The Russian people have a great spiritual thirst, a thirst to hear the Word of God. The Lord is also giving me many opportunities to preach the gospel in Russia.

December 3

GEORGE V. VOINOVICH, governor of Ohio since 1991; chairman, Midwestern Governors' Conference; chairman, Council of Great Lakes Governors; chairman, Republican Governors' Association; mayor of Cleveland, 1979–89, longest of any mayor in the city's history; he led Cleveland to three-time National Municipal League All-America City status.

Come unto me, all ye that labour and are heavy laden, and I will give you rest. Take my yoke upon you, and learn of me; for I am meek and lowly in heart: and ye shall find rest unto your souls. For my yoke is easy, and my burden is light. (Matthew 11:28–30, KJV)

The life that is not Christ-centered struggles to find meaning. Those without faith experience a longing and an emptiness that worldly pursuits and treasures "of this earth" simply cannot fulfill. I see evidence of that spiritual hunger almost every day in my job as governor. Without my personal acceptance of Jesus Christ and the Holy Spirit into my life, I could not keep going. Every day, I offer up my prayers, works, joys, and sufferings to the Lord in reparation for my sins and ask Him to help me carry the crosses He sends me. I try to understand that whatever we encounter is redemptive and helps us toward our goal. Every day, I ask God to open my eyes to the opportunities He gives me to be of service to my fellow citizens.

December 4

ICHIRO WACHI, president, Prime Interface, Inc., Tokyo-based company importing housing materials into Japan.

You did not choose me, but I chose you and appointed you to go and bear fruit—fruit that will last. (John 15:16, NIV)

About five years ago, I suddenly sensed that I wanted to be baptized. Later I learned that my wife, Yasuko, had been praying for me with Christian friends in a church in San Diego and with my business friends, Bob and Audrey Dorney in Pennsylvania—praying for so many years that I would be saved. Although Jesus had been showing me His deep love, I did not know that. But with many brothers and sisters praying for me, I suddenly became aware of the Living Christ, our Lord Jesus. I now have two Japanese business friends who recently became aware of Jesus' love and were baptized after a similar experience of being prayed for—by me and many other Christian friends. They told me it was so easy for them to accept Jesus because they both had the feeling they had been helped by somebody they did not know. They found out it was Jesus Himself, who said, "You did not choose me, but I chose you."

December 5

YASUKO WACHI, assistant professor of anthropology, Department of Comparative Culture and Society, International Christian University, Tokyo, Japan; wife of Ichiro Wachi.

> ... *"I am the way, the truth, and the life. ..."*
> *(John 14:6, NKJV)*

I teach anthropology at a Japanese university where people sometimes doubt and wonder how I keep my faith and maintain a high academic standard, because they are of the opinion that Christians do not possess balanced intelligence. But to me, my faith in our Lord Jesus Christ has no conflict with my endeavor to maintain a high academic standard, which is to seek the truth. Our Lord says He is the truth. To some people, being scientific can leave no room for religion. On a superficial level, they can improve their knowledge, but on the deeper level, they need to experience the truth of our Lord Jesus.

In the university where I now work, full-time faculty members are required to be Christian. This is called the "Christian clause" of the university's "Bylaws to the Act of Endowment." This clause, also known as the "Christian code," has been attacked by some of the faculty members. They ask, Is not the Christian code irreconcilable with the nature of academic inquiries? Does not the Christian code present an impediment to maintaining the academic standard of the faculty? Does not the Christian code make the university an exclusive community where only like-minded people are gathered? Is not the Christian code a form of discrimination based on creed as defined and prohibited by United States civil rights legislation? Some academics test us by asking, Why Christianity in this age of globalization? Is the university engaged in proselytism? If you really believe and have faith, why not abandon the Christian code and see what will happen? If you want this university to be Christian, you only need 51 percent Christian, but not 100 percent.

In responding to these critics, we must pray more and let them know the goodness of the Lord and what a great blessing His salvation is, that our Lord Jesus Christ is the way, the truth, and the life. Our responsibility is great because if we do not maintain a high academic standard, they will repeat the charge that the Christian clause is an impediment to maintaining the superb academic standard of the faculty.

December 6

KEN WALES, executive producer, CBS's *Christy* series, based on the late Catherine Marshall's best-selling 1967 novel with the same title; his other producing credits include the Golden Globe– and Emmy-winning miniseries, *John Steinbeck's East of Eden;* the theatrical films *Islands in the Stream* with George C. Scott, *Wild Rovers* with William Holden, *Revenge of the Pink Panther* with Peter Sellers, and *The Tamarind Seed* with Julie

Andrews; TV's *Cagney and Lacey;* and *The Prodigal,* released by the Billy Graham Evangelistic Association; former vice president of production, The Disney Channel; as an actor, he has appeared in twenty-four films and seven TV series, beginning with *Father Knows Best* as Betty's boyfriend.

> *You have heard that it was said, "You shall love your*
> *neighbor and hate your enemy." But I say to you, Love*
> *your enemies and pray for those who persecute you, so*
> *that you may be sons of your Father who is in heaven; for*
> *he makes his sun rise on the evil and on the good, and*
> *sends rain on the just and on the unjust. . . .*
> *(Matthew 5:43–45, RSV)*

I think of my father, Dr. Wales Smith, a Disciples of Christ pastor for fifty-three years who died in 1992, who was such an example of more than turning the other cheek. He was able to truly love those who were unkind to him—sincerely, genuinely love those who attempted to do him in, who were thoughtless, uncaring, hurtful, untruthful, backstabbing. As happens in our lives, we pattern our behavior after our parents' models, and I know that one of the gifts my dad gave to me was the encouragement to do just what this verse says, to really love your enemies. It's a hard thing to do and I fall far short, but hopefully somewhere in my life I can begin to achieve a small amount of that. It is so easy to want revenge and have motives of "I'll get even" with those who hurt us. It probably takes every ounce of strength and courage to do the opposite, from a Christian perspective, because our human lives seem to function so much on action and reaction. But if there can be forgiveness even before action happens, that's an ultimate achievement. As life goes on, we gather more friends, but I suppose time allows us to have even more enemies. And what a wonderful way if we could make friends of all the enemies. Simply turning the other cheek is easy. But to extend a deep sense of love, to love a person beyond his or her unkindness, is extraordinary. What a victory if that kind of love can ever be approached.

December 7

SUSAN WALES, wife of *Christy* producer Ken Wales; her involvement in the series' production has ranged from music coordination to public relations; author of five cookbooks, including a 1995 revised edition of *'Tis the Season* and *50 Ways to Feed Your Lover: A Romantic Guide to Entertaining;* founder and former president, Chrane Group, Inc., Atlanta management consulting firm.

> *. . . for I know whom I have believed, and am persuaded that he is able to keep that which I have committed unto him against that day. (2 Timothy 1:12, KJV)*

I remind myself of this verse each morning and whenever I run into trials and tribulations. I have it taped to my desk and I carry it on an index card in my calendar as a constant reminder. For years, it's always been right there. It's been great in carrying me through difficult times. Sometimes I'll just pull it out and stare at it and read it over and over. And then I'll sing it. Then I'll say it. I've had weak points when I've wondered, like everyone wonders, "God, have you forgotten about me?" And as I repeat the verse, it gives me the strength I need and the belief that, yes, He really is there through the rough times.

This verse says so many things to me about Christ. He is able to handle everything we give Him. He does bear our burdens. We just have to keep remembering that, yes, He is a sovereign God and is fully able to work out what we trust Him with. We don't always see that He's doing it; a lot of times we have to walk by faith when things are not going the way we had hoped or thought they should. God may not do specifically what we want Him to do, but we know that He has a greater purpose and a greater plan than we as human beings sometimes see. The word *know* in this verse is a verb of incredible knowledge of God—to know He is God, to know it from inside out, to the tip of your toes, to the top of your head, to the bottom of your heart. Even when circumstances may seem grim, He is a powerful, sovereign God and His will shall be done.

December 8

MICHAEL WARREN, creator and executive producer with Bill Bickley of ABC's *Family Matters* and *Step by Step;* executive producer with Bickley of ABC's *Hangin' with Mr. Cooper* and, earlier, *Perfect Strangers;* the duo began as a team in 1975, writing scripts for *Happy Days, Laverne and Shirley,* and *Welcome Back Kotter,* later becoming executive consultants for *Happy Days.*

> *Hear, O Israel: The LORD our God, the LORD is one.*
> *Love the LORD your God with all your heart and with*
> *all your soul and with all your strength. These command-*
> *ments that I give you today are to be upon your hearts.*
> *Impress them on your children. Talk about them when*
> *you sit at home and when you walk along the road,*
> *when you lie down and when you get up. Tie them as*
> *symbols on your hands and bind them on your foreheads.*
> *Write them on the doorframes of your houses and on*
> *your gates. When the LORD your God brings you into*
> *the land he swore to your fathers, to Abraham, Isaac and*
> *Jacob, to give you—a land with large, flourishing cities*
> *you did not build, houses filled with all kinds of good*
> *things you did not provide, wells you did not dig, and*
> *vineyards and olive groves you did not plant—then when*
> *you eat and are satisfied, be careful that you do not forget*
> *the LORD, who brought you out of Egypt, out of the land*
> *of slavery. (Deuteronomy 6:4–12, NIV)*

The Exodus story has taught me much about God. He is loving and desires to give more to His children than they are ever able to comprehend. It has allowed me to ask much from Him. Unfortunately, I am most often like the Israelites who got comfortable and decided that they didn't need all of the promised land and settled for less than God desired for them.

These verses also have taught me much about myself. Pride is always at hand. Given the slightest prompting, it will spring up and take credit for what in fact God has given to us. The entertainment business is full of people who have been "given much" but believe it is from their power and the might of their own hands that they have made their success.

These verses have taught me about forgiveness. Even after the children of Israel failed God so many times. Even when they did not believe Him when He said they could take the land, and when they fell short of possessing it, then forgot Him and acted as if they had built the cities and dug the wells and planted the vineyards He had given them. Even then, He forgave them when they turned to Him and asked for forgiveness.

Moses and the Exodus, Joshua and his faithfulness, Caleb and his courage—this story has grandeur and scope; it is the huge canvas of life and history upon which God paints the story of His dealings with humanity and His creation. I return to it often and gain strength and a closeness to God.

December 9

SHEILA WEST, president, chief executive officer, ACI Consolidated, Inc., Monroe, Michigan, a multiple-company corporation that began with a retail store she and her husband opened in 1981; ACI's Archery Center International has been listed twice on the *INC.* 500 list of America's fastest-growing privately owned companies. She has been profiled in *INC., USA Today,* and Tom Peters's book *On Achieving Success* and is the author of *Beyond Chaos: Stress Relief for the Working Woman.*

Let us fix our eyes on Jesus, the author and perfecter of our faith, who for the joy set before him endured the cross, scorning its shame, and sat down at the right hand of the throne of God. Consider him who endured such opposition from sinful men, so that you will not grow weary and lose heart. (Hebrews 12:2–3, NIV)

As we live in the midst of chaos—and it's here to stay—we can look beyond the chaos, or the cross we're having to bear, to our reason for being: to become more like Jesus, to make Him more meaningful in our spheres of influence. This passage gives us all we need to do that. It says to set our sights on Jesus. We have to adjust what we're focusing on in life, not let our focus stay on what's easiest. It says Jesus is the author and finisher of our faith. That is so stress-relieving; it's not our responsibility to write out what our life is going to be like—that's already been worked out for us. All we have to do is respond to the call. We don't have to have all the answers; we can respond in many steps, just day by day as we face life's choices. And it says to consider Him who endured so many things. That tells me I'm not alone. If I've got to compare myself with someone, it doesn't have to be someone who is doing better than I am or someone who's doing worse than I am, because I'll become either overwhelmed or egotistical. I should consider Jesus, that He endured these things with a power and strength that had eternal significance. That gives me the ability to feel that even behind the seemingly meaningless situations of life, there is a purpose.

December 10

LISA WHELCHEL, actress who played Blair on *The Facts of Life* NBC sitcom nine years and has been featured in numerous other TV, film, and stage roles; vocalist whose *All Because of You* debut received a Grammy nomination for Best Inspirational Album.

Are you so foolish? Having begun in the Spirit, are you now being made perfect by the flesh?
(Galatians 3:3, NKJV)

Recently my life is being transformed by Paul's letter to the Galatians. If I were to try to pinpoint a verse, it would be Galatians 3:3. Having served the Lord all my life and having a strong personality by nature, I sometimes get caught up in striving to be perfect. The goal is good, but the means is often works. I am being reminded that anything of eternal value will come by "faith working through love."

December 11

HEATHER WHITESTONE, Miss America 1995; her five-point "STARS" (Success Through Action and Realization of your DreamS) emphasis as Miss America and as a profoundly deaf woman calls for having a positive attitude, believing in your dream, facing your obstacles, working hard, and building a support team; Executive Committee member, President's Committee on Employment of People with Disabilities; former member, Alabama Governor's Task Force for the Deaf and Hard-of-Hearing; subject of *Yes, You Can, Heather!*, biography by her mother, Daphne Gray, with Gregg Lewis.

Come to Me, all you who labor and are heavy laden, and I will give you rest. . . . (Matthew 11:28, NKJV)

For years, I had struggled with not only my deafness, but other obstacles as well. I was very demanding of myself to overcome them on my own. I was very disappointed with myself, but one day I saw a picture of Jesus holding a young man, who had a disappointed face, in His arms. Jesus comforted him. On the bottom of the picture was a Bible verse, Matthew 11:28. I realized that no one on this earth can overcome the obstacles he or she faces without His help. He is the only way to heaven. What has touched my heart the most is His unconditional love that holds me safe and secure.

December 12

DALLAS WILLARD, professor of philosophy, University of Southern California, since 1984 and associate professor there, 1969–84, assistant professor, 1965–69; author of several books, including *In Search of Guidance: Developing a Conversational Relationship with God.*

> *But you have come to Mount Zion and to the city of the living God, the heavenly Jerusalem, and to innumerable angels in festal gathering, and to the assembly of the first-born who are enrolled in heaven, and to God the judge of all, and to the spirits of the righteous made perfect, and to Jesus, the mediator of a new covenant, and to the sprinkled blood that speaks a better word than the blood of Abel. (Hebrews 12:22–24, NRSV)*

It was this Scripture, with its "you have come" (expressing a state of completion), that helped me to understand my precise position in life now and my current and continuing relationship to God and His world, including all the great saints and my own family members who had moved beyond the veil of the visible. It gave substance, for me, to *the heavens* and to the kingdom, which in the Gospels—Matthew 4:17, etc.—Jesus announces has come (again, a state of completion). My faith went from something that I hoped would please God to a vision of reality by which I lived.

December 13

DENIECE WILLIAMS, singer who has won three Grammys; her pop/rhythm-and-blues hits include "Let's Hear It for the Boy," which also received an Oscar nomination, and "Too Much, Too Little, Too Late," a duet with Johnny Mathis; songwriting and a children's lullaby album are among her other credits; her career began as a backup singer with Stevie Wonder, with her solo debut as the opening act for Earth, Wind, and Fire.

I can do all things through Christ who strengthens me.
(Philippians 4:13, NKJV)

As a minister for Christ, a mother, singer, songwriter, publisher, and author, I am faced with so many challenges. It seems that just when I get one "fire" put out, up jumps another. Before I know it, I'm running around in circles like a chicken with my head cut off. Thank God for His Word! When I run out of strength, it's a comfort to know that through Christ I have an inexhaustible supply. Christ's power will sustain me in every difficulty.

December 14

KAREN L. WILLOUGHBY, freelance writer and editor, Lemoore, California; former editor and publisher, *The Beacon,* Christian newspaper in New York City; former volunteer journalist covering Baptist work in fifteen western states and, earlier, staff writer for the *Fort Worth Star-Telegram.*

Now go, write it on a tablet before them
And inscribe it on a scroll,
That it may serve in the time to come
As a witness forever. (Isaiah 30:8, NASB)

It was late one muggy summer's night in Fort Worth, Texas, when I stumbled across these words that convinced me it really was God's will for me to quit a secure job that I loved to go out as an itinerant volunteer journalist. I turned to these words often during the following two years and they, plus many other Isaiah passages, kept me focused and surely more faithful than otherwise I would have been. They comforted me when I felt alone. They encouraged me when I didn't think I was doing much good. They prodded me when I rested too long.

December 15

JOEL K. WILSON, president, Detroit Mailers Union No. 2040 of the International Brotherhood of Teamsters, 1977–91; pastor, Hilton Road Baptist Church, Ferndale, Michigan, 1981–92; now retired in Panama City, Florida.

> *Then said Jesus, Father, forgive them; for they know not what they do. . . . (Luke 23:34, KJV)*

When I doubt whether God loves me or hears my prayers, or whether He's even real, I just remember what He said, "Father, forgive them; for they know not what they do," and I remember that God's love was settled for me at Calvary.

December 16

KEMMONS WILSON, founder, Holiday Inns, who opened the first Holiday Inn in 1952 in Memphis, Tennessee; among honors he has received for leading the company's growth nationally and internationally, induction into *Fortune* magazine and Junior Achievement's National Business Hall of Fame and the American Society of Travel Agents' Travel Hall of Fame; after leaving Holiday Inns, he founded Orange Lake Country Club, 1,100-unit time-share resort near Disney World, Wilson World Hotels, and Wilson Inns.

> *Let the words of my mouth, and the meditation of my heart, be acceptable in thy sight, O LORD, my strength, and my redeemer. (Psalm 19:14, KJV)*

I'm eighty-two years old now, and Psalm 19:14 has been my favorite verse for the last seventy-five years. If you'll just think about what it says—the words of my mouth and the thoughts of my heart being acceptable in God's sight—if you can do that, you're going to be all right. I first heard it in Sunday school when I was a little boy, though I don't think it made too much of an impression back then. But as I got older, I realized just how much that verse really meant. It works almost every day on something.

December 17

MIMI WILSON, former missionary in Quito, Ecuador; co-author, with Mary Beth Lagerborg, of family mealtime activity book, *Table Talk*, and cookbook, *Once-a-Month Cooking;* her parents and grandparents were missionaries among the Pygmies of Zaire, Africa, for more than fifty years.

> . . . *and if you spend yourselves on behalf of the hungry*
> *and satisfy the needs of the oppressed,*
> *then your light will rise in the darkness,*
> *and your night will become like the noonday.*
> *The LORD will guide you always;*
> *he will satisfy your needs in a sun-scorched land*
> *and will strengthen your frame.*
> *You will be like a well-watered garden,*
> *like a spring whose waters never fail.*
> *(Isaiah 58:10–11, NIV)*

Even though these verses were spoken to the children of Israel, I have found them very helpful in my life as well. I have used these verses to motivate me with my interaction with my family, in hospitality, and in my work with the handicapped or those in need.

December 18

HAL C. WINGO, retired international editor and assistant managing editor, *People Weekly;* as international editor, he supervised *People* editions in Australia and Taiwan; member of the Time Inc. team that developed the format and focus for *People*'s 1974 debut; as a senior editor with *Life* from 1963 to 1972, his roles included Far East regional editor, directing the magazine's coverage of the Vietnam War, 1968–70; brother of Nancie Wingo, English teacher in Gaza and, previously, Lebanon.

> *. . . for I know whom I have believed and I am convinced that He is able to guard what I have entrusted to Him until that day. (2 Timothy 1:12, NASB)*

I first came to appreciate this verse as a child when I learned it at summer church encampments as the text of a gospel hymn. Many years later I look at the verse as a reminder of my personal understanding that Christian belief is not a matter of knowledge, but of choice. This verse speaks to the choice I make every day to believe that God will be faithful to the trust and hope I place in Him. I do not know and I do not worry about how or when He will do it, but I choose to believe He will ultimately honor my sometimes-feeble trust and often-mediocre faith. In my life's occupation, I have been called on frequently to tell the stories of individuals at times of tragedy or great misfortune in their lives. In those moments, I am invariably reminded that even in such circumstances we can choose to believe that God is out ahead of every difficulty we may encounter and that the one thing that will not fail is His embracing grace—whenever it finally finds us. Believing that, I can also say that no story is complete until it reaches that happy ending.

December 19

NANCIE WINGO, retired English teacher who worked in Gaza from 1987 to 1996 and in West Beirut, Lebanon, from 1964 to 1987; featured in *Life* magazine in 1984 and *People Weekly* in 1987 in coping with Lebanon's civil war; sister of Hal C. Wingo, retired international editor and assistant managing editor, *People*.

> *[God] is able to do immeasurably more than all we ask or imagine, according to his power that is at work within us. (Ephesians 3:20, NIV)*

When I went to Beirut in 1964, one out of every seven people in the world was a Muslim. Now close to one in five is a Muslim. Missionaries in the Middle East have had to be evacuated at times, some Christian ministries have closed, and others have been disrupted repeatedly during these thirty years. Islam has grown in numbers and in political power. It is hard to know how God is using our work in the Arab world. Certainly we see lives being blessed by Christian ministries and we are grateful to be able to live and work here. However, Ephesians 3:20 reminds me that God will act to redeem the vast Muslim world in ways beyond anything I can think of or ask Him to do. Muslims are people God acted miraculously to preserve, and He loves them and wants good for them and works faithfully toward that end.

December 20

JAMES WINN, landscape painter with works on display at the Art Institute of Chicago and some thirty other public collections in the United States; featured in solo exhibitions at the Sherry French Gallery in New York, the Struve Gallery in Chicago, and other notable galleries and in fourteen catalogs and such periodicals as *Art Forum, American Artist,* and *U.S. Art.*

The heavens declare the glory of God; and the firmament sheweth his handywork. (Psalm 19:1, KJV)

In my life on the prairie I have often stood in awe of the unfolding drama in the skies above. In the sublime vastness of a clear day or beneath the towering grandeur of approaching thunderheads, I am stilled by a sense of Presence. The psalmist was apparently similarly transfixed. This passage has become a touchstone for my work as it has been my intent, my focus, to convey in some measure that glimpse of the Creator in His good works.

December 21

CLAUDE M. WITT, executive director, Temperance League of Kentucky, since 1986; elected president of the American Council of Alcohol Problems in 1996; at age thirteen, he lost his father to a drunken driver and, at age six, an uncle.

> . . . if my people, who are called by my name, will humble themselves and pray and seek my face and turn from their wicked ways, then will I hear from heaven and will forgive their sin and will heal their land.
> (2 Chronicles 7:14, NIV)

In one Old Testament verse, we have the Good News and a call for discipleship. As I look upon the vast horizon of our society and see the decline of moral standards, as I witness the hurt and the horror that the drug alcohol spreads like an infection trying to devour God's people, and as I see the hollow and deceptive philosophy of the gamblers, 2 Chronicles 7:14 just jumps off the page and demands attention.

December 22

LARRY WOIWODE, author of five novels, beginning with *What I'm Going to Do, I Think,* 1969, William Faulkner Award winner for best first novel of the year, *Beyond the Bedroom Wall, Poppa John, Born Brothers,* and *Indian Affairs,* two collections of short stories, a book of poetry, and *Acts: A Writer's Reflections on the Church, Writing, and His Own Life* based on the New Testament Book of Acts; his short stories and poems have appeared in *The New Yorker, Harper's, Atlantic Monthly, Esquire,* and other periodicals; former writer-in-residence, University of Wisconsin, and director of the creative writing program, State University of New York, Binghamton.

For we are his workmanship, created in Christ Jesus unto
good works, which God hath before ordained that we
should walk in them. (Ephesians 2:10, KJV)

This verse first struck me when I began to take the Bible seriously, now nearly twenty years ago. As I have grown, I hope, as a Christian, the implications of the verse continue to grow. Wrapped up in it is the heart of all biblical theology: we are God's workmanship, His creation, and as His people we are created in Christ, who has shown us the Way we should walk. God, meanwhile, in His infinite and sovereign wisdom, ordained before time began how each of His own, formed in Christ, is to fashion his or her own walk. The verse also invites us to rest in entire faith and hope on Christ, because this, too, has been ordained by God, as indeed Jesus' walk was. And it is a lovely exhortation that leaves few loopholes for the shirker. It commends *good works*. We need more acts of active love for one another.

December 23

MARTHA S. WOOD, mayor, Winston-Salem, North Carolina, elected in 1989 and reelected in 1993, the first woman to hold the office; member of the Winston-Salem Board of Aldermen the previous eight years before her election as mayor.

. . . Much is required from the person to whom much is
given; much more is required from the person to whom
much more is given. (Luke 12:48, TEV)

Too frequently we ignore or omit the second half of Luke 12:48. Many of us are richly blessed in a number of ways that we too often take for granted. We become blind to the duty that those blessings impose upon us. This verse helps me remember to be patient and to persevere in fulfilling that duty.

December 24

DUDLEY WOODBERRY, dean and professor of Islamic studies, Fuller Theological Seminary's School of World Mission, Pasadena, California; former Christian worker in Pakistan, Afghanistan, and Saudi Arabia; author of several books on Christian-Muslim relations.

> . . . *you meant evil against me, but God meant it for good.* . . . *(Genesis 50:20, NASB)*

These words by Joseph to his brothers in Egypt have been especially meaningful at two times in my life. The first was when I returned to Kabul, Afghanistan, after the government had torn down our new church building. The second was in Riyadh, Saudi Arabia, when the government informed our congregation that we could no longer meet in one place for worship. In both situations my first sermon to our people explored this verse; we looked at the "evil," then at our God who was not caught by surprise, and finally at the "good" that could come out of the situation. In both cases we developed more flexibility to go where the people were, and more leadership developed in the congregation. God meant it for good.

December 25

JOHN WOODEN, the only member of the National Basketball Hall of Fame inducted both as a player and as a coach; head basketball coach, UCLA, twenty-seven seasons; his forty-year head coaching record of 885–203 is the winningest in sports history; he led UCLA to a record ten NCAA championships, four undefeated seasons, thirty-eight-game NCAA tournament win streak, and eighty-eight-game win streak over four seasons; college Player of the Year on Purdue University's 1932 NCAA championship team.

Though I speak with the tongues of men and of angels, and have not charity, I am become as sounding brass, or a tinkling cymbal. And though I have the gift of prophecy, and understand all mysteries, and all knowledge; and though I have all faith, so that I could remove mountains, and have not charity, I am nothing. And though I bestow all my goods to feed the poor, and though I give my body to be burned, and have not charity, it profiteth me nothing. Charity suffereth long, and is kind; charity envieth not; charity vaunteth not itself, is not puffed up. Doth not behave itself unseemly, seeketh not her own, is not easily provoked, thinketh no evil; Rejoiceth not in iniquity, but rejoiceth in the truth; Beareth all things, believeth all things, hopeth all things, endureth all things. Charity never faileth: but whether there be prophecies, they shall fail; whether there be tongues, they shall cease; whether there be knowledge, it shall vanish away. For we know in part, and we prophesy in part. But when that which is perfect is come, then that which is in part shall be done away. When I was a child, I spake as a child, I understood as a child, I thought as a child; but when I became a man, I put away childish things. For now we see through a glass, darkly; but then face to face: now I know in part; but then shall I know even as also I am known. And now abideth faith, hope, charity, these three; but the greatest of these is charity. (1 Corinthians 13, KJV)

The "Love Chapter," 1 Corinthians 13, would solve all problems if truly followed.

December 26

DAN WOODING, founder and international director, ASSIST Ministries (Aid to Special Saints in Strategic Times), Garden Grove, California, with such projects as "Bridge of Friendship" pen-pal discipleship of new believers in the former Soviet Union; former reporter for the *Sunday Mirror* in London and other British newspapers and former London-based *National Enquirer* correspondent; cohost of *The Hollywood Connection* cable TV show, radio commentator, and author of more than thirty books, including *Blind Faith,* coauthored with his eighty-eight-year-old mother, a former missionary to the blind in Nigeria.

> *At the present time your plenty will supply what they need, so that in turn their plenty will supply what you need. Then there will be equality. . . .*
> *(2 Corinthians 8:14, NIV)*

When I first read this verse back in 1988, I was just starting ASSIST (Aid to Special Saints in Strategic Times), which now has offices in the United Kingdom, Canada, Australia, New Zealand, and Brazil. I have long felt that the church in America needs to be part of an "equal opportunity" body of Christ. This verse says that our "plenty" should be assisting the rest of the church in the underprivileged countries of the world. That "plenty" is mainly financial and could help supply tools to help those Christians grow in their faith, so that they can go on to make disciples in their own countries.

Because so many of them have been through "the fire," they can, in turn, help us by sharing the secrets of how they have survived victorious through so much suffering and persecution. At present, things are rather lopsided, with them doing most of the suffering and we here in the United States doing much griping in the midst of our relative ease. This verse has inspired me, as the head of a ministry and a journalist and broadcaster, to rededicate my waking hours to alerting the American church that we are part of a worldwide family—and we need to focus on that family. Otherwise, both groups are missing out on the best that God wants for us!

December 27

CHARLES WUORINEN, composer of some 200 musical works for orchestra, chorus, chamber ensemble, soloists, ballet, and stage; youngest composer to win the Pulitzer Prize in music, 1970, at age thirty-two; member of Rutgers University faculty and formerly composer-in-residence for the San Francisco Symphony and faculty member at Columbia University and Manhattan School of Music; first composer commissioned to compose works for Christoph von Dohnanyi of the Cleveland Orchestra and Michael Tilson Thomas's New World Symphony.

> *In the beginning was the Word, and the Word was with God, and the Word was God. The same was in the beginning with God. All things were made by him; and without him was not any thing made that was made. In him was life; and the life was the light of men. And the light shineth in darkness; and the darkness comprehended it not. . . . He was in the world, and the world was made by him, and the world knew him not. He came unto his own, and his own received him not. But as many as received him, to them gave he power to become the sons of God, even to them that believe on his name: . . . And the Word was made flesh, and dwelt among us, (and we beheld his glory, the glory as of the only begotten of the Father,) full of grace and truth. . . . And of his fullness have all we received, and grace for grace.*
> *(John 1:1–5, 10–12, 14, 16, KJV)*

These are among the most profound and beautiful of any verses in the Bible, and they have an immeasurable richness. They are both philosophical and personal; abstract and concrete; majestic and intimate. Certainly they sum up Christianity.

December 28

KAY YOW, women's basketball head coach, North Carolina State University, whose teams have won four Atlantic Coast Conference championships and recorded more than 500 wins during her twenty years there; coach of the 1988 Olympic gold medalist women's basketball team; assistant coach of the 1984 Olympic gold medalist team; 1991 Converse Women's Basketball Coaches Association Coach of the Year.

I can do all things through Christ which strengtheneth me. (Philippians 4:13, KJV)

As a coach, I believe physical strength is an important factor in determining success in basketball as well as other sports. It takes an inner strength, however, to be successful in life. This inner strength is available through the power of the Holy Spirit to each person who has made the choice to accept Jesus Christ as Savior and Lord. I praise the Lord for providing a means of strength and victory in times of trials and difficulties.

December 29

KERMIT ZARLEY, PGA Tour golfer, 1964–82; current Senior Tour competitor; 1970 Canadian Open champion; NCAA golf champion, 1962; author of four books on Christian themes.

For God so loved the world, that he gave his only begotten Son, that whosoever believeth in him should not perish, but have everlasting life. (John 3:16, KJV)

When I was thirteen my Sunday school teacher had the class memorize ten Bible verses and John 3:16 was one of them. It impacted me when I understood that a person could perish because he or she did not believe in Jesus, God's Son. I wanted eternal life, everlasting life. That's when I believed and my

Sunday school teacher led me in a prayer; I just thanked Jesus Christ for coming into my life. That's when I think I became a real Christian.

December 30

NORMA ZIMMER, "Champagne Lady" soloist on *The Lawrence Welk Show.*

> *But O my soul, don't be discouraged. Don't be upset. Expect God to act! For I know that I shall again have plenty of reason to praise him for all that he will do. He is my help! He is my God! (Psalm 42:11, TLB)*

For ten years I struggled with a terrible affliction—tic douloureux, trigeminal facial neuralgia (a nerve condition involving severe facial pain). As I lay in bed, I repeated the comforting promises of Psalm 42:11 over and over. I never got discouraged, for I knew that in God's own perfect timing I would be healed. Praise God, He directed me to a marvelous doctor, Peter J. Jannetta, from Presbyterian University Hospital in Pittsburgh, Pennsylvania, who performed brain surgery, and I'm free of pain! I give God the glory!

December 31

ELIZABETH ZIPF, president, American Scientific Affiliation, 1993–94, 2,000-member organization dedicated to fidelity to Scripture and integrity in the practice of science; retired technical consultant to the president, Biosciences Information Service, Philadelphia, thirty-two-year staff member and former head of its editorial department.

> *God is my strength and power: and he maketh my way perfect. (2 Samuel 22:33, KJV)*

I was brought up in a Christian home and always considered myself a Christian. After I left graduate school, I went up to Princeton as a researcher and that's where I really found the Lord. I came to know Him intimately and became a committed Christian; it was when Billy Graham was at Madison Square Garden. I had been wondering whether I should stay in research or what I should do with my life. And the whole thing just sort of fell together. I began to really devour the Bible, reading it as if I had never read it before. That was such a surprise to me, because I had always read the Bible from Sunday school in church to family devotions at home. Yet when I really committed my life to the Lord, it was as if I had to devour the Bible again. I kept turning to 2 Samuel 22:33 again and again. And I said, "That's terrific to know that the Lord will make my way perfect."

PEOPLE INDEX

Ruth Graham Dienert, 74
James C. Dobson, 76
Shirley Dobson, 77
Phil Downer, 78
Diet Eman, 86
Irene M. Endicott, 89
Carol Everett, 90
Bob Fenn, 93
Linda Caldwell Fuller, 96
Millard Fuller, 97
George Gallup, Jr., 98
Fritz Glaus, 103
Finley Hays, 121
Melissa Himes, 127
Jim Hodges, 129
Donna Rice Hughes, 137
Bill Irwin, 141
Joe Ivey, 144
Dawn Smith Jordan, 152
Jeff Kemp, 157
Mary Beth Lagerborg, 165
Vicki Harrell Leavell, 171
Robbie Maroney, 182
Robin Y. McDonald, 187
Bryant Millsaps, 193
Annie M. Morgan, 199
Elisa Morgan, 200
Patrick Morley, 201
Hattie Newell, 207
Fern Nichols, 209
Rosa Parks, 222
Rose Price, 236
Naomi Rhode, 244
Vonda Kay Van Dyke Scoates,
    261
Herbie Shreve, 265
Shepherd Smith, 273
Allan A. Swenson, 283

Joni Eareckson Tada, 284
Jerry Thacker, 288
Sue Thacker, 288
Debbye Turner, 290
Pam Veteto, 294
Heather Whitestone, 305
Claude M. Witt, 312

Media
Forrest Boyd, 29
Bob Briner, 35
James "J.B." Brown, 37
Richard G. Capen, Jr., 44
Frank Haley, 115
Valerie Hancock, 117
Finley Hays, 121
Jo Kadlecek, 153
Rudy Kalis, 154
Michael J. McManus, 189
Christi Myers, 204
Deborah Norville, 212
Curtis Peck, 225
Joanna B. Pinneo, 231
Wesley G. Pippert, 232
Barbara Reynolds, 243
Robert Rieth, 245
Willard Scott, 262
Sandy Smith, 272
Wayne Stayskal, 277
Adon Taft, 285
Karen L. Willoughby, 307
Hal C. Wingo, 309
Dan Wooding, 315

Medicine
Ben Carson, 45
Kenneth H. Cooper, 58
Maria Daoud, 66
Grace Ketterman, 160

George Hamilton IV, 116
Bill Mack, 180
Barbara Mandrell, 182
Paul Overstreet, 219
Stu Phillips, 227
LuLu Roman, 249
Ricky Van Shelton, 264

Music, Popular
Pat Boone, 26
Billy Davis, Jr., 67
Rick Dees, 72
Dion DiMucci, 75
Marilyn McCoo, 186
Bob Singleton, 269
Noel Paul Stookey, 278
Deniece Williams, 306
Norma Zimmer, 319

Science
Francis S. Collins, 54
Raymond Damadian, 65
Calvin B. DeWitt, 73
David Dockery, 78
Susan Drake, 79
Charles Duke, 81
Owen Gingerich, 102
Rodney D. Ice, 141
David Larson, 168
Dave Leestma, 171
Shannon W. Lucid, 180
Henry M. Morris, 202
Donald W. Munro, 203
Steve Nagel, 205
Nina Parushev, 223
Parush Parushev, 224
Ghillean T. Prance, 235
Hugh Ross, 250
Arthur L. Schawlow, 259

Ruth Scott, 261
Elizabeth Zipf, 319

Sports, Baseball
Sid Bream, 30
Tim Burke, 39
Brett Butler, 43
Gary Carter, 46
Glenn Davis, 69
Dave Dravecky, 80
Carl Erskine, 89
Brian Harper, 118
Jack Howell, 136
Scott McGregor, 188
Bobby Richardson, 245
Jim Sundberg, 282
Andre Thornton, 290

Sports, Basketball
Jennifer Azzi, 12
Mark Eaton, 83
Heidi Gillingham, 102
Dan Issel, 142
Bobby Jones, 149
Roger Schweickert, 260
John Wooden, 314
Kay Yow, 318

Sports, Football
Jay Barker, 14
Ann Bowden, 27
Bobby Bowden, 28
Terry Bowden, 29
Bill Brooks, 36
James "J. B." Brown, 37
Chris Godfrey, 104
Darrell Green, 112
Archie Griffin, 113
Bobby Hebert, 121
Tom Landry, 166

THEME INDEX

Faithfulness of God: Anderson, 6;
    Bevill, 20; Dienert, 74; Elliot,
    86; Gleave, 103; Powers, 235
Faithfulness to God:
    Cheeseborough, 50; Miller,
    192; Shepherd Smith, 273
Fear: Ashcroft, 11; George, 101;
    K. Phillips, 227; Schweickert,
    260
Fellowship: Gallup, 98; Parks,
    222
Finances: Anthony, 8; Burkett,
    40; Lavelle, 169; MacLeod,
    181; Merrival, 191
Forgiveness: J. Carter, 47; Cruz,
    64; Everett, 90; Merrival, 191;
    Monk, 196; Price, 236;
    Singletary, 268; Warren, 302;
    J. Wilson, 308

God's plan: Everett, 90; Hancock,
    117; K. Hillin, 126; Hughes,
    137; B. Jones, 149; Keith,
    155; Maroney, 182; Simon,
    267; Sandy Smith, 272. *See
    also* Will of God
Great Commission: B. Bright, 30
Greatness of God: Boyd, 29;
    Gregory, 113; Keane, 155
Greed: Anthony, 8; L. Fuller, 96
Guidance from God: Bream, 30;
    C. Davis, 69; Gossett, 108;
    Hodges, 129; Hood-Phillips,
    134; Hutto, 138; Ice, 141;
    Jenkins, 145; Landry, 166;
    MacLeod, 181; Mohr, 194;
    Naylor, 207; Offerdahl, 216;
    Page, 220; Saint, 255; Scoates,
    261

Healing: Court, 62; Cruz, 64
Holy Spirit: Boone, 26; L. Harris,
    120; Keith Thibodeaux, 289
Hope: Alcorn, 5; Hughes, 137;
    Offerdahl, 216; Parks, 222;
    Stephens, 277
Humility: S. Carter, 47; Gensel,
    100; Martin, 185; Quie, 241;
    Sloan, 270; L. Smith, 270
Humor: Bolton, 26; Burns, 42

Incarnation: Wuorinen, 317
Integrity: Coats, 54

Justice: S. Carter, 47; Coats, 54;
    Kadlecek, 153; Martin, 185;
    Pippert, 232

Kindness: Coats, 54
Knowing God: Hines, 128;
    Strudwick, 280; Turner, 290;
    Zipf, 319

Law of God: Homer, 132;
Loneliness: Mack, 180
Love for God: Balbach-Taylor,
    13; McDonald, 187; Morley,
    201; Newell, 207; Rieth, 245
Love for others: Bird, 22; Coats,
    54; Daugherty, 67; B. Davis,
    67; T. Decker, 72; Dees, 72;
    Gandy, 99; Gatlin, 100; Gore,
    108; D. Harris, 118; Hatfield,
    120; Kadlecek, 153; Kiel, 160;
    Lennon, 172; Nickles, 210;
    Nunn, 213; Rieth, 245;
    Schundler, 259; Simon, 267;
    Stanley, 276; K. Wales, 299;

M. Wilson, 309; Woiwode,
312; Wooden, 314
Love of God: Anderson, 6; Bias,
21; Boyd, 29; Burke, 39; Day,
71; M. Fuller, 97; Gillingham,
102; B. Graham, 109; Haley,
115; Hatfield, 120; James,
144; Largent, 168; E. Morgan,
200; Perkins, 226; Prance,
235; Roman, 249;
Schweickert, 260; Taft, 285;
Warren, 302; Whitestone,
305; M. Wilson, 309

Making a difference: T. Bowden,
29; DiMucci, 75; Swenson,
283
Marriage: L. Fuller, 96;
McManus, 189
Mercy: S. Carter, 47; Kalis, 154;
Pippert, 232
Missions: Andrew, 7; B. Bright,
30; Burks, 41; Wooding, 315
Moral decline: B. Armstrong, 9;
Baehr, 12; Damadian, 65;
Shepherd Smith, 273; Witt,
312
Morality: R. Ross, 251;
Singletary, 268

New birth: Blanchard, 23; Burke,
39; G. Carter, 46; B. Davis,
67; B. Graham, 109; Hood-
Phillips, 134; Langer, 167;
Lilly, 174; Merrival, 191;
Monk, 196; N. Parushev, 223;
Reynolds, 243; Roberts, 246;
R. Rogers, 248; H. Ross, 250;

Rutigliano, 253; Ryun, 254;
Strobel, 279; I. Wachi, 297

Parenting: A. Bowden, 27;
Endicott, 89; C. Fuller, 95;
Merrival, 191
Peacemaking: P. Parushev, 224;
W. Scott, 262; Stookey, 278
Peace of God: S. Decker, 71; J.
Dobson, 76; Gregory, 113;
Issel, 142; Joanne Kemp, 157
Perfection: Whelchel, 304; Zipf,
319
Perseverance: B. Armstrong, 9;
Buckley, 38; Dravecky, 80;
Kenyon, 158; Loos, 177;
Offerdahl, 216; Wooding, 315
Placing God first: Blanchard, 23;
Chernoff, 50; Eckerd, 84;
Godfrey, 104; Howell, 136;
Hybels, 139; Kerr, 159;
Largent, 168; Lavelle, 169;
Lennon, 172; McCartney,
186; Moore, 197; Ogilvie,
217; Osborne, 218; Pinneo,
231; Rahjes, 242; Rote, 252;
Stanley, 276
Positive attitude: T. Bowden, 29
Possessions: Burkett, 40; Coors,
59
Power of God: Carson, 45;
Lindsey, 174
Prayer: Barker, 14; Barnard, 15;
Beasley, 18; Brown, 37; A.
Cooper, 57; G. Davis, 69; S.
Dobson, 77; D. Harris, 118;
Horne, 135; Jenkins, 145;
Joanne Kemp, 157; Koop,

Singletary, 268; Kathy
Thibodeaux, 289; H. Wingo,
309; Zimmer, 319
Trust in God: Anthony, 8;
Barrett, 17; V. Bright, 32;
Brooks, 36; Bryant, 38; Burns,
42; Cliburn, 52; Daoud, 66;
C. Davis, 69; Duke, 81;
Erskine, 89; Fenn, 93; L.
Fuller, 96; Gonzales, 106;
Graves, 111; Haggai, 114;
Hebert, 121; Herlong, 124;
Hodel, 129; Howell, 136;
Irwin, 141; L. Jones, 149;
Jordan, 152; Leestma, 171;
Lewis, 173; Mandrell, 182;
McGregor, 188; McGrew,
188; Plantinga, 232; Ryan,
253; Senter, 263; Stan Smith,
275; Sundberg, 282; Vernon,
291; S. Wales, 301; H. Wingo,
309; N. Wingo, 310
Truth: Collins, 54; Kalis, 154;
Ku, 164; Pippert, 232;
Shepherd Smith, 273; Y.
Wachi, 298

Victory: Cornelius, 60; S.
Thacker, 288

Will of God: K. Cash, 49;
Clower, 53; Eaton, 83; Jack
Kemp, 156; Leavell, 171;
Lucid, 180; Mims, 194; Mohr,
194; Root, 249; Satcher, 258;
Teaff, 286; Teets, 287; Turner,
290; Vernon, 291; Vins, 296;
Woodberry, 314
Wisdom: Collins, 54; B. Hillin,
126; Myers, 204; A. Purcell,
238; K. Wilson, 308
Witness for God: Azzi, 12; Beaty,
19; Bird, 22; Burrows, 42;
Carson, 45; Clower, 53; K.
Cooper, 58; R. Davis, 70;
Downer, 78; Everett, 90;
Fetterolf, 94; Fletcher, 95;
Haberer, 114; Henry, 124;
Holmes, 131; Ivey, 144; Koop,
162; Lindsey, 174; McGrew,
188; Merrival, 191; Millsaps,
193; Morley, 201; Page, 220;
Plaugher, 233; Rhode, 244; F.
Rogers, 247; Shreve, 265; P.
Smith, 271; Stanley, 276
Worship: Barker, 14; Butts, 44

Psalm 139:1–14, 23–24:
Strudwick, 280
Psalm 139:7–12: Lagerborg, 165
Psalm 139:9–10: Bevill, 20
Psalm 139:14: Gillingham, 102
Proverbs 1:7: Goode, 107; Ku,
164
Proverbs 3:3: Kalis, 154
Proverbs 3:5: B. Hillin, 126
Proverbs 3:5–6: Bream, 30;
Brooks, 36; Burns, 42;
Carson, 45; Cliburn, 52; C.
Davis, 69; Gonzales, 106;
Gossett, 108; Herlong, 124;
Jordan, 152; Jack Kemp, 156;
Leestma, 171; McCoo, 186;
Naylor, 207; Senter, 263; Stan
Smith, 275; Vernon, 291
Proverbs 3:5–7: Hebert, 121
Proverbs 3:5–8: Duke, 81
Proverbs 9:10–11: Larson, 168
Proverbs 11:14: Hodges, 129
Proverbs 15:15: Bolton, 26
Proverbs 16:1–9: Page, 220
Proverbs 22:1: Cathy, 49
Proverbs 30:8: Anthony, 8
Proverbs 31:10–11, 25–28: A.
Bowden, 27
Ecclesiastes 11:9, 12:7: N.
Parushev, 223
Isaiah 9:6: Haley, 115
Isaiah 26:3: Ryan, 253
Isaiah 30:8: Willoughby, 307
Isaiah 40:11: E. Morgan, 200
Isaiah 40:28–31: David Johnson,
147
Isaiah 40:29–31: Jonrowe, 150
Isaiah 40:31: B. Armstrong, 9;

Azzi, 12; Buckley, 38;
Ketterman, 160
Isaiah 41:9–16: Everett, 90
Isaiah 43:2–3: Elliot, 86
Isaiah 43:18–19: Kruse, 164
Isaiah 45:2–3: Lindsey, 174
Isaiah 55:8–9: Teets, 287
Isaiah 58:6–8: Kadlecek, 153
Isaiah 58:10–11: M. Wilson, 309
Isaiah 60:1–2: Stephens, 277
Isaiah 64:4: Graves, 111
Jeremiah 1:6, 9–10: R. Davis, 70
Jeremiah 9:23–24: Ogilvie, 217;
Rote, 252
Jeremiah 18:1–6: Marshall, 183
Jeremiah 29:11: Alcorn, 5;
Hancock, 117; Maroney, 182;
Veteto, 294; Vins, 296
Jeremiah 29:11–13: Sandy Smith,
272
Jeremiah 32:27: Roman, 249;
Kathy Thibodeaux, 289
Jeremiah 33:3: Beasley, 18;
Horne, 135; Koop, 162
Lamentations 2:19: Nichols, 209
Lamentations 3:22–23: Dienert,
74
Ezekiel 2:3–6: Shreve, 265
Ezekiel 37:26–28: Balbach-
Taylor, 13
Daniel 3:17–18: Lucid, 180
Amos 5:24: Martin, 185
Micah 6:8: S. Carter, 47; Coats,
54; Drake, 79
Habakkuk 2:3: Keith, 155
Zechariah 4:6: Bryant, 38
Matthew 4:4: Roberts, 246
Matthew 5:9: W. Scott, 262

Romans 8:19–22: R. Scott, 261
Romans 8:28: Barker, 14;
    Cornelius, 60; K. Hillin, 126;
    Jeff Kemp, 157; Lewis, 173;
    Mandrell, 182; D. Rogers,
    247; Satcher, 258; Scoates,
    261
Romans 8:28–29: Hughes, 137
Romans 8:29–30: Turner, 290
Romans 8:35–39:
    Cheeseborough, 50
Romans 8:37–39: Schweickert,
    260
Romans 12:1–2: Hamilton, 116;
    B. Jones, 149; Teaff, 286
Romans 12:4–6: Dwelle, 82
Romans 15:21: Saint, 255
1 Corinthians 1:25: F. Rogers,
    247
1 Corinthians 9:19–23: Bird, 22
1 Corinthians 10:12: Gensel, 100
1 Corinthians 13: Wooden, 314
1 Corinthians 13:4–7: Dees, 72
1 Corinthians 15:10: Glaus, 103
1 Corinthians 15:57: S. Thacker,
    288
1 Corinthians 15:58: Hays, 121;
    Norton, 212; Paddon, 219
2 Corinthians 1:20: Tada, 284
2 Corinthians 2:14: Henry, 124
2 Corinthians 4:1: Hestenes, 125
2 Corinthians 5:7: S. Dobson, 77;
    Irwin, 141
2 Corinthians 5:17–21: Danforth,
    65; Price, 236
2 Corinthians 5:19–20: Morley,
    201

2 Corinthians 8:14: Wooding,
    315
2 Corinthians 10:3–5: Baehr, 12
2 Corinthians 12:7–10:
    Halverson, 115
2 Corinthians 12:9: Erskine, 89
2 Corinthians 12:9–10: McGrew,
    188; Parkening, 222
Galatians 2:20: Hellinger, 122;
    Perkins, 226
Galatians 3:3: Whelchel, 304
Ephesians 2:4–5, 10, 14:
    Tarrants, 285
Ephesians 2:8–10: Mohr, 194;
    Simon, 267
Ephesians 2:10: Capen, 44;
    Woiwode, 312
Ephesians 3:20: N. Wingo, 310
Ephesians 4:32: J. Carter, 47
Ephesians 5:21: McManus, 189
Ephesians 6:12: A. Clark, 51
Philippians 1:6: Komp, 162;
    Mims, 194
Philippians 2:1–5: M. Graham,
    111
Philippians 2:3: Sloan, 270;
    Stanley, 276
Philippians 2:12–13: Boone, 26
Philippians 2:14–16: Briner, 35
Philippians 3:4–9: McGregor,
    188
Philippians 3:10–11: Fleming, 94
Philippians 3:12–14: Dravecky,
    80
Philippians 4:4–7: Issel, 142;
    Richardson, 245
Philippians 4:6–7: S. Decker, 71;

Joanne Kemp, 157
Philippians 4:11–13: Colson, 56
Philippians 4:12: J. Dobson, 76
Philippians 4:13: B. Bowden, 28;
T. Bowden, 29; Court, 62;
Diaz, 74; Holmes, 131; Hutto,
138; Dave Johnson, 147;
Landry, 166; Newell, 207;
Norville, 212; Williams, 306;
Yow, 318
Philippians 4:19: Daoud, 66;
Fenn, 93
Colossians 1:16–17: Munro, 203
Colossians 1:18: Burrows, 42
1 Thessalonians 2:4: Ice, 141
1 Thessalonians 4:1, 11–12:
Eaton, 83
1 Thessalonians 5:11: Gallup, 98
1 Thessalonians 5:24: Burks, 41
1 Timothy 1:15–16: Monk, 196
1 Timothy 4:8: K. Cooper, 58
1 Timothy 6:15: Moorhead, 198
2 Timothy 1:7: Ashcroft, 11
2 Timothy 1:12: S. Wales, 301;
H. Wingo, 309
2 Timothy 2:21–22: Reynolds,
243
Hebrews 11:1: Howard, 135;
Rutigliano, 253
Hebrews 12:1–2: Kenyon, 158
Hebrews 12:1–3: Offerdahl, 216
Hebrews 12:2: Thornton, 290

Hebrews 12:2–3: West, 303
Hebrews 12:22–24: Willard, 306
Hebrews 13:5: Gleave, 103;
Powers, 235
Hebrews 13:6: Hodel, 129
James 1:2–3: Luchsinger, 179
James 1:2–5: A. Purcell, 238
James 1:2–8: Myers, 204
James 1:5: Collins, 54
James 1:12: Singletary, 268
James 1:25: Homer, 132
James 5:15: D. Harris, 118
1 Peter 2:9–10: Stookey, 278
1 Peter 3:3–4: K. Cash, 49
1 Peter 3:15: Ivey, 144
1 Peter 4:10: C. Fuller, 95
1 Peter 4:10–11: P. Smith, 271
1 Peter 5:5–9: L. Smith, 270
1 Peter 5:6: Stayskal, 277
1 Peter 5:7: V. Bright, 32; Burke,
39; Melancon, 190
2 Peter 3:3–6: Morris, 202
1 John 3:16–18: Merrival, 191
1 John 3:21–22: Poland, 234
1 John 4:7–8: Schundler, 259
3 John 4: R. Ross, 251
Jude 24: Singleton, 269
Revelation 3:2: Andrew, 7
Revelation 3:7–8: Jepsen, 146
Revelation 3:8: H. Ross, 250
Revelation 3:20: Butler, 43

PERMISSIONS

AMPLIFIED BIBLE. *The Amplified Bible:* Old Testament. Copyright © 1962, 1964 by Zondervan Publishing House. Used by permission. *The Amplified New Testament.* Copyright © 1958 by the Lockman Foundation. Used by permission.

ASV. *Authorized Standard Version.*

CEV. *The Contemporary English Version.* Copyright © 1991 by the American Bible Society. Used by permission.

JERUSALEM BIBLE. *The Jerusalem Bible.* Copyright © 1966 by Darton, Longman, & Todd, Ltd., and Doubleday & Co., Inc. Used by permission.

KJV. *King James Standard Version.*

NASB. *The New American Standard Bible.* Copyright © 1960, 1962, 1963, 1968, 1971, 1972, 1973, 1975, 1977 by the Lockman Foundation. Used by permission.

NEB. *The New English Bible.* Copyright © 1961, 1970 by the Delegates of the Oxford University Press and the Syndics of the Cambridge University Press. Reprinted by permission.

NIV. *The Holy Bible: New International Version.* Copyright © 1978 by the New York International Bible Society. Used by permission of Zondervan Bible Publishers.

NKJV. *The New King James Version.* Copyright © 1979, 1980, 1982 by Thomas Nelson, Inc., Publishers.

NRSV. *The New Revised Standard Version* of the Bible. Copyright © 1989 by the Division of Christian Education of the National Council of the Churches of Christ in the U.S.A. All rights reserved.

PHILLIPS, J. B. J. B. Phillips, *The New Testament in Modern English, Revised Edition.* Copyright © 1958, 1960, 1972 by

J. B. Phillips. Used by permission of Macmillan Publishing Co., Inc.

RSV. *Revised Standard Version* of the Bible. Copyright © 1946, 1952, 1971, 1973 by the Division of Christian Education of the National Council of the Churches of Christ in the U.S.A. Used by permission. *Revised Standard Version* Bible, Catholic Edition. Copyright © 1965, 1966 by the Division of Christian Education of the National Council of the Churches of Christ in the U.S.A. Used by permission.

TEV. *Good News Bible.* Old Testament. Copyright © 1976 by the American Bible Society. New Testament. Copyright © 1966, 1971, 1976 by the American Bible Society. Used by permission.

TLB. *The Living Bible.* Tyndale House Publishers, Wheaton, IL, 1971. Used by permission.